1997

BEYOND INSTRUCTION

BEYOND INSTRUCTION

Comprehensive Program Planning for Business and Education

William J. Rothwell
Peter S. Cookson

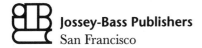

Jossey-Bass Publishers
San Francisco

Substantial discounts on bulk quantities of Jossey-Bass books are available to corporations, professional associations, and other organizations. For details and discount information, contact the special sales department at Jossey-Bass Inc., Publishers: (415) 433–1740; Fax (800) 605–2665.

For sales outside the United States, please contact your local Simon & Schuster International Office.

Jossey-Bass Web address: http://www.josseybass.com

Library of Congress Cataloging-in-Publication Data
Rothwell, William J.
    Beyond instruction : comprehensive program planning for business
and education / William J. Rothwell, Peter S. Cookson. — 1st ed.
       p.   cm. — (The Jossey-Bass business & management series)
    Includes bibliographical references and index.
    ISBN 0-7879-0328-0
    1. Employees—Training of.   2. Instructional systems—Design.
I. Cookson, Peter S. II. Title. III. Series.
HF5549.5.T7R657   1997
658.3'12404—dc21   96-53566

FIRST EDITION
HB Printing   10 9 8 7 6 5 4 3 2 1

THE JOSSEY-BASS BUSINESS & MANAGEMENT SERIES

From William J. Rothwell

This book is dedicated to my soul mate and wife,
Marcelina V. Rothwell, my teenage daughter, Candice S. Rothwell,
and my son, Froilan Perucho. Without their support
this book could not have been written.

From Peter S. Cookson

I dedicate this book to my wife, Judith, and my children,
Ammon, Sarah, and Esther, and their families. I am deeply
grateful for their patience, forbearance, and prayers over the
years that this book has been in the making. I also dedicate this book
to the two outstanding academicians who served as my mentors:
Wesley W. Craig Jr., formerly at Brigham Young University, and
the late William S. Griffith, formerly at the University of Chicago.
Their lives of dedicated service to students and colleagues will be an
unceasing source of inspiration to me in my own academic career.

CONTENTS

PREFACE

Plans are useless, but planning is essential.

GENERAL DWIGHT DAVID EISENHOWER

Learning occurs everywhere. As adults grapple with the challenges of their daily lives, they learn informally through experience. Informal learning is, however, notoriously inefficient and time-consuming. It is rarely sufficient to help adults meet the demands of dynamically changing work requirements. Moreover, many workers resent being thrust into sink-or-swim experiences without preparation. To avert the problems that can stem from total reliance on informal learning, organizations sponsor planned programs to support, facilitate, and accelerate work performance mastery and to improve the ability of the workforce to meet or exceed customer requirements.

Unfortunately, in too many organizations program planning activities are assigned without regard to sound practice or to the essential competencies needed for effective program planning. One result is that much time, money, and effort are wasted. Business and academic institutions could save resources if the competencies of program planners were enhanced. Enhancing those competencies is the primary goal of this book.

Purposes

Beyond Instruction: Comprehensive Program Planning for Business and Education has three purposes: (1) to familiarize readers with the essential components of effective program planning, (2) to examine program planning in unique learning situations or work environments, and (3) to explore the myriad ways in which program planners may formulate program plans while remaining carefully attuned to the learners and to the work environment in which learning will be applied. It is important to understand that the process presented in the book is *contingency based*. By focusing on the program planning process, the book also supports the opening quotation by General Eisenhower, which emphasizes the importance of the planning process over the plans themselves.

Audience

This book is written for those who have program planning responsibilities, including trainers, educators, and managers. Some readers will be familiar with the many themes discussed in the book. For them, it will review and affirm what they already know, while also evoking new insights and providing current references. Other readers will not be familiar with the issues discussed here. The book will introduce them in a comprehensive way to key issues in program planning as practiced in business and educational settings.

Research Foundations

We decided to provide this book with a research-based foundation to set it apart from other program planning texts. To do that we took several steps.

First, we conducted a literature search on program planning. We looked for recent descriptions of program planning activities in business and educational settings. Our aim was to base the book on what is known about state-of-the-art program planning practices.

Second, we conducted four separate surveys. One survey focused on training needs assessment practices (Rothwell, 1995a). Sent out in May 1995 to 350 randomly selected members of the American Society for Training and Development (ASTD), it is the only study in some time to describe typical training needs assessment practices in business. The results were compiled in August 1995. A second survey that focused on program planning practices was distributed in July 1995 to 300 randomly selected continuing education professionals employed by academic institutions (Cookson and Rothwell, 1995). The results were compiled in January 1996 and are published for the first time in this book. A third survey, constructed to parallel the second survey, was sent out in July 1995 to 300 randomly selected human resource development (HRD) professionals in business

(Rothwell and Cookson, 1995). The fourth survey focused on training evaluation. Mailed in May 1995 to 350 randomly selected members of ASTD (Rothwell, 1995b), its results serve as a counterpoint to the training needs assessment study by presenting information about typical training evaluation practices in business. The survey results were compiled in August 1995.

Third and finally, early drafts of this book were field-tested and used in classes by Cookson over several years in graduate classes on lifelong education program planning held in North America, Central America, and Africa. The book has thus been enriched through review in diverse cultures and by an international audience.

Taken together, these steps provide a research-based grounding that is rare in most current books that address program planning practice for a professional audience. Our aim is to ensure that this book provides a comprehensive, up-to-date treatment of program planning practices for business and education.

Overview of the Contents

The chapters in Part One introduce program planning and explain why it is important. Chapter One opens with two brief vignettes to dramatize the challenges in program planning. It defines key terms used throughout the book and explains why program planning is important. It also introduces two foundational models for the book: the Lifelong Education Program Planning (LEPP) model, which describes *what* program planners do, and the Contingency-Based Program Planning (CBPP) model, which describes *how* program planners approach their work activities.

Chapter Two provides background information on the time-honored program planning models designed by Cyril Houle, Malcolm Knowles, Patrick Boyle, and Leonard Nadler. By examining these four models, we quickly introduce readers to many of the key issues affecting program planning practice, as well as give them a historical foundation for understanding the issues examined in the book. This chapter also introduces the authors' survey results on program planning practices in business and education.

The chapters in Part Two focus on Quadrant 1 of the LEPP model. Chapter Three reviews how program planners can organize themselves and their work by applying effective approaches to time management and project planning. Chapter Four describes traditional and emerging roles for program planners. It offers suggestions for magnifying their impact even as their workloads increase and their numbers decrease. It also reviews the authors' research results on the importance of program planning roles.

Chapter Five helps both aspiring and experienced program planners to articulate their working philosophies. If, according to the view espoused by Socrates, "the unexamined life is not worth living," then program planners should examine what they believe. To assist in such an examination the chapter defines *working philosophy*, reviews six functions of such a philosophy, helps program planners to develop and articulate a working philosophy, and offers two examples of such philosophies. Chapter Six reviews common ethical dilemmas faced in program planning. It also recommends how program planners can resolve those dilemmas.

Since program planning is not carried out in a vacuum, it is influenced heavily by the environments in which program planners work. The chapters in Part Three focus on Quadrant 2 of the LEPP model and examine those relevant environments. Chapter Seven defines what is meant by the term *external environment*, describes its key aspects, introduces open systems theory, and suggests ways that program planners can monitor changes in the external environment. The chapter also reviews relevant portions of the authors' surveys to show how program planners are monitoring the external environment for changes that affect programs. Chapter Eight serves as a counterpoint to Chapter Seven. It defines the term *internal environment*. It also suggests ways in which program planners can examine internal environmental conditions, and reviews selected results of the authors' surveys to describe how program planners are monitoring the internal environment for changes that affect programs.

Chapter Nine offers suggestions for program planners who seek information about targeted participants. The first part of the chapter offers ideas about *what* to look for; the second part offers ideas about *how* to look. Chapter Ten directs attention to assessing learning needs and negotiating stakeholder interests. It defines *interests, needs,* and *learning needs.* It also reviews methods for assessing learning needs. Finally, it summarizes the results of a 1995 study conducted by Rothwell about what human resource development (HRD) professionals in U.S. businesses perceive to be the most commonly used and most effective training needs assessment methods.

The chapters in Part Four examine Quadrant 3 of the LEPP model and thus focus on program design. Chapter Eleven explains how to prioritize learning needs, formulate program purposes, and establish goals and objectives. Chapter Twelve defines evaluation, explains why it is worthwhile, reviews four approaches to program evaluation, describes measurement issues associated with evaluation, and summarizes the results of a 1995 survey conducted by Rothwell on what HRD professionals in U.S. businesses perceive to be the most commonly used and most effective training evaluation methods.

Chapter Thirteen reviews two important models for guiding instructional design in terms of their appropriateness for applying the directive, collaborative, and nondirective approaches described in the CBPP model. The first model is the ADDIE model; the acronym is formed from the first letters of the words *analysis, design, development, implementation,* and *evaluation.* The second model is the Action Learning (AL) model. Chapter Fourteen reviews possible learning formats available to program planners, stakeholders, and learners.

Part Five is organized according to Quadrant 4 of the LEPP model. It examines administrative aspects of program planning. Chapter Fifteen answers three questions: (1) How can program participants be recruited effectively? (2) How can program participants be retained successfully? and (3) What practical suggestions can help improve program recruitment and retention? Each question is, of course, essential in establishing appropriate program administration.

Chapter Sixteen describes strategies for program promotion and marketing. Chapter Seventeen reviews basic budgeting principles, explains how to calculate program costs and benefits, and provides advice on program budgeting in higher education. Chapter Eighteen offers recommendations for program planners who must select, supervise, evaluate, and develop full-time and part-time instructors.

An Afterword offers advice on ways to apply the LEPP and CBPP models in business and education. Finally, two appendixes appear at the end of the book. The first appendix gives program planners a tool for assessing their own competencies using the LEPP model. The second appendix is a code of ethics for adult educators and program planners.

As you read this book, bear in mind that the program planning method presented here is contingency based. That means that the LEPP model can be applied in many ways and started or ended at many points. Indeed, many approaches to program planning are possible and appropriate. One approach, however, may be more appropriate than another for a particular situation, targeted learner group, or work environment. Since the approach suggested in this book reflects a decidedly North American worldview, it may or may not be appropriate for other cultures. The authors assume, however, that many of the principles described in the book may be adapted and applied in *any* culture—with the assistance of one or more cultural informants. Principles that cannot be adapted should prompt investigation to find out why.

Acknowledgments

Writing a book is more work than it appears to be. Many people influenced the making of this book. This is our opportunity to thank them.

First, we are grateful to the graduate research assistants who, like good detectives, helped track down myriad books and articles on program planning and undertook the tiresome chore of tallying survey responses. Rothwell's graduate assistants were Dawn Holley, Mark Ning-Li, and Jean Pritchard; Cookson's graduate assistant was Doreen Lyons. We thank them all. Second, we owe our thanks to the students who read earlier versions of this book in the many courses taught by Cookson on different continents over several years. They offered invaluable suggestions for improvement that were refined over time and incorporated into this book. Third, we would like to thank our five manuscript reviewers for their valuable advice. Fourth and finally, we would like to express our appreciation to our editor, Bryon Schneider, for his help and advice during the formative stages of this manuscript and after the initial reviews were in.

February 1997

William J. Rothwell
University Park, Pennsylvania, USA

Peter S. Cookson
Athabasca, Alberta, Canada

THE AUTHORS

William J. Rothwell is associate professor of education at the University Park campus of The Pennsylvania State University. He leads a graduate emphasis in training and human resources in the Department of Adult Education, Instructional Systems, and Workforce Education and Development. He also directs Penn State's Institute for Research in Training and Development, which conducts research and offers consulting services on training-related issues for business, government, and nonprofit organizations around the world.

Before entering the academic world in 1993, Rothwell had been a training director in the public and private sectors since 1979. He planned countless instructional programs. His experience with program planning in business and government forms one foundation for this book. He has authored, coauthored, and edited numerous books, book chapters, and articles. He most recently authored *The ASTD Models for Human Performance Improvement: Roles, Competencies and Outputs* (1996), *Beyond Training and Development: State-of-the-Art Strategies for Enhancing Human Performance* (1996), *The Just-in-Time Training Assessment Instrument and Administrator's Handbook* (1996), and *The Self-Directed On-the-Job Learning Workshop* (1996).

Rothwell completed a B.A. degree in English at Illinois State University in 1974, an M.A. degree (and all courses for the doctorate) in English at the University of Illinois at Urbana-Champaign in 1978, an M.B.A. degree at Sangamon State University (now the University of Illinois at Springfield) in 1982, and a Ph.D.

degree with a specialization in employee training at the University of Illinois at Urbana-Champaign in 1985.

Peter S. Cookson is professor of distance education in the Centre for Distance Education at Athabasca University, Athabasca, Alberta, Canada. From 1984 to 1996 he was with the Adult Education Program at The Pennsylvania State University, teaching at the Harrisburg, University Park, and Monroeville campuses. For nine of those twelve years he served as professor-in-charge of the Adult Education Program. Prior to 1984 he was a professor of adult education at the University of British Columbia in Canada (1979 to 1984) and what is now known as Texas A & M University at Kingsville (1976 to 1979).

One of the courses he has taught most frequently is program planning. Since 1977 Cookson has also taught seminars, workshops, and courses in Venezuela, Panama, Mexico, Costa Rica, and Nicaragua. In 1991 he was awarded a Fulbright Central American Republics Research Fellowship to conduct research on education and training programs and organizations in Nicaragua and Costa Rica. The same year he was named visiting researcher at the National Autonomous University of Nicaragua-Managua, the Polytechnic University of Nicaragua, and the State Distance Education University of Costa Rica. Cookson edited *Recruiting and Retaining Adult Students* (Jossey-Bass, 1989). His experience with program planning in educational settings is one of the foundations for this book.

A native of Liverpool, England, Cookson emigrated as an adolescent with his family to California in 1955. He received his B.A. and M.S. degrees in sociology and Latin American studies from Brigham Young University in 1968 and 1969. In 1977, he was awarded a Ph.D. degree in adult education from the University of Chicago.

PART ONE

CONCEPTUAL FOUNDATIONS

The chapters in Part One provide essential background information on program planning. Chapter One opens with two vignettes that dramatize the challenges facing program planners. It defines key terms used in the book and explains why program planning is important. It also introduces the Lifelong Education Program Planning (LEPP) model and the Contingency-Based Program Planning (CBPP) model, the two foundational models on which subsequent chapters in this book are based. Chapter Two reviews four time-honored program planning models. It also introduces the authors' 1995 survey research results on program planning practices in business and education.

CHAPTER ONE

THE MEANING OF PROGRAM PLANNING

Program planning can be a challenging endeavor. The following vignettes are presented to give you an appreciation for those challenges. They are not intended to be complete case studies; rather, they are meant to stimulate your thinking about the challenges that can confront program planners. As you ponder the vignettes, consider this question: *What key program planning issues are raised?*

Vignette 1

The leaders of a professional association find their organization faced with the need to comply with new government regulations within six months. To initiate action, members of the association's executive committee are planning a conference to be held in three months. The conference will focus on regulatory compliance. All association members will be invited. The association's chief conference planner has been asked to prepare a program plan for the conference. She must present it to the board of directors for review.

Vignette 2

The training director of a manufacturing company has been asked to organize an executive retreat to formulate the company's strategic business plan. The chief executive officer has asked that the meeting be held at a glamorous golf resort on a popular Caribbean island. It should last no more than two days.

Definitions of Key Terms

In each of the vignettes just presented, someone needed to plan a program. In the first vignette, an association's program planner was confronted with the need to plan a conference. In the second vignette, a training director was asked to design an executive retreat. Each vignette thus dramatizes different program planning challenges.

At this point it may be useful to address several important questions: What is a program? What is program planning? What is a program planner? What is lifelong education?

What Is a Program?

A program is a set of organized learning activities that are systematically designed to achieve planned learning outcomes in a specified period. It constitutes the outcomes resulting from the deliberative interaction of one or more learners and a program planner. Educators occasionally use the term *curriculum,* based on the Latin meaning "the course of a race" (Egan, 1978), to denote a program. However, the authors find the term *program* preferable to *curriculum* when referring to planned learning experiences. One reason is that the term *curriculum* is burdened with educational overtones that may confuse managers in business settings. Another reason is that the meaning of *curriculum* is often unclear to many people. *Program,* however, is a recognizable term. When we use the term *curriculum* in this book we limit its meaning to the design of instructor and learner interactions and to the resources intended to accompany those interactions. *Instruction* is the step in program planning that focuses on the interaction between a learner and a trainer or educator that is intended to help learners acquire new knowledge, skills, or attitudes. Both instruction and curriculum can be viewed as steps in program planning.

What Is Program Planning?

In this book, program planning is a comprehensive process in which program planners, exercising a sense of professional responsibility, designate specific strategies to engage relevant contexts, design specific sets of learning outcomes, and plan relevant administrative aspects. Like any planning, program planning is forward-looking. In most cases it seeks to craft effective learning experiences before action is taken to achieve desired results.

What Is a Program Planner?

Program planners are individuals who are responsible for preparing planned learning experiences, for collaborating with others in the preparation of planned learning experiences, or for helping others prepare their own planned learning. They may be employed full-time or part-time. They may serve as employees or contractors. They may occupy high-level or low-level positions in an organization. They may have received specialized education or training in program planning, or they may have been thrust into the program planner role with little or no preparation. Whatever their status or background, they bear responsibility for establishing and achieving planned learning outcomes. In this book, we follow the example set by Cervero and Wilson (1994) and "use *planners* as shorthand for a broad array of people who are involved in deliberating about the purposes, content, audience, and format of educational programs for adults" (p. 6).

Program planners serve under myriad job titles. They are variously called trainers, human resource development (HRD) professionals, training and development professionals, continuing education professionals, program planners, meeting planners, conference planners, staff development specialists, employee developers, and team facilitators. They are also called "administrators and program or curriculum developers in for-profit and nonprofit businesses, community agencies, and public school and higher education institutions" (Cervero and Wilson, 1994, p. 6). Program planning is also occasionally—and increasingly—a responsibility borne by supervisors, managers, executives, and team leaders who are expected to plan and facilitate meetings, set the tone for team-based organizations, and build high-performance and learning organizations (Senge, 1990).

What Is Lifelong Education?

Lifelong education is the sum of organized learning activities available to men and women in a geographical area. The focus of this book is on the *process* that such activities share. Accordingly, lifelong education may also be defined as "the process whereby men and women (alone, in groups, or in institutional settings) seek to improve themselves or their society by increasing their knowledge, skill, or sensitivity. Or alternatively, it is the process whereby individuals, groups, or institutions seek to help men and women grow in those ways" (Houle, 1972, p. 26).

Four key issues in Houle's definition warrant emphasis. First, lifelong education is a *process* of systematic, organized, and intentional learning. Second, the lifelong learning process involves men and women acting in socially accepted roles appropriate to their culture. Third, men and women participate in the process as individuals or as members of teams, groups, communities, or institutions. Fourth, the process results in individual, institutional, or societal development.

Program planners actively encourage lifelong education. The learning activities they plan constitute part of lifelong education both geographically and temporally. Geographically, any education or training program is one instance of the organized learning experiences available to men and women in a particular area. Temporally, any education or training program is an opportunity for program planners to encourage men and women to engage in lifelong responsiveness and openness to learning, in growth and development in all facets of life. All program planners, whether positioned in education or business institutions, are thus engaged in a common lifelong education enterprise.

Two implications can be drawn from viewing lifelong education as a process. First, such a view permits program planners to probe beneath the surface (and superficial) reality of diverse organizational settings to disclose what Houle (1972, p. 26) called "the basic unity of process" shared by the multifarious forms of education and training available to adults. Second, the lifelong education process involves various technologies in which learning needs, resources, organizational structures, and activities are acted upon to achieve learning outcomes.

Lifelong education is not a frill—nice to have but not essential. To survive and remain competitive during this time of dynamic change, global markets, and fierce competition, organizations must encourage lifelong education. Individuals, who have learned through many (and continuing) organizational downsizings that job security and the traditional employer-employee contract are things of the past, must adopt a mind-set for lifelong education if they are to remain employable.

The Importance of Program Planning

Systematic program planning is probably more the exception than the rule in many organizations (Rothwell and Kazanas, 1988). In too many cases programs are conducted without determining the desired results in advance. As a consequence, decisions are made about learning experiences without adequate information. Program planners sometimes remain unaware of the costs or benefits of what they do. Successful programs result from happy coincidence rather than planned design. Programs that turn out well are repeated. Those that do not turn out well are discarded.

At the same time, human resource development (HRD) and continuing education professionals are under increasing pressure to deliver quick and infallible results while they witness dwindling resources to support their efforts. One consequence is that systematic program planning is becoming more challenging.

Another consequence is growing interest in real-time programs that are planned just in time for—and even during—implementation.

Planned programs, however, bear distinct advantages over unplanned ones. Planned programs are targeted for particular results. Since the desired results are clear, accountability for achieving those results can be assigned. Amid the chaotic pressures of modern organizations, however, current conditions call for flexibility rather than rigidity in program planning. Such flexibility takes into account differing corporate, national, and ethnic cultures, value systems, and available resources. Program planning of this kind is contingency based in that "phases overlap, and some activities fit equally well in several different phases. Program development represents a synergistic process. The sum equals more than the parts. It consists of a system made up of several subsystems" (Overfield, 1994, p. 26).

This contingency-based approach is consistent with what is known about the actual practices of program planners, who do not apply all steps of any program planning model at all times (Wedman and Tessmer, 1993). Indeed, "Zemke (1985) found that only 10 percent of respondents [to a survey he conducted] claimed to follow the entire instructional design process. It would seem, then, that neither novices nor experienced practitioners proceed exactly as instructional design models suggest" (Winer and Vázquez-Abad, 1995, p. 62). To explain this phenomenon, Wedman and Tessmer (1990, 1991) posit what they call a *layers of necessity model* in which program planners select instructional design steps according to perceived necessity. Some activities are viewed as more important than others, depending on the situation. That view is consistent with Brookfield's (1986) observation that "years of experience dealing with organizations [reveals that] personality conflicts, political factors, and budgetary constraints alter neatly conceived plans of action" (p. 202). In support of this view, research conducted by Winer and Vázquez-Abad (1995, p. 60) revealed common reasons why program planners do not perform typical steps in program planning. They found that the most common reasons were (in order from most to least important): (1) the program planner lacked expertise; (2) the step was not supported by such stakeholders as learners and managers; (3) a decision had already been reached without taking the step; (4) the step was viewed as unnecessary; (5) insufficient time existed; and (6) money was not available to support taking the step.

Two flexible program planning models will serve as the organizing schemes for this book. Each model is a practical aid for program planners as they confront work challenges. Neither model is intended to be applied sequentially; rather, each is intended to be applied with versatility. The first model is called the Lifelong Education Program Planning (LEPP) model. It focuses on *what* program planners do. The second model is the Contingency-Based Program Planning (CBPP) model. It focuses on *how* program planners enact their roles.

The Lifelong Education Program Planning Model

What do program planners do? The LEPP model helps answer this difficult question. The model orients program planners to the lifelong education program planning process. Providing guidance but not prescriptions about what should be done, it describes the complexity of program planning activities.

The LEPP model, illustrated in Figure 1.1, is comprised of four quadrants: (1) exercising professional responsibility, (2) engaging relevant contexts, (3) designing the program, and (4) managing administrative aspects. Each quadrant, in turn, consists of four subquadrants. All quadrants are related to each other, as depicted in the figure by the doubleheaded arrows connecting the quadrants. Reciprocal and continuous influences exist across quadrants. *No single point of entry or fixed sequence exists in the model, so program planners are free to begin and end wherever they wish as circumstances require.* The planning process has multiple entry points and may follow divergent sequences, as depicted by the doubleheaded arrows within each quadrant.

Quadrant 1: Exercising Professional Responsibility

Carved above the Temple of the Delphic Oracle in ancient Greece was the inscription "Know thyself." That is also the central message of Quadrant 1. Successful program planners exercise professional responsibility by demonstrating the competencies necessary to work effectively, magnify their roles, articulate a working philosophy, and enact a sense of ethical responsibility.

To *work effectively*, program planners exercise effective time management and project management skills. In spite of the stress created by restructured and reengineered organizations, successful program planners perform multiple and complex tasks while satisfying the increasing demands of learners, managers, and other stakeholders.

To *magnify their roles*, program planners regard themselves as professionals. They do more than their written job descriptions specify. They are driven to achievement out of a sense of personal pride in their craft rather than by prospects of personal or financial gain. Assuming a positive and proactive stance, they seize the initiative to ensure that programs support their sponsoring organizations, program participants, and other stakeholders.

Program planners are capable of describing what they believe and why they believe it, and thus to *articulate a working philosophy*. That is the starting point for self-reflection and self-awareness. A program planner's personal philosophy provides an anchor for holding fast amid the ebbs and tides of organizational events.

FIGURE 1.1. THE LIFELONG EDUCATION PROGRAM PLANNING (LEPP) MODEL.

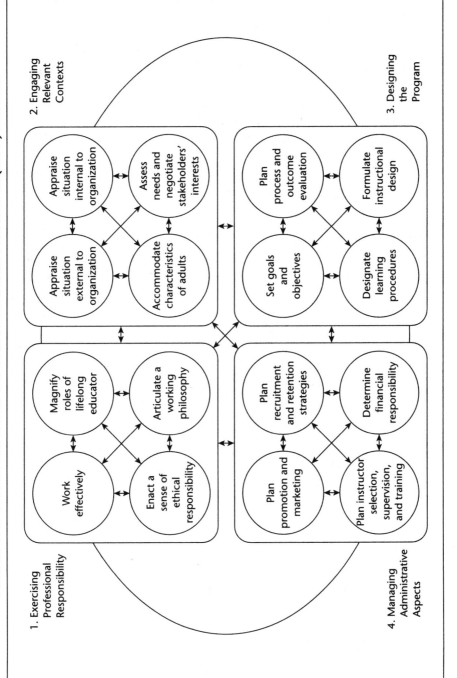

To *enact a sense of ethical responsibility,* program planners recognize the moral dimension of what they do. They know their own values. Planned learning experiences are never apolitical or amoral. Values are the underpinning of every planning decision and action. Program planners are thus prepared to balance organizational demands for productivity and performance enhancement against such counterbalancing issues as individual equity and fairness.

Of course, there are differences in how these activities are carried out in business and educational settings. These differences often amount to differences in degree. For example, those performing in business settings may find it especially important to meet or exceed deadlines and to increase their impact in downsized settings. Conversely, those performing in educational settings may find different pressures to perform because results are more difficult to measure objectively.

Quadrant 2: Engaging Relevant Contexts

Program planners do not work in a vacuum. For that reason, they take into account the environmental conditions affecting their work. Such conditions include the external environment, the internal environment, learning needs, and learner characteristics. Successful program planners engage the relevant contexts by demonstrating the competencies needed to appraise situations external to the organization, to appraise situations internal to the organization, to assess learning needs and negotiate stakeholders' interests, and to accommodate adult characteristics during planned learning experiences. These competencies are equally important in both business and educational settings.

To *appraise situations external to the organization,* program planners are sensitive to what is happening in the world around them and their organizations. They thus identify and monitor trends and adapt planned learning experiences to match emerging challenges.

To *appraise conditions internal to the organization,* program planners determine how much these conditions affect the program planning process. As Cervero and Wilson (1994) have noted, program planning is a political process. Indeed, program planners negotiate with others while establishing, achieving, and following up on objectives. Cervero (1994) combines the concepts of power, interests, negotiation, and responsibility in explaining how adult educators can simultaneously nurture a democratic process and confront power relations that support or threaten it throughout the program planning process. The organization's formal structure (as represented by the organization chart) and informal culture (as represented by the values and beliefs of organizational members) significantly determine what is and what is not appropriate. The policies, purposes, goals, objectives, restrictions, and problems that an organization faces can encourage or discourage program success. Effective program planners stay abreast of conditions internal to their organizations, consider those conditions when planning, and seek to influence them while pursuing program goals.

To *assess learning needs and negotiate stakeholders' interests,* program planners distinguish the need for learning-oriented action from the need for management-oriented action and pinpoint issues of genuine concern to stakeholders. Not all problem situations should be solved by training or education. For instance, no amount of training will help typists improve their skills if management does not provide the equipment necessary for typing. Successful program planners are able to analyze existing problems, anticipate future problems or opportunities, and identify appropriate solutions from a range of possibilities. Once performance problems or learning needs have been identified, program planners subject them to more intensive analysis to determine precisely what needs should be met and how they should be met.

To *accommodate adult characteristics,* program planners design programs that are congruent with what is known about effective adult learning experiences. Indeed, most adults share some physical, psychological, and mental characteristics. These characteristics must be accommodated to achieve success in planned learning experiences. At the same time, other characteristics arising from program participants' national, regional, local, cultural, ethnic, or geographical contexts should also be considered during program planning.

Quadrant 3: Designing the Program

Program design encompasses the activities necessary to shape effective planned learning experiences. When designing programs, successful program planners demonstrate the competencies needed to set goals and objectives, plan process and outcome evaluation, formulate instructional design, and designate learning procedures. These competencies are equally important in both business and educational settings.

To *set goals and objectives,* program planners clarify desired program results or outcomes. Goals specify the general results to be achieved, though they typically do not lend themselves to measurement. Objectives, however, are derived from goals; they lend themselves to measurement and provide a basis for measuring program achievement. What will learners be able to do after a program that they were not able to do before it? What will they know that they do not already know? Answering these questions provides a foundation for developing planned learning experiences while satisfying learning needs and stakeholders' interests. Goals and objectives derived from learning needs and stakeholders' interests are assumed to have greater practical value than goals and objectives derived in other ways. Goals and objectives illuminate and guide all subsequent actions in program design.

To *plan process and outcome evaluation,* program planners convert program goals and objectives into program targets. In other words, goals and objectives are the basis for evaluation, the process of placing value on program results. Evaluation is directed to assess simultaneously the outcomes of planned learning experiences and the processes used to achieve them. In the LEPP model, evaluation pervades program planning because evaluation enables program planners to assume a critically reflective perspective from which to examine each component of the program planning process.

To *formulate instructional design,* program planners select, modify, or prepare materials and experiences to achieve desired results. Alternatively, program planners may help learners and other stakeholders to select, modify, or prepare their own materials and experiences. Program planners can organize experiences so they will be effective with learners who are initially unfamiliar with the subject matter.

To *formulate learning procedures,* program planners select appropriate ways to deliver planned learning experiences. Various ways may be used, of course. In our discussion of designing the learning process, we will focus on the effectiveness of methods, techniques, and devices—and on the delicate balance between delivering planned learning experiences quickly and delivering them in ways that are most effective for encouraging learning.

Quadrant 4: Managing Administrative Aspects

To manage the administrative aspects of program planning, successful program planners create an environment that supports planned learning experiences. Toward that end, they demonstrate the competencies needed to recruit and retain program participants, promote and market programs, budget and finance programs, and select, supervise, train, and evaluate instructors. These competencies are equally important in both business and education settings.

To *recruit and retain participants,* program planners must often induce the targeted learners to participate. Recruiting is important because many lifelong learning opportunities are voluntary, and retaining participants is important because sustained participation in programs is rarely mandatory. Participant retention is thus key to eventual program success.

To *promote and market programs,* successful program planners establish credibility for their efforts. A positive image promotes programs. Promotion communicates to targeted participants how programs will help them meet their needs. Promotion and marketing also help stakeholders to see how programs contribute to organizational plans and goals.

To *budget and finance programs,* program planners work within existing resource constraints. The financial bases for programs vary, of course. Budgetary and financial restrictions stem from the accounting systems of the sponsoring organization, from registration fees paid by participants, and from contracts or agreements with businesses, government agencies, or nonprofit foundations. This book focuses on two types of financing: programs that must be self-financed and programs financed by sponsoring organizations. Although we offer suggestions about budgeting that planners can apply in any setting, we do not consider budgeting policies to be the most important aspect of exercising financial responsibility.

To *select, supervise, train, and evaluate instructors,* program planners find people who can deliver instruction or facilitate planned learning experiences. Program planners are also able to supervise, train, and evaluate those instructors. The LEPP model recognizes that program planners may vary in how much responsibility they bear for these activities. If program planners themselves deliver the instruction they have designed, obviously they will not be responsible for selecting, supervising, training, or evaluating instructors. However, if the programs they plan and coordinate are delivered by an organization's trainers or by external vendors, program planners may bear responsibility for contracting with internal or external instructors. The ability to supervise full-time or part-time instructors is growing more important as many business organizations outsource their work and as many educational institutions rely on adjunct faculty and part-time instructors.

The LEPP model describes but does not prescribe what program planners should do when they encounter situations that warrant planned learning experiences. The model captures in economical form the many activities and responsibilities that confront program planners. It must be applied, however, in a way that is geared to the particular situation. For that reason, it should be applied in a way that recognizes contingencies.

The Contingency-Based Program Planning Model

The CBPP model helps program planners apply the LEPP model and enact their roles. Depicted in Figure 1.2, the model suggests that program planning can be carried out directively, collaboratively, or nondirectively. These distinctions are critically important.

Directive Approaches

According to the CBPP model, directive approaches rest heavily on program planners acting as *directors of learning*—they control and direct what others learn. Such

FIGURE 1.2. THE CONTINGENCY-BASED PROGRAM PLANNING (CBPP) MODEL.

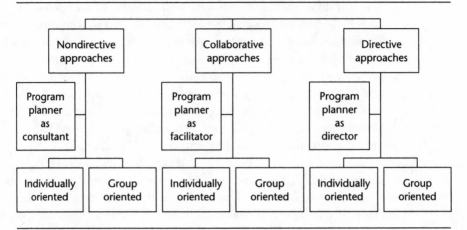

program planners oversee each step of the planning process, which often means that they permit learners limited involvement in the process. Program planners are called upon to meet a need, to conduct a needs assessment, to formulate objectives, to make or buy instruction tied to the objectives, to test the instruction, to deliver it, and to evaluate the results. Directive approaches place the primary burden for program planning squarely on program planners.

Directive approaches are exemplified in many traditional Instructional Systems Design (ISD) models and in pedagogical practices in which professional educators or trainers make decisions for the learners (Rothwell and Kazanas, 1992). While one program planner can make decisions about needs quicker than a group of learners, directive approaches may also work at cross-purposes with the goal of building employee involvement, participation, and teamwork.

Perhaps an example of a directive approach would be helpful. Suppose a bank is experiencing an increasing number of complaints. Using a directive approach, program planners would take initiative to distinguish needs best met through instruction from needs best met by other management actions, to assess which groups have the most customer contact and what kind of contacts they have. During this process they would likely examine complaints to pinpoint their causes, as well as how many and what kinds of employees were affected. Program planners would then identify what behaviors were associated with effective customer service, prepare training to show employees how to demonstrate those behaviors, and establish methods to follow up with participants to see how well they apply on their jobs what they learned in training.

Collaborative Approaches

Collaborative approaches are participatory. They call for negotiation, dialogue, and cooperation among program planners, learners, and other stakeholders. Program planning is a joint venture. All interested parties work together to identify when needs exist. They also work as partners to conduct needs assessments, to formulate objectives, to make or buy instruction keyed to the objectives, to test instruction, to deliver instruction, and to evaluate results. Program planners act as *learning facilitators,* whose primary focus is on the learning process rather than on instructional content. As Hart (1992) explains, "the facilitator must know the group members' attitudes, commitment, skills and experience. The content of the group's experience is the group itself. Its objective is to accomplish its chosen goal. Thus the facilitator does not have a set design but must instead have many methods and techniques available to use with the group as it goes through the five stages of [small group] development" (pp. 2–6). Program planners who act collaboratively aim to build learner ownership in the planned learning experiences in which they participate.

Consider how a collaborative approach would be applied. In the example of the bank experiencing an increasing number of complaints, program planners who adopt a collaborative approach would work with managers and employees to distinguish instructional from management needs, to assess which groups have the most customer contact and what kind of contacts they have. In this process they would help the managers and employees as they examined complaints to pinpoint their causes, and to determine how many and what kinds of employees were affected. Program planners would then help managers and employees to identify what behaviors are associated with effective customer service. They might offer training to help managers and employees design training to show their peers how to improve behaviors linked to customer service, and to establish methods to follow up with participants to see how well they apply on their jobs what they learned in training.

Nondirective Approaches

Nondirective approaches to program planning are carried out by the learners themselves. Learners assume responsibility for their own instructional, personal, and professional development and learning. They identify occasions when they experience a learning need, conduct their own needs assessments as appropriate, formulate their own objectives, make or buy learning experiences tied to the objectives, test instruction, pursue planned learning activities they have chosen, and evaluate results.

Nondirective approaches place the primary burden for program planning on the learners. Program planners become resource and enabling agents as well as learning consultants. They may, however, bear responsibility for monitoring learner progress, evaluating learning outcomes, and reporting results to relevant audiences. Their primary role is to advise learners and other stakeholders about how they should proceed. The responsibility for program planning, however, rests largely with the learners.

Examples of nondirective approaches include action learning (AL), problem-based learning, the goal-based scenario, and self-directed learning (Boud and Felleti, 1991; Campbell and Monson, 1994; Casey, 1993; Collins, Brown, and Newman, 1989; Cunningham, 1994; Inglis, 1994; McGill and Beaty, 1992; Piskurich, 1993; Usher, Simmonds, and Earl, 1991). In one approach to AL, the organization forms a team to solve a problem, crystallize a vision, achieve a goal, or grapple with a pressing issue. Team members are briefed about the problem, vision, goal, or issue. They are supplied with constraints on time, money, and people. However, team members—not program planners—are responsible for clarifying the objectives, identifying the learning strategies, finding the learning resources, and experimenting with solutions to difficult problems. Eventually, team members are individually and collectively debriefed about what they learned from the experience and what they feel they need to learn in the future. Program planners in this process serve as consultants to build team cohesiveness.

Self-directed learning may share many of these features. Learners are empowered to identify their own learning needs, craft their own objectives, determine their own learning resources and strategies, establish their own schedules, and in many cases evaluate their own results. Against this backdrop, program planners become consultants, helping the learners to apply the LEPP model on their own. That means they help learners to (1) exercise responsibility for their learning, (2) magnify their own roles in the learning process, (3) articulate a working philosophy of lifelong education and program planning, (4) enact their roles with a sense of ethical responsibility, (5) assess learning needs and negotiate stakeholder interests, (6) demonstrate the ability to design their own programs, (7) set goals and objectives, (8) establish measurement criteria by which to judge program success, (9) formulate their own effective designs for planned learning, and (10) designate appropriate learning procedures.

Consider for a moment how a nondirective approach is applied. In the example of the bank experiencing an increasing number of complaints, program planners adopting a nondirective approach would likely begin by helping stakeholders such as managers and employees to define the problem they are trying to solve, the best approach to solve it, and the best ways to implement and evaluate the solution. The stakeholders themselves would actually plan programs, while program planners would teach them ways to do that—and to stay focused in the process.

Selecting an Approach

How do program planners know which approach to select from the CBPP model and apply to carrying out the steps depicted in the LEPP model? There is no simple answer to that question. However, program planners can obtain clues from multiple sources:

1. *Corporate culture.* Do most decisions flow from the top down or from the bottom up, or are they negotiated? A directive approach is often advisable if most decisions flow from the top down; a nondirective approach is recommended if most decisions flow from the bottom up; and a collaborative approach is best if most decisions are negotiated.

2. *Project constraints.* Do sufficient time, money, people, and other resources exist to permit collaborative or nondirective approaches? If not, a directive approach may have to be used. It is, after all, the fastest.

3. *Stakeholder preferences.* How much do the learners, their immediate supervisors, or others want to assume responsibility for learning? If they do not want to take that responsibility, then a directive approach may be necessary.

4. *Program planners' values and preferences.* How skilled and capable are program planners in applying directive, collaborative, and nondirective approaches? If program planners lack the ability to apply all approaches, then they are limited to the ones in which they are skilled. Of course they may also call upon external assistance as needed to supplement their own abilities.

5. *Nature of the learning experience.* How knowledgeable are the learners about the subject? A directive approach is often most efficient when learners lack experience, but collaborative and nondirective approaches are usually more effective when the learners possess their own base of knowledge and experience.

6. *The importance of predictable outcomes.* How important is it to ensure predetermined outcomes? If learners must comply with safety regulations or job certification requirements, for example, a directive approach may be most appropriate because program planners must develop instruction that is consistent with meeting those demands. However, if the aim is to encourage creative problem solving (or problem finding), then collaborative or nondirective approaches will be more suitable because they encourage group interaction, build learner motivation, and create learner commitment to new ways of thinking and acting.

Linking LEPP and CBPP

It is worth emphasizing that each program planning activity presented in the LEPP model can be carried out either directively, collaboratively, or nondirectively. The

LEPP model, while descriptive rather than prescriptive, provides program planners with flexibility in deciding what to do, and the CBPP model provides flexibility in deciding how to do it. Taken together, the two models provide program planners with a range of strategies for enacting their roles and meeting their responsibilities.

Deciding what to do and how to do it, however, depends on an in-depth understanding of many program planning issues. One way to summarize these issues succinctly is to review the most influential program planning models. That is the subject of the next chapter.

Summary

This chapter defined *program* as a set of organized learning activities that are systematically designed to achieve planned learning outcomes within a specified period. *Program planning* is a comprehensive process in which program planners, exercising a sense of professional responsibility, designate specific strategies to engage relevant contexts, design specific sets of learning outcomes, and plan relevant administrative aspects. *Program planners* are individuals responsible for preparing planned learning experiences or for helping others prepare their own planned learning.

The chapter described two flexible program planning models that will serve as the organizing schemes for this book. The LEPP model focuses on *what* program planners do. It is comprised of four quadrants: (1) exercising professional responsibility, (2) engaging relevant contexts, (3) designing the program, and (4) managing administrative aspects. Each quadrant in turn is comprised of four subquadrants. The model is descriptive rather than prescriptive.

The CBPP model focuses on *how* program planners enact their roles. Three approaches may be used: directive, collaborative, and nondirective. Directive approaches rest heavily on program planners acting as directors of learning. Collaborative approaches are participatory, and program planners act as learning facilitators. Nondirective approaches are carried out by the learners themselves, while program planners serve as consultants to participants in building their own programs. To select an approach from the CBPP model and apply it to carrying out the flexible steps of the LEPP model, program planners are well-advised to look to clues obtained from the corporate culture, the project constraints, the stakeholder preferences, their own values and preferences, the nature of the learning experience, and the importance of predictable outcomes.

CHAPTER TWO

THE CONTEXT FOR COMPREHENSIVE PROGRAM PLANNING

Program planners can familiarize themselves quickly with the background of program planning and the important issues raised in Chapter One by the LEPP and CBPP models by reviewing four time-honored models of program planning. The term *model,* as it is used here, refers to an ideal design. The abstraction of a theoretically ideal program provides practical reference points with which to compare real programs.

As Cervero and Wilson (1994) point out, ideas about program planning can be categorized into three schools of thought: *the classical viewpoint, the naturalistic viewpoint,* and *the critical viewpoint.* Adherents of the *classical* viewpoint base their thinking primarily on the work of Ralph Tyler. According to Tyler (1949, p. 1), four major questions guide educational program development: (1) What educational purposes should the instructor seek to attain? (2) What educational experiences can be provided that are likely to attain these purposes? (3) How can educational experiences be effectively organized? and (4) How can the instructor assess whether the purposes were achieved? Program planners who believe in the classical viewpoint attempt to answer these questions, which are practical reference points to use in considering any program, whether in business or education. Applied to business, the first question focuses on the purposes of the training function or training experience, the second question focuses on the best means to achieve those purposes, the third question focuses on the best way to organizing the means, and the fourth question focuses on the evaluation of results. These questions are as practical today as they were in the 1940s.

Adherents of the *naturalistic* viewpoint, as Cervero and Wilson (1994) point out, share one major characteristic: they emphasize that "planning systems do not make choices in the real world, planners do" (p. 19). They focus attention on making program decisions and on the specific context in which those decisions are made; they believe that values drive programs.

Adherents of the *critical* viewpoint emphasize the role that program planners play in improving and changing society and in unleashing human potential. Critical theorists examine "the central role played in the planning process by interpersonal, organizational, and societal relationships of power" (Cervero and Wilson, 1994, p. 22). They believe that political issues drive programs as much as business, institutional, or individual needs.

The four program planning models reviewed in this chapter were chosen because they have weathered the test of time. They may also be viewed as prototypical because they were among the first models proposed. They have exerted profound influence on program planning practices in the United States.

Before delineating the models, this caveat is offered: each model represents a simplification of the program planning process. Only key steps or activities in the process are included in the summaries of these models.

Cyril Houle's Model

More than twenty years ago Cyril Houle (1972) posed an educational framework as a systematic way to design, conduct, and evaluate educational programs for adults. Presented as a descriptive rather than a prescriptive model, Houle's framework summarizes key decision points for building systematic program planning. The model is composed of four parts. This discussion, however, will focus on only two of those parts.

Categories of Educational Situations

Program planners have typically devoted most of their attention to working with groups. Houle's model, however, illustrates other ways to conceptualize program planning. Each way can be helpful to program planners as they struggle to make sense of how to offer a program, and to determine who the target audience might be.

Houle identified eleven categories of educational design situations. According to these categories, learners may be organized in four ways: as individuals, as groups, as institutions, or as a mass. There are two ways to view educational situations for individuals (Houle, 1972, p. 44): they can design their own activities, or they can design activities for other individuals. There are four ways to view educational situations for groups: (1) a group of learners can design an activity for an individual, (2) a teacher or group of teachers can design an activity for and/or with a group of learners, (3) a committee can design an activity for a larger group, or (4) two or more groups can design an activity that will enhance their combined programs. There are also four ways, according to Houle, that educational situations may be categorized at the institutional level: (1) a new institution can be designed, (2) an institution can design an activity in a new format, (3) an institution can design a new activity in an established format, and (4) two or more institutions can design an activity that will enhance their combined programs. Finally, there is one way that a "mass" educational situation can be categorized: an individual, group, or institution can design an activity for a mass audience.

The Educational Framework

Houle (1972) also focused attention on the decisions involved in program planning. He described seven key components, or decision points, of an adult education framework:

1. *A possible educational activity is identified.* This activity is a response to a perceived need. For example, a course may be added to an existing sequence of instructional programs offered by a university, a government ministry, a private enterprise, or a professional association.

2. *A decision is made to proceed.* The feasibility and practicality of conducting the educational activity are assessed. Once decision makers are confident that the educational activity is worthwhile, they authorize additional planning.

3. *Objectives are identified and refined.* The objectives express the results desired from planned learning experiences. They are in turn linked directly to meeting identified needs. The objectives should be practical while also sufficiently broad to cover the episodes that will collectively constitute a program.

4. *A suitable format is designed.* The program components should constitute a coherent whole. A suitable form is chosen after resources, leaders, methods, schedule, sequence, social reinforcement, individualization, roles and relationships, criteria of evaluation, and clarity of design are considered:

- *Resources* include instructional materials, electronic media, and human resources such as participants' previous experience and knowledge.

- *Leaders* spearhead the program planning process. During the design and implementation stages, leadership is critical to determining the format's adequacy. Although one or more participant representatives may serve on a program planning team, someone must eventually assume decision-making responsibility.
- *Methods* are ways of organizing participants to meet needs. To be successful, methods must be consistent with the culture of the sponsoring organization and with the learning tasks.
- *Techniques* are the arrangements within a method by which participants are organized in relation to the learning task.
- *Schedule* is the time during which the program is to be delivered. Each program requires sufficient time for design and implementation. Some programs are designed so that participants may use them at times of their own choosing; other programs occur only once.
- *Sequence* is the order of activities within a program. Sequencing is possible once desired outcomes have been identified. Depending on the activity, planned learning experiences may be sequenced from simple to complex, from specific to general, or from general to specific. For example, sequencing from general to specific might involve presenting a model that depicts all steps in a process, such as strategic planning. Each part or step in the model is then discussed. Sequencing from specific to general works exactly opposite of that. Participants may also, on occasion, decide sequencing.
- *Social reinforcement* is the support learners receive both during and after the learning event. Program planners should examine symbolic material and other rewards to ensure that participants will find the program worthwhile both during and after delivery. Examples of social reinforcement may include providing manageable and achievable learning tasks within a unit of instruction, making encouraging comments, rapidly correcting and returning participants' assignments in correspondence courses, and reasonably orienting first-time participants in audio or computer teleconferencing courses.
- *Individualization* is the selection of program format to reduce participants' social isolation. Although many programs are delivered in group formats, they should be designed to allow individual exploration while avoiding individual isolation, which may require using small group and individual activities.
- *Roles and relationships* are participants' expectations about how they should behave in planned learning experiences. Since conduct is determined primarily by experience and most people have participated in many learning experiences, roles and relationships should be clarified early in any planned program. Both participants and program planners may enact such roles as designer, producer, content specialist, tutor or instructor, adviser, and colearner.

- *Criteria of evaluation* are the means by which program participants' performance is judged in relation to the program objectives. When participants are aware of these criteria, they can assess their own progress. Clear objectives stated at the outset should also help participants to understand what is expected of them and how their performance will be judged.
- *Clarity of design* affects how well participants understand what is expected of them. Having a clear idea of the learning design can assure and motivate participants. Also important is the clarity with which the program planner communicates expectations about participants' responses and provides feedback on those responses.

5. *The format is fitted into the larger pattern of participants' lives.* Participants have more to do than immerse themselves in a program, of course. Thus, to be effective any program should begin with a participant orientation that spells out desired expectations and participant benefits. Programs should also be consistent with participants' lifestyles, economic resources, and modes of interpretation.

6. *The plan is implemented.* Program planners must orchestrate participants and other stakeholders' efforts. They should also be prepared to make quick modifications to deal with unforeseen events.

7. *The results are measured and appraised.* Evaluation is essential if program success is to be determined and future improvements are to be made. There are four kinds of evaluation: (1) formative evaluation provides information about ways to improve a program before it is offered; (2) concurrent evaluation provides information about ways to improve a program as it is offered; (3) summative evaluation provides information about how well the program's objectives were attained; and (4) follow-up or impact evaluation provides information after a program has concluded about the persistence of desired performance over time.

By categorizing educational situations and guiding program planning practices, Houle's educational framework can be as helpful to trainers or human resource development (HRD) professionals in business settings as to academically based continuing education professionals.

Malcolm Knowles's Model

Malcolm Knowles's (1980) program planning model is probably the most distinctive of the four models presented in this chapter. Knowles builds on four principles that distinguish *pedagogy*, which he defines as the art and science of teaching, from *andragogy,* which he defines as the art and science of helping others to learn. These principles distinguish between pedagogical and andragogical assumptions in such areas as the concept of the learner, the role of the learner's experience, the learner's readiness to learn, and the learner's orientation to learning:

1. *The concept of the learner.* For Knowles (1980, pp. 43–44), adherents of pedagogy—called *pedagogues*—conceive of the learner as dependent upon the instructor. The instructor is expected to assume full responsibility for making decisions about what is to be learned, when it is to be learned, how it is to be learned, and how well it has been learned. In contrast, adherents of andragogy—called *andragogues*—conceive of the learner as moving from dependency toward increasing self-directedness, but at different rates for different people and in different dimensions of life. Andragogues believe that instructors should encourage this movement. Adults have a deep psychological need to be self-directing, although they may be dependent in particular temporary situations.

2. *The role of the learner's experience.* Pedagogues and andragogues also differ in their perspectives on the role of the learner's experience. Pedagogues think that the learner's experience has little value. They believe that while experience may be a starting point, learners actually gain more from instructors, textbook writers, or other experts. As a result, pedagogues prefer transmittal techniques such as lecture, assigned reading, and audiovisual presentation. Andragogues, however, believe that as learners develop they accumulate a rich reservoir of experience that is a resource for learning for themselves and others. Moreover, they believe that learners gain more from experience-based learning than from transmittal techniques. For that reason, they feel that appropriate approaches to adult learning include laboratory experiments, discussions, problem-solving cases, simulations, and field experiences.

3. *The learner's readiness to learn.* Pedagogues and andragogues differ in how they regard the readiness of the learner to learn. Pedagogues believe that learners are and should be prepared to learn whatever others—such as society or an organization—indicate they should learn. They believe that individuals of approximately the same age are ready to learn about the same things, and that learning should therefore proceed in assembly-line fashion, with everyone learning about the same things in the same way in a consistent progression. Andragogues, however, believe that individuals are ready to learn only when they experience a need to learn stemming from immediate and pressing work-related or life-related tasks or problems. They believe, therefore, that instructors should create an environment conducive to learning, and tools and procedures for helping learners discover their own learning needs, and that planned learning experiences should

be organized around work-related or life-related problems to increase learners' motivation to learn.

4. *The learner's orientation to learning.* Pedagogues and andragogues differ in how they view the learner's orientation to learning. Pedagogues, Knowles believes, think that learners regard instruction as a process of giving and receiving subject matter. They believe that learners understand that the value of much of what they learn will not be apparent to them until much later in life, and they believe that the curriculum should be organized by logically sequenced courses. Andragogues, conversely, see education as a way to help learners increase their life-related and work-related competence, and they believe that learners want to apply what they learn immediately. Accordingly, learning experiences should cultivate increased competence.

On the basis of the principles of andragogy, Knowles draws important conclusions about program planning. For example, to be effective, program planners must work collaboratively with adult learners. In that way, program planning harnesses what Knowles believes to be the inherent desire of most adults for self-direction in their learning initiatives. Knowles also concludes that learning activities should be designed to emphasize the practical application of what is to be learned. One way to do that is to center program content around important life issues encountered by adults, such as those identified by Havighurst (1961) for middle-class North Americans in mid-century, which Knowles adapted. Of course, appropriate developmental tasks corresponding to each life stage will vary by gender, time, and culture. Havighurst's contribution was to emphasize the importance of linking central life stages and tasks to program planning efforts. Program planners should thus organize learning activities to address problems warranting solutions rather than to address general topics.

Knowles offers seven steps for carrying out program planning. Program planners should (1) establish a climate conducive to adult learning; (2) create an organizational structure for participative planning; (3) assess learning needs; (4) formulate learning directions—that is, establish objectives; (5) design learning activities; (6) carry out the activities; and (7) reassess learning needs—that is, evaluate results.

The implications of Knowles's model for program planning should be apparent. The principles of the model have been widely applied in both academic continuing education programs and job training for business settings. They provide a starting point for pondering the philosophical issues of program planning as well as offering practical suggestions for basing programs on experiential principles.

Patrick Boyle's Model

Patrick Boyle (1981) made a valuable contribution by describing three program planning models, which he called the *developmental model*, the *institutional model*, and the *informational model*. Although he was thinking of university agricultural extension efforts and continuing education programs in the United States when he formulated these models, his views can also be applied in other settings. Table 2.1 compares the three models based on such factors as their primary goals, source of objectives, use of knowledge, involvement of the learner, role of the program planner, and standards of effectiveness. The table captures the key issues associated with each model.

Each model offers different steps from which to choose in carrying out the program planning process. In the developmental model, Boyle (1981, pp. 51–54) lists eight steps by which programs should be planned. Program planners should (1) identify the basis of the program, (2) analyze the situation affecting the community and clientele, (3) identify the desired outcomes, (4) identify the resources and support necessary to carry out the program, (5) design an instructional plan, (6) prepare a plan of action, (7) establish accountability for resources, and (8) communicate the value of the program to such stakeholders as learners, managers, and others who stand to gain from it. To apply the institutional model, program planners should take five steps: (1) define the targeted learners and other clients, (2) clarify program content, (3) identify the instructional approach, (4) provide instruction, and (5) evaluate the results (pp. 55–57). To apply the informational model, program planners should take three steps: (1) "determine what content is available, needed or desired" (pp. 55), (2) "provide information or knowledge" (p. 56), and (3) "determine the extent of the distribution of content" (p. 57).

Note that the developmental model most closely resembles the program planning models proposed by Houle and Knowles. In both the developmental and institutional models, instruction is only one step in program planning. The developmental model encompassing different steps for program design and instructional planning—with slight variations from the eight steps listed earlier—is presented in more detail in Table 2.2.

Leonard Nadler's Model

Leonard Nadler's (1982, 1985) program planning model is intended for workplace training applications, but it may be adapted to accommodate other program planning situations. Nadler believes that identifying all of the steps in program planning

TABLE 2.1. BOYLE'S THREE PROGRAM PLANNING MODELS.

Factors	Program Types		
	Developmental	Institutional	Informational
Primary goal	Define and solve individual, group, or community problems.	Growth and improvement of an individual's basic abilities, skills, knowledge, competencies.	Exchange of information.
Source of objectives	Developed primarily out of needs or problems of the clients.	Developed primarily from the discipline or field of knowledge and from the educator.	Derived primarily from new information available from research findings, new laws, or new regulations.
Use of knowledge	Knowledge or content is used to aid in the solution of the problem; it is a means to an end.	Mastery of content or knowledge is the focus. Programs are focused on how to achieve this end.	Content is transferred to the client for immediate use.
Involvement of the learner	Involved in determining problem or need and the scope and nature of the program.	Involved in implementing the learning experiences.	Involved primarily as a recipient of the knowledge.
Role of the programmer	Facilitating the entire educational process from need identification through the evaluative process. Other roles include promotion, legitimation, and communicating the results.	Disseminates knowledge through instructional process.	Provides answers to requests for information.
Standards of effectiveness	Effectiveness determined by the quality of the problem solution and the degree to which individuals, groups, and communities developed problem solving skills.	Effectiveness determined by how well the client mastered the content or desired competencies.	Effectiveness determined by the number of persons reached, and by how much information was distributed.

Source: Boyle, P. *Planning Better Programs.* New York: McGraw-Hill, 1981, p. 7. Used by permission of The McGraw-Hill Companies.

TABLE 2.2. BOYLE'S DEVELOPMENTAL MODEL.

Suggested Phases	Details
1 Establish organizational and individual commitment	The organization's philosophy and procedures for program development should influence each professional's behavior on the job. They also affect the role and involvement of people in your programs. The organizational philosophy and procedures become the framework within which specific actions will take place. Before developing a major program, understand your role and responsibilities, the role of local persons involved in your programs, the organization's program focus, and the relationships with other agencies, groups, and institutions.
2 Analyze the situation of the community and the clients	Start with some basic information about the people and the community. This situational analysis will reveal the need for the program, the potential barriers and sources of support, and your own ability to handle the program.
3 Identify broad program objectives	State the results expected from your program: What will be changed or improved in the economic, social, cultural, or environmental situation, and what evidence will help you to identify those results? Also consider the expected impact of each objective on different types and numbers of people affected by the problem. More specific objectives will come in the program design and instructional plan phases.
4 Determine needed resources and support	Major programs usually need resources (people, time, money, materials) and support from several professionals, citizen leaders, and other agencies and groups. Find out what resources you will need to carry out your program; make sure they will be available when you need them.
5 Design the program	Unite your broad program objectives with the specific audiences you want to reach and decide how to approach them. Define the general content (appropriate to the problem or need) that best fits the needs of the audiences. Choose methods to fit each audience type's learning style and build combinations of these methods in a logical sequence so that one learning experience builds on another.
6 Prepare the instructional plan	Instructional plans are developed for each specific activity or event. They include learning opportunity, time, specific objectives, target clientele, planned learning experiences, content outline, instructional resources, and evaluation.
7 Take action	Your most challenging effort will be to promote and actually carry out the program and its related activities. This requires good program communication, promotion, and time and resource management, and checking to see whether things are going as planned. Make sure that the different activities and events are in proper sequence and integrated; change them if they are not.
8 Determine the program's value	The program's value is judged by participants and others whom the results affect. No matter what personal judgment you make about the program's success, you will need evidence such as participants' reactions,

TABLE 2.2. BOYLE'S DEVELOPMENTAL MODEL, cont'd.

Suggested Phases	Details
	actions taken, objectives met, problems solved, and needs satisfied. The program's value to you can be judged by its implications for your future programs.
9 Communicate results	Report the program's results to key resource people, participants, leaders, advisory groups, colleagues, administrators, and the public. Such reports may take different forms for different audiences—from word of mouth to formal documents. No matter what form they take, reports should include the need for the project; an explanation of what was done; the agency's role; major results, benefits, and action; and reactions of people and participants.

Source: Boyle, P. *Planning Better Programs.* New York: McGraw-Hill, 1981, pp. 29–32. Used by permission of The McGraw-Hill Companies.

is futile because issues outside the model may influence the planning process. He also believes, however, that it is possible to identify critical program planning events. Nadler's model, shown in Figure 2.1, highlights the relationship between each critical event and evaluation and feedback.

Identify Organizational Needs

The first step in applying Nadler's model is identifying organizational needs. When approaching situations in which program planning appears to be appropriate, program planners should pose three important questions: (1) Do performance problems exist? (2) Can the causes of performance problems be distinguished from their symptoms? and (3) Are the cause(s) of performance problems traceable to deficiencies of knowledge, skill, or attitude; deficiencies of management; or a combination of the two?

Because resources generally are scarce, programs should not be designed when problems do not exist, when symptoms are indistinguishable from causes, or when problems stem from management rather than performer deficiencies. Performance problems that are traceable to management deficiencies should be solved by management action, and performance problems traceable to deficiencies of performers' knowledge should be solved by planned learning experiences. If instruction is designed and delivered to address problems caused by management deficiencies, the problems may actually be intensified rather than solved. One reason is that instruction can build individual skills, but without management support those skills cannot be applied by individuals in their work settings. Another reason is that instruction cannot by itself solve problems stemming

FIGURE 2.1. NADLER'S CRITICAL EVENTS MODEL.

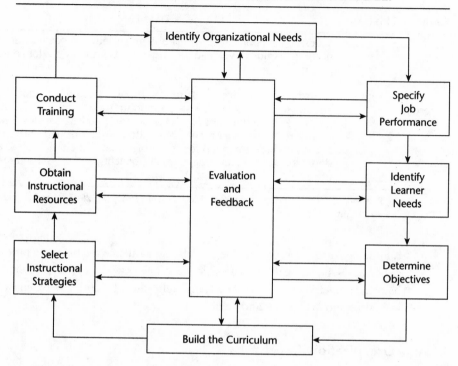

from such management deficiencies as failing to plan or to provide inadequate feedback, or providing inappropriate tools, equipment, and other resources for doing the work. Performance problems stemming from these practices can only be addressed through deliberate management action (Rothwell, 1996b).

Specify Job Performance

Nadler suggests that program planners should undertake at least one form of job analysis to obtain information about job-related performance. At least three forms of job analysis are possible:

1. *Task analysis based on observation.* Workers are observed while performing. Different tasks are recorded and the knowledge, skills, and attitudes necessary

for success are analyzed. The value of task analysis is that it is very detailed and is based carefully on the work.

2. *Analysis based on task simulation.* Performers competent in a job are asked to perform in an artificial setting. What they do is observed, recorded, and subsequently analyzed. Such an approach may be easier to arrange and less obtrusive than task analysis. Unfortunately, it is also less realistic.

3. *Analysis based on interview.* Performers describe to a program planner what they do, how they do it, and how successful performance is measured. This method is often combined with other methods because performers sometimes forget to mention or may even be unaware of critically important activities, behaviors, or outcomes. However, analysis based on interview may also serve to validate the results of other methods.

Identify Learner Needs

While specifying job actions is important, so too is identifying learner characteristics and needs. Who performs the work? What must they know, do, or feel to perform successfully? To answer these questions, program planners should collect information about how many learners are likely to participate in the program; where they are located; how much experience, education, training, and work they have had related to the program topic; and what requirements have been specified for successful job performance, as well as information on participants' cultural and language proficiencies, level of motivation to learn, physical and mental characteristics, and interests and prejudices (Wiggs, 1985). Once this information has been collected, program planners can compare actual to desired levels of learner knowledge, skills, and attitudes. Such analysis can distinguish deficiencies that are fundamental, important, and useful from those that are not.

Determine Objectives

Based on the deficiencies identified and classified in the previous step, program planners can then decide on general program, instructional, and learner objectives:

General program objectives justify investing resources to solve performance problems. They clarify what purpose is to be served by designing and delivering a planned learning experience. They also communicate to managers the importance of the program so they will support the effort and supply the resources necessary to make it successful.

General instructional objectives are the basis for designing planned learning activities. They guide the program planning process by focusing on the results to be achieved. They are useful whether the program is designed inside the organization by a program planner, selected externally from the offerings of vendors, or designed and delivered by learners themselves.

Learner objectives clarify why the instruction is to be offered, and they channel learner energy and attention toward achieving desired results. Learner objectives include three fundamental elements: (1) tasks to be achieved that are stated as observable actions, (2) conditions in which learners are to demonstrate successful performance, and (3) standards to indicate how acceptable performance will be assessed in terms of quantity, quality, cost, or time.

Build the Curriculum

Sometimes program planners, acting as instructional design experts, can work with subject matter experts to organize the sequence of what is to be learned. Planned instruction can be sequenced in different ways, such as in psychological order, job-related (procedural) order, logical order, or problem-oriented or issue-oriented order. If instruction is organized in *psychological order*, the content is sequenced to facilitate learning from past to present, simple to complex, known to unknown, concrete to abstract, practical to theoretical, or present to future. If instruction is organized in *job-related order*, the content is presented to learners in the same order in which work tasks or decisions are performed on the job. *Logical order* means that content is sequenced in building blocks, perhaps based on limited assumptions about what learners already know. If instruction is organized in a *problem-oriented* or *issued-oriented* order, the content is usually described inductively, that is, beginning with a practical problem so that learners can discover the problem's solution.

Select Instructional Strategies

Having formulated *what* is to be learned, program planners can then decide *how* the learning process can best be facilitated. They should select methods and materials that can be used to achieve the objectives. They should consider seven issues when selecting these methods and materials:

1. *The objectives.* Objectives are the most important consideration when selecting learning activities. The reason: instructional methods and materials should support and be harmonious with the desired learning results.
2. *The content.* What is to be learned will affect the choice of methods and materials.
3. *The instructors.* The number, experience, and competence of the instructors will limit the methods and materials to be used. If programs are delivered in ways that do not require instructors, the media used will place limitations on the

level of participant interaction. For instance, video teleconferencing substitutes direct face-to-face interaction for interaction that is affected by the medium in which it is presented.

4. *The targeted learners.* The learners' education, experience, age, strength, and other characteristics will affect the effectiveness of the methods and materials that are used.

5. *The facilities and equipment.* The environment should be appropriate to support learning. Obviously, limitations on location will impose limitations on methods and materials. Computer-based or computer-assisted instruction cannot be used, for instance, if computers are not available.

6. *Time.* Sufficient time must be available to complete learning tasks. Some methods and materials take more time for learners to use than others. For this reason, time is an important constraint on the choice of methods and materials.

7. *Costs.* Adequate financial resources must be available to support program expenses. Of course program benefits—financial or otherwise—must outweigh the costs. However, the financial support available will influence program planning decisions about methods and materials.

In some cases program outcomes do not correspond to those that were planned. One reason: program planners or instructors use whatever methods, techniques, or devices might be available, or those that are least costly, rather than those designed to achieve the desired outcomes. Another reason: program planners or instructors may use methods or materials with which they are familiar rather than other, perhaps more effective ones. For programs to be effective, methods and materials must be used that are intended to achieve the desired results.

Obtain Instructional Resources

Developing a detailed program budget is not possible before this step, though it is possible to establish a general budget. Once program planners have developed the program plan, sequenced content, and chosen methods and materials, they are ready to garner the resources necessary to deliver planned learning experiences.

Conduct Training

This step is the last one we shall discuss from Nadler's model. However, program plans should remain flexible to be responsive to contingencies. Continuous program improvement should be an aim. From the outset, programs should be planned to provide a foundation for accountability for program planners, instructors, learners, and other stakeholders.

Although Nadler's model emphasizes the importance of correcting human performance deficiencies—an issue of increasing interest in business and industry training (Rothwell, 1996b)—it can also be applied to future-oriented efforts to build competence in an occupation, field, or subject area.

Research on Program Planning Practices

In writing this book, the authors undertook research to assess program planning practices in business and educational settings. In July 1995, Cookson and Rothwell constructed a survey questionnaire to assess the status of program planning practices in academic continuing education programs. A second, parallel survey questionnaire was constructed to assess the status of program planning practices in business-based human resource development (HRD) and training programs.

Study Objectives and Pretesting

The objectives of the study were (1) to assess typical program planning practices, and (2) to compare educational and training practices. The surveys were reviewed for clarity and content by two groups: two continuing education professionals reviewed the survey questionnaire designed for continuing education professionals, and two experienced trainers in business reviewed the survey designed for business and industry trainers. Based on the recommendations of the reviewers, the surveys were revised to improve their clarity.

Sample Selection and Survey Administration and Analysis

The names of three hundred continuing education professionals were randomly selected from *The Higher Education Directory* (1994) and a sample of three hundred trainers was randomly selected from the membership directory of the American Society for Training and Development (1994). A letter was written to invite participation in the study; it was sent to the continuing education directors and HRD professionals approximately two weeks before survey distribution. The surveys were then mailed. Approximately two weeks later the researchers sent postcards to prospective respondents requesting that they complete and return their surveys.

By October 1995, fifty-two surveys were returned from the continuing education directors. The response rate was thus 17 percent, which is consistent with similar survey responses. By October 1995, however, only twenty-two surveys were returned from the HRD professionals. The response rate was thus (a disappointing) 7 percent. The surveys were then statistically analyzed. No effort was made to follow up with nonrespondents.

Limitations

While these studies were limited by low response rates and possible systematic bias stemming from the sources of the samples, they do shed light on program planning practice and are useful because they inform such practice. They also provide better data than are extant from any other source as this book goes to press.

Selected Survey Results

Who were the respondents? Fifty academic respondents provided job titles. Of these, nineteen (38 percent) held the title of dean, seventeen (34 percent) held the title of director, and fourteen (28 percent) held another title. Twenty-one HRD professional respondents provided job titles. Of these, eight (38 percent) were managers, two (10 percent) were owners, and the remaining respondents had other titles.

What were the respondents' institutional affiliations? Forty-seven academic respondents provided information about their institutional affiliations. Of these, nineteen (40 percent) represented community colleges, twelve (26 percent) represented private universities, eight (17 percent) listed their affiliations as public universities, and eight (17 percent) cited other higher educational institutions. Twenty-one HRD professional respondents provided information about the industries in which they worked. Of these, three (14 percent) represented education, two (10 percent) represented utilities, two (10 percent) represented government agencies, two (10 percent) represented health care organizations, and twelve (57 percent) represented diverse industries.

Additional survey results will be presented in future chapters to support the discussion. The results of two other independent surveys of HRD professionals are also reported in this book. Survey results about training needs assessment practices are reported in Chapter Ten; results about training evaluation practices are reported in Chapter Twelve.

Summary

This chapter reviewed four time-honored program planning models as a means to summarize the key issues confronting program planners. The term *model*, as used here, refers to an ideal design. This background information introduced readers in more detail to the important program planning issues raised by the LEPP and CBPP models in Chapter One.

The four models reviewed in the chapter were those of Cyril Houle, Malcolm Knowles, Patrick Boyle, and Leonard Nadler. Houle's chief contribution was to pose an educational framework as a systematic way to design, conduct, and evaluate educational programs for adults. He also focused attention on the decisions involved in program planning, and described seven key decision points: (1) identifying a possible educational activity, (2) making a decision to proceed, (3) identifying and refining objectives, (4) designing a suitable format, (5) fitting the format into larger patterns of life, (6) implementing the plan, and (7) measuring and appraising results.

Knowles's program planning model builds on four principles that distinguish *pedagogy*, which he defines as the art and science of teaching, from *andragogy*, which he defines as the art and science of helping others to learn. Knowles distinguishes between pedagogical and andragogical assumptions in such areas as the concept of the learner, the role of the learner's experience, the readiness to learn, and orientation to learning. Knowles offers seven steps for program planning: (1) establishing a climate conducive to adult learning, (2) creating an organizational structure for participative planning, (3) assessing learning needs, (4) establishing instructional objectives, (5) designing learning activities, (6) carrying out the activities, and (7) reassessing learning needs, that is, evaluating results.

Boyle described three program planning models: developmental, institutional, and informational. Each model offers different steps from which to choose in carrying out the program planning process. The developmental model, which most closely resembles the program planning models proposed by Houle and Knowles, lists eight steps by which programs should be planned: (1) identifying the basis of the program, (2) analyzing the situation affecting the community and clientele, (3) identifying the desired outcomes, (4) identifying the resources and support necessary to carry out the program, (5) designing an instructional plan, (6) preparing a plan of action, (7) establishing accountability for resources, and (8) communicating the value of the program to such stakeholders as learners, managers, and others who stand to gain from it.

Nadler believed that describing all steps in program planning is futile because issues outside the model may influence it. However, he also believed that it is possible to pinpoint critical program planning events. Among them are: (1) identifying organizational needs, (2) specifying job performance, (3) identifying learner needs, (4) determining objectives, (5) building the cirriculum, (6) selecting instructional strategies, (7) obtaining instructional resources, and (8) conducting training.

PART TWO

EXERCISING PROFESSIONAL RESPONSIBILITY

The chapters in Part Two focus on what program planners, as professionals, can do to orient themselves to their program planning responsibilities. Chapter Three addresses the key question, *How should program planners organize themselves to work effectively?* thus emphasizing the importance of organizing work. It also highlights key issues in time management and project planning. Chapter Four reviews the roles that may be played by program planners in business and education. It suggests ways that program planners can magnify their impact in the face of increasing needs and decreasing staff. The first section of Chapter Five defines the term *working philosophy* and reviews six functions of such a philosophy. The second section helps program planners to develop and articulate a working philosophy, and the third section offers two examples of working philosophies. Chapter Six emphasizes the importance of ethical decision making in program planning. The chapter reviews common ethical dilemmas facing program planners and offers advice for resolving those dilemmas.

CHAPTER THREE

WORKING EFFECTIVELY

Working effectively means using time productively and coordinating projects successfully. As organizations are restructured, budgets are slashed, and decision makers become more insistent on seeing quick but effective results, few competencies are growing more important to program planners than this one. Time has become a strategic advantage. Working effectively is a means to harness that advantage.

But what is time management? How can program planners use time most productively? What is project planning and management? How can program planning projects be organized and managed successfully? This chapter addresses these important questions. By doing so it gives program planners valuable clues about ways to work effectively.

Time Management

Time management means using time to achieve optimal results and to accomplish worthwhile tasks. *Why is time management important for program planners?* The authors interviewed a program planner in business:

> I have so much to do that I do not know where to begin. I devote more than one hundred hours per week to my work. All I do is work. My family and

friends have forgotten what I look like. I have no time for community, religious, or professional activities. I use my weekends to prepare for assignments due next week or to resolve problems from last week. Worse yet, I am not alone: many colleagues are experiencing the same problem, since I can call them in their offices on Sunday morning and find them at work. And I do not see how I can better manage the time I have. For example, I have learned how to use time in my car to make phone calls, how to rely on voice mail to help me screen and prioritize calls, and how to reach people by electronic mail at odd times on routine matters. What can I do to improve my time management skills?

These words dramatize the growing importance of time management. Many people can relate to the dilemma described by this program planner.

Time management is important to program planners for many reasons. If time is not used effectively, work will not be completed. If the work remains undone, the program planner performs poorly. If program planners continually sacrifice their family lives to their work, they risk family disintegration. If other aspects of life are sacrificed, the program planner becomes a candidate for burnout, depression, alcoholism, drug abuse, or other self-defeating behaviors.

The authors have found that inexperienced program planners often have difficulty learning to make the best use of their time. Unlike their more experienced counterparts, they do not know how to juggle several tasks at once or take advantage of predictable delays on one task or project to push forward on others. Instead, they handle time in linear fashion, expecting each step of a project to follow neatly what precedes it, which rarely happens. Planners learn to use time effectively by watching other planners, by following the directions of their supervisors, or by being forced into effective time management to meet tight deadlines.

What does research reveal about program planners' time management challenges? The authors' 1995 surveys of continuing education directors and human resource development (HRD) professionals shed light on how much time they devote to the steps described in the Lifelong Education Program Planning (LEPP) model (discussed in Chapter One). The authors posed the following questions to both groups: *The process of planning can be broken down into a number of interrelated and often iterative sequences of program planning practices. When you plan programs, how often do you see that such practices are implemented?* While this question is not directly linked to time usage, it does yield responses that can be associated with it. The collective responses are summarized in Figures 3.1 and 3.2.

Although self-reports of time usage are not always reliable due to faulty memories, the survey results suggest that continuing education professionals are

FIGURE 3.1. TIME DEVOTED TO PROGRAM
PLANNING ACTIVITIES BY CONTINUING EDUCATION DIRECTORS.

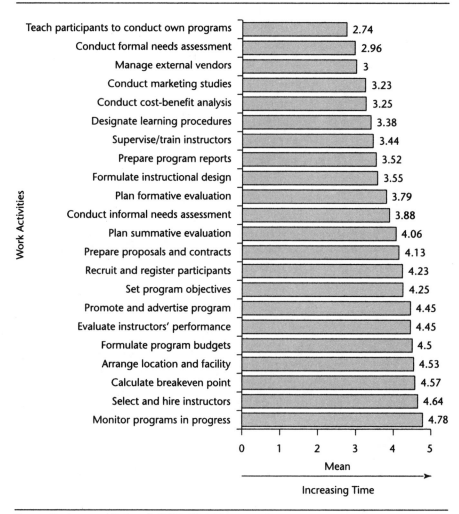

FIGURE 3.2. TIME DEVOTED TO PROGRAM PLANNING ACTIVITIES BY HRD PROFESSIONALS.

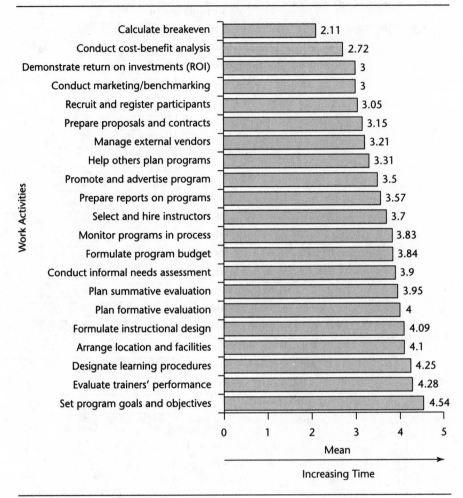

Increasing Time

devoting most of their time to such steps as monitoring programs in progress, selecting and hiring instructors, calculating break-even points for programs, arranging locations and facilities, formulating program budgets, evaluating instructors' performance, and promoting and advertising programs. If these survey results are to be believed, then academically based continuing education professionals are focusing their time and energies on managing administrative aspects of programs, and not on such other important activities as designing the program, engaging relevant contexts, or exercising professional responsibility.

HRD professionals, conversely, claim to be focusing more on designing the program. As Figure 3.2 illustrates, they say they devote most of their time to setting goals and objectives, evaluating designated learning procedures, arranging location and facilities, formulating instructional design, planning formative evaluation, planning summative evaluation, and conducting informal needs assessment. All of these activities—except arranging location and facilities (an administrative activity) and conducting informal needs assessment (an "engaging relevant contexts" activity)—fall into the "designing the program" quadrant of the LEPP model.

If accurate, these survey results may have three important implications. First, because each group seems to be devoting time to different activities, the survey results may suggest different time management challenges for HRD professionals and academically based continuing education professionals. For instance, HRD professionals may perceive themselves to be focusing more on achieving program results, while continuing education professionals may perceive themselves to be devoting more time to servicing clients' predetermined needs. Second, the survey results provide a benchmark against which to prepare program planners in training for the challenges awaiting them in practice. And third, the results provide a reference point for improving time management usage. Program planners may examine their own time use and then compare how they spend their time to how others say they are spending their time. If they find differences, they may ask useful questions about why such differences exist.

Why are program planners vulnerable to time management problems? Working with people can be extraordinarily time-consuming. Although individuals can usually make up their minds quickly, groups typically do not reach immediate decisions. Program planners often work with managers, learners, and other stakeholder groups who have varied and occasionally conflicting expectations. As a result, program planners find that much of what they do is delayed as group members process decisions. In fact, the more collaborative or nondirective the approach they use, the lengthier the decision-making process can become.

How can program planners use time most effectively? There are no silver bullets for managing time. About the best that can be hoped for is that program planners will set clear work priorities within a larger context of life priorities. They should then allocate time according to these priorities, master creative ways to use the time available to accomplish multiple tasks (what some call *multitasking*), identify the most common time stealers they face and take active steps to overcome them, and seek a dynamic balance between their work and their personal lives, however difficult that may be.

Since most program planning is conducted as project work, perhaps the best way to make more productive use of time is to improve project planning and project management.

Project Planning and Project Management

A *project* is a work assignment of limited duration. It has a discernible beginning, middle, and ending. Projects vary in scope and duration, of course, but they share common features. Examples of program planning projects include conducting needs assessments, designing courses or orchestrating other planned learning experiences, delivering instruction, facilitating learning, and evaluating results.

Project planning means preparing for a work assignment of limited duration; *project management* means implementing the project plan and evaluating results. By understanding project planning—and by understanding how to write project proposals based on project steps—program planners can help themselves to manage their time and work effectively. They are also more likely to achieve project goals and objectives.

When planning and managing projects, program planners will usually seek answers to the following questions:

- Why does the project exist? More specifically, what need, goal, issue, vision, or problem prompted the project?
- Who are the stakeholders of a project, and what results do they seek from it?
- Who should be assigned to a program planning project to meet the requirements for expertise stemming from project requirements?
- What goals, objectives, and results are sought?
- How can the goals, objectives, or outcomes be most efficiently and effectively achieved?
- When are the final project results sought? What interim results are sought, and when are they sought?
- What tasks must be completed to achieve project goals, objectives, and results?
- In what order should project tasks be completed? Do some tasks lend themselves to being carried out concurrently with others?
- Where will the project tasks be carried out?

What project problems are commonly encountered by program planners? Common project planning problems stem from several predictable sources. First, stakeholders and program planners occasionally enter a project without clear goals, objectives, and expectations. (Common stakeholders include the targeted learners and their immediate supervisors. Other stakeholders may also exist, however, and may include society, a particular community, an industry, a customer or client group, an organization's supplier, an organization's distributors, and even an organization's competitors.) Different groups may expect different, perhaps conflicting, results. Failure to clarify goals can lead to unsatisfactory project performance. Program planners who wish to avert this outcome may send out an open-ended survey to participants in advance. Participants may be asked for their individual expectations and project goals. These can then be shared immediately at the opening of the first meeting about the new project as a way to clarify goals, as well as to surface conflicting expectations to be worked out.

Second, program planners may enter a project lacking sufficient information. Much time can be wasted simply learning what prompted a project, who is supporting it, and how much commitment they have to it. To avert this problem, program planners are well-advised to collect information before an initial meeting on a new project. This can be accomplished by phone calls, electronic mail messages, or face-to-face interviews.

Third, resource constraints going into a project are sometimes unclear or unrealistic, creating unique project coordination problems or other constraints. For instance, a large company or community college district may demand a comprehensive needs assessment to be performed in a short time, such as a week. In most cases, that goal would be unrealistic unless project parameters are carefully limited.

Fourth, inexperienced program planners take one project step at a time in linear fashion instead of successfully managing multiple and concurrent steps. One-step-at-a-time project management practices can unduly delay a project. They may also give stakeholders the erroneous impression that program planners are not proceeding with a sense of urgency to meet their needs. To cite one example, it may be possible to identify off-the-shelf training materials to meet a need while simultaneously lining up participants to evaluate materials. In short, multiple steps can be accomplished at once, which short-circuits project time lines and makes maximum use of the available time.

Many other problems may arise while operating program planning in a project format. For example, program planners may juggle too many projects for the staff available to carry them out. To avert that problem, program planners should set strict project priorities and follow them. They should also make it a practice to avoid taking on more than they know they can reasonably handle.

How should program planning projects be managed? Three different approaches may be used. They are not mutually exclusive, however. Indeed, one project step may be carried out using one approach, while another approach may be used on another step. These approaches are based on the approaches offered in the Contingency-Based Program Planning (CBPP) model (described in Chapter One). Projects may thus be managed directively, collaboratively, or nondirectively.

The Directive Approach

When program planners use the directive approach to project program planning, they assume the role of director. They oversee the project closely. They delegate few, if any, project steps. Such an approach to project planning and management is akin to the pedagogical approach to instruction discussed by Knowles (1980). A directive approach is typically faster than collaborative or nondirective project management approaches because fewer people are involved in decision making. However, the directive approach reduces participation by stakeholders in the project, which limits their project ownership. Such an approach is usually most appropriate when a program is to be designed and implemented on an emergency basis and when the cost of delay is likely to be high.

Hennessy and Hennessy (1989) have recommended steps in project planning based on the instructional systems design (ISD) model (Rothwell and Kazanas, 1992). They suggest that program planners should manage projects in three distinct phases: analysis, design, and development. During the analysis phase, program planners would answer such journalistic questions as who is involved, what do they need, why do they need it, when do they need it, where is it needed, and what resources are available to support the effort? During the design phase, project planning steps would be devised that would provide program planners with a detailed blueprint at the beginning of the project. They would focus attention on actions to be taken by program planners rather than by stakeholders, and would thus be consistent with a directive approach. During the development phase, program planners make, buy, or buy and modify instructional materials to meet program objectives.

A simple example may help readers understand how the directive approach may be appropriately used. A large but rural community college was racked by a scandal when the president and the board chairperson were accused of sexually harassing subordinates. After a lengthy, well-publicized, and sordid investigation had nearly destroyed the college's community image and faculty morale, the director of staff development was asked to design and deliver sexual harassment avoidance training for all college administrators, faculty, and staff. The project was time-sensitive, since board of trustees members believed that the project was essential to reviving the college's tarnished community image and demoralized faculty after the forced removal from office of the president and board chairperson.

As a first step, the director of staff development, functioning as a program planner, examined the college's policy on sexual harassment. It was so vague that it did not provide adequate policy guidance, especially when the highest-level decision makers stood accused. The director of staff development immediately launched a benchmarking effort to review the sexual harassment policies of other colleges and universities. She then drafted a new, improved policy. With the full support of a new president and a new board chairperson, she then designed and delivered instruction on how to apply the new policy to administrators, faculty, and staff. In less than three months, working alone, she trained all administrators, faculty, and staff. She was so successful that the board voted unanimously to promote her.

The point of this example is that emergency circumstances demanded a swift, strong response. Decision makers felt that a committee could not act quickly enough. Instead, one competent person, acting alone, designed and delivered the program successfully in record time with the full support of key decision makers and stakeholders. That is the hallmark of a directive approach.

The Collaborative Approach

In the collaborative approach, program planners work closely with participants to craft a project plan that is responsive to organizational and individual needs. Projects are divided into key steps reflecting the action research model that is the underpinning of organization development (Rothwell, Sullivan, and McLean, 1995). Participants and program planners manage the project as a joint venture.

The first step is *initial client contact*. An organization, group, or individual (known as the *client*) experiences a performance problem or a program need. The client may or may not understand the cause of the problem. In either case, initial client contact begins as a response to the client's help-seeking behavior. The client seeks a program planner who is perceived to possess expertise in clarifying the problem's cause, solving the problem, or meeting identified needs. During the initial contact, program planners help the client clarify the problem or need and identify who is affected by it, how they are affected, what actions can be taken to solve the problem or meet the need, and how that corrective action can be taken.

The second step is *assessment*. Working closely with the client, program planners craft a strategy by which to discover the precise needs of a targeted group. The group may consist of the entire organization, one job category, one department or function, or an individual. Alternatively, the group may consist of participants who are to attend conferences, continuing education programs, or educational institutions. During assessment the focus is on clarifying what needs should be met through instruction. Program planners work closely with client representatives—perhaps in an advisory council or project team that encourages participation—to clarify the educational or work requirements to be met by a program.

The third step is *feedback, clarification, and priority-setting.* At this point program planners provide feedback to participants about differences of opinion on goals and objectives. In this way, problems or needs are brought clearly into focus through a collaborative process, which lays the foundation for establishing project priorities.

The fourth step is *action planning.* Although program planners usually take the lead to develop a project proposal to achieve the goals desired by program participants, the proposal is revised after careful review by the participants. Most proposals cover at least the issues listed in Table 3.1. Proposals can, of course, be used in approaches other than the collaborative. What is noteworthy is that in the collaborative approach participants have an equal say in setting directions and in planning for action.

The fifth step is *implementation.* Program planners implement the proposal in partnership with the client. In other words, they carry out the action plan. Members of affected groups should be clear about the desired goals to be achieved, the steps required to achieve them, the outcomes expected, and the *project deliverables* (final products or outcomes) desired.

The sixth and final step is *evaluation and continuous improvement.* Program planners and stakeholders assess how well the program solved the performance problems it was intended to solve or met the learning needs it was intended to meet.

The key to the collaborative approach is, of course, collaboration. Program planners, decision makers, participants, and other stakeholders work closely as partners throughout the project. Ownership is broadly shared. However, achieving project results through a collaborative approach is usually more time-consuming than a directive approach. The reason is that as more people are involved in decision making the time required increases.

A simple example should illustrate the collaborative approach in action. A large public utility was about to install team-based management, and an external consultant was brought in to help. She began by providing basic awareness instruction to inform managers, supervisors, and employees about teams. She also took groups from the organization to other public utilities to see firsthand how they had installed teams, what training they gave team members, and how they were using teams. Once that phase was concluded, she solicited information from managers, supervisors, and employees about problems confronting the organization. She analyzed that information and provided a summary to those who had sup-

TABLE 3.1. ISSUES TO BE COVERED IN PROJECT PROPOSALS.

Issue	Questions to Be Answered by Proposal
Statement of the problem, need, issue, or goal	What prompted the project?
Background (if appropriate)	What is known about the problem, need, issue, or goal at the outset?
	What is known about the client?
Statement of the proposed solution	What actions should be taken to solve the problem, meet the need, address the issue, or achieve the goal?
Action plan	What steps (tasks) should be taken to solve the problem, meet the need, address the issue, or achieve the goal?
Time line	When should the steps (tasks) be carried out?
	What are the project milestones (interim points marking achievements)?
	What are the project deadlines (final points to deliver final project deliverables)?
Budget	What resources, financial and otherwise, are necessary to carry out the project?
	When will the resources be needed?
Project staffing	Who will oversee the project on a policy level?
	Who will oversee each task in the project?
	What are the qualifications of the project staff, and how well do they match project requirements?

plied the information. She then led managers, supervisors, and employees in a structured process to formulate the approach to team-based management that the organization could use to solve its business problems. The information gathered earlier became the basis for establishing team responsibilities and assessing needs for team training. In this way, the consultant, operating as a program planner, demonstrated a collaborative approach.

The Nondirective Approach

When using the nondirective approach, program planners serve as learning consultants, resource people, and enabling agents. They do not function directively or collaboratively. Instead, they help people to plan and manage their own learning projects and to design, deliver, and evaluate their own planned learning experiences.

In this approach, program planners focus their attention on helping decision makers, participants, and other stakeholders to carry out the program planning process on their own.

As in the directive and collaborative approaches, learning projects are divided into several key steps. The first step is *issue or problem clarification*. The organization, individual, or group experiences a performance problem or need. Program planners may help them clarify what the problem or need is and what action should be taken to address it. Participants and other stakeholders maintain control, however. They guide the project. Program planners may, if invited, facilitate discussions and small- or large-group decision making. If the participants and other stakeholders choose not to investigate an issue or problem, program planners help them debrief, reach closure, and turn to issues that are more deserving of attention and action.

The second step is *information sharing, needs assessment, and objective setting*. Program planners help participants and other stakeholders, as individuals or as team members, to investigate a problem, situation, learning need, or other issue. The learners then conduct their own self-directed search for information. If the learners are working in a team, this step culminates in a team-managed needs assessment and the articulation of clear objectives. If the learners are working individually, this step culminates in clear objectives for an individualized learning project. In contrast to their role in other approaches, program planners using the nondirective approach merely help learners to function cohesively and to crystallize their thinking, while the responsibility for program planning remains in the learners' hands.

The third step is *experimentation*. Learners select, develop, or select and modify their own materials consistent with the project's objectives. They then conduct their own formative evaluation, deliver the instruction (or pursue learning projects), and evaluate results. Program planners provide expert assistance on program design when their help is requested. For the most part, however, they simply help learners identify, organize, and carry out their tasks. Program planners thus function as developmental coaches for the learners or other stakeholders in the learning project.

The fourth and final step is *evaluation and continuous improvement*. If the learning project is carried out in a team, program planners collect information from individual team members about the experience. The planners provide the team members with developmental feedback about the team collectively and about team members' individual functioning on the team. That information is then used to improve future team-based program planning efforts. If the learning project is carried out individually, program planners debrief individual learners about the results of their learning.

Two simple examples may illustrate how this process works. In one case, top managers in a business setting decided that the company needed an orientation program for new employees. With the advice of a program planner brought in from a local community college, they formed a twelve-member team representing top, middle, and supervisory management and hourly workers. The program planner briefed the team on the LEPP model. Then, working with the program planner, who served as a team facilitator and coach, the team members assessed employee needs for an orientation program, prepared the instructional materials, rehearsed the presentation of the materials, delivered the orientation, and evaluated results. At the end of the project, the program planner debriefed the team members on what they had learned from the experience both collectively and individually. A new team was then formed to deliver the orientation program on a continuing basis. The program planner helped the new team members to understand their roles and improve their presentation skills. She did not, however, design or deliver instruction.

In another case, an employee was about to be transferred to another country. She did not know the culture or language. With the help of a program planner, the employee developed an organized plan to guide her preparations for the transfer and to clarify what she would need to learn. After meeting with the program planner, the employee implemented the learning plan. She read extensively about the culture, and spoke to others who had worked in the culture. She learned to converse in the language. By the conclusion of the learning project, she was as ready as she could possibly be for making the move.

Summary

This chapter defined *working effectively* to mean using time productively and coordinating projects successfully. *Time management* was defined as using time to achieve optimal results and to accomplish worthwhile tasks. *Project* was defined as a work assignment of limited duration. *Project planning* was defined as preparing for a work assignment of limited duration, and *project management* was defined as implementing the project plan and evaluating results.

The chapter pointed out that time management is important to program planners for many reasons. If time is not used effectively, work will not be completed. If the work remains undone, the program planner performs poorly.

The authors' 1995 surveys of continuing education professionals and HRD professionals revealed that continuing education professionals perceive themselves as devoting most of their time to monitoring programs in progress, selecting and hiring instructors, calculating break-even points for programs, arranging locations and facilities, formulating program budgets, evaluating instructors' performance, and promoting and advertising programs. HRD professionals, conversely, claim to be focusing more time on setting goals and objectives, evaluating designated learning procedures, arranging location and facilities, formulating instructional design, planning formative evaluation, planning summative evaluation, and conducting informal needs assessment.

Since most program planning work is conducted as project work, perhaps the best way to make more productive use of time is to improve project planning and project management. Examples of program planning projects include conducting needs assessments, designing courses or orchestrating other planned learning experiences, delivering instruction, facilitating learning, and evaluating results.

Three different approaches may be used to manage program planning projects. These approaches are based on the CBPP model. Hence, projects may be managed either directively, collaboratively, or nondirectively. Each approach, in turn, can be helpful in magnifying the roles of the program planner—the topic of the next chapter—by first helping to clarify the nature of that role in each project.

CHAPTER FOUR

MAGNIFYING THE ROLES
OF THE PROGRAM PLANNER

All organizations are under increasing pressure to do more with less. That pressure is manifested in work restructuring, downsizing, and a growing emphasis on achieving cost-effective results. It calls for creative responses by program planners, who are as vulnerable to this pressure as others yet are expected to achieve more results than they once did with larger staffs and more plentiful resources. Program planners may achieve extraordinary outputs from ordinary (or less than ordinary) inputs by magnifying their roles and thus optimizing the impact of program planning work.

Before program planners can magnify their impact, however, they must be clear about what they do—that is, they must be clear about their roles. *Roles*, of course, are the parts played by program planners as they carry out their work. Roles are not identical to job titles, work activities, or responsibilities; rather, they are how people carry out their activities.

What, then, are the roles of program planners? How can they magnify their impact to ensure that what they do has a lasting impact on such stakeholders as managers and employees in the organizations they serve? This chapter answers these important questions. The first part of the chapter reviews various ways to think of program planners' roles. The second part suggests strategies by which program planners can magnify their impact.

The Roles of Program Planners

How can the roles of program planners be conceptualized? One way is to view them against the backdrop of the lifelong education field in general; a second way is to consider them as they are affected by organizational placement; a third way is to consider them as they are described in various competency studies; and a fourth way is to review the roles that program planners themselves say they are enacting.

Program Planning Roles and the Lifelong Education Field

Over three decades ago, Houle (1970) analyzed the leadership structure of lifelong education. At the base of what he called the *pyramid of leadership* are volunteers who share their knowledge, skills, and values with others. They derive little or no personal financial benefit from what they do. They are driven by a deep sense of dedication and include association trainers and unpaid teachers who devote their time to training and educating others. For example, volunteers may provide instruction on first aid and drug abuse prevention; they may provide a range of services, such as literacy tutoring and instruction on organizational leadership. They work for a variety of organizations, including educational institutions, the Boy Scouts, the Girl Scouts, CARE, USAID, and the YMCA and YWCA. Occupying the middle of the adult education leadership pyramid are full-time administrators or instructors. Among the many duties they are assigned within their respective organizations is planning or delivering educational activities for other organizational members or for other adults who are served by their organization. Because often so much of their time and attention are devoted to noneducational activities, they seldom define their roles as relating to either training or education. Although some who occupy this middle level might begin to form an identity with lifelong education and engage in graduate studies in such diverse fields as instructional systems design, adult and continuing education, extension education, or distance education, most are content to supplement their on-the-job training with intensive, short-term training specifically aimed at responding to immediate programming needs.

At the top of the pyramid are the program planners who exert leadership. They work full-time on planning, implementing, and evaluating instructional activities. Similar to those who occupy the middle level of the pyramid, they are often prepared for their responsibilities through on-the-job experience in the field of professional expertise for which they are now serving as program planner, but they now regard themselves as lifelong educators by occupation. They have extended their loyalty beyond their specialized fields and aligned themselves with the broader field of lifelong education, training, and human performance enhancement. Despite their links with other fields, leaders at the apex of the pyramid have forged a professional identity oriented to lifelong education. While they may occupy different organizational positions, they usually maintain a central allegiance to lifelong education.

Houle (1972) convincingly showed that the placement of program planners on the lifelong education pyramid of leadership influences how they are oriented toward and developed for what they do. Volunteers are oriented to their roles in program planning by participating in conferences, seminars, short courses, or workshops. These short-term orientation programs are usually focused on the organizations in which the volunteers will work. Volunteers are qualified by hours of service or by completion of training. Certificates symbolize achievement.

Program planners positioned on the pyramid's second level are prepared by work experience and by short-term training activities that are more intensive than those conducted for volunteers at the first level. In contrast, program planners on the third level of the pyramid participate more often in advanced studies in lifelong education or such related fields as training and development, human resource development, human performance enhancement and improvement, or adult and continuing education. They hold specialized degrees in these fields. They also attend conferences, read journals, and network with peers who share their occupational orientation and professional interests.

Program Planning Roles and Placement in the Organizational Hierarchy

Houle's pyramid of leadership highlights the differential time commitments and professional development needs of human resource development and continuing education professionals. Those with primarily voluntary and part-time roles (those at the first two levels) might benefit greatly from participation in professional development activities, but such activities can be dispensed on an intensive and short-term basis. Those with full-time roles who define themselves in terms of their major training or education program planning role often need to engage in professional development activities as part of a career-long perspective toward lifelong education. While Houle's pyramid of leadership provides a useful way to understand differences in the status and preparation of program planners, it does not explain differences in their roles—that is, in how they carry out their activities. According to Knowles (1980), who was the first to posit this view, these differences may be determined by their placement in an organizational hierarchy.

(*Hierarchy* refers, of course, to the organization chart.) Traditionally, there have been three levels of program planning:

1. *Program planners-instructors* usually interact with learners face-to-face. Among the many duties of program planners functioning in this role are helping learners to diagnose learning needs, planning a sequence of experiences to produce desired results, creating motivating conditions to stimulate learners, selecting the most effective instructional or developmental methods and techniques and providing the resources necessary to produce desired learning, and helping learners to measure their learning outcomes.

2. *Program directors* serve as committee directors, training directors, evening school directors, university extension deans, and other administrators. Among their many functions, they supervise assessments of individual, institutional, and societal needs for adult learning in organizational settings; create organizational units to carry out educational programs; formulate objectives to meet identified needs; design objectives intended to meet the needs; and institute and supervise procedures required for effective program operations, such as recruiting and training leaders and teachers, managing facilities and administrative processes, recruiting students, financing program initiatives, and assessing program effectiveness.

3. *Program leaders and visionaries* center their careers in lifelong education. They establish strategic plans for human resource development or continuing education efforts, develop new knowledge, prepare instructional materials, invent new techniques, provide leadership to others in the field, train and mentor less experienced colleagues, and promote the fields of program planning and lifelong education.

Program Planning Roles and Competency Studies

Many studies have been conducted to assess the roles and competencies of program planners who function as human resource development specialists in business and industry. These studies can be immensely helpful to those aspiring to enter the program planning field and to experienced program planners seeking professional development, because they provide information about what program planners do—or should do. Examples of such competency studies include the work of Leonard Nadler (1962), the U.S. Civil Service Commission (1976), the Ontario Society for Training and Development (1976; Dixon, Conway, Ashley, and Stewart, 1995), the American Society for Training and Development (Pinto and Walker, 1978; McLagan and McCullough, 1983; McLagan, 1989), and the International Board of Standards for Training, Performance and Instruction (Foshay, Silber, and Westgaard, 1986; Hale, 1989; Stein and Hutchison, 1988). *Role* in this context means "a common grouping of competencies" (McLagan,

1989, p. 77), and *competency* means "an area of knowledge or skill that is critical for producing key outputs. Competencies are internal capabilities that people bring to their jobs; capabilities which may be expressed in a broad, even infinite array of on-the-job behaviors" (McLagan, 1989, p. 77).

Nadler conducted groundbreaking work about the competencies of training directors in his doctoral dissertation (1962). He found that training directors enact three roles: learning specialist, administrator, and consultant. Learning specialists design and deliver instruction, administrators oversee the training function, and consultants assist line managers, learners, and others to identify training needs and evaluate program results. Nadler's study has profound implications for program planners; like trainers, program planners often serve as consultants, learning specialists, and administrators.

The American Society for Training and Development has commissioned four competency studies of training and development professionals since 1978. The results of the most recent of these studies has just been published (Rothwell, 1996a). One of the best known of the studies is *Models for HRD Practice* (McLagan, 1989). A team led by Patricia McLagan conducted several rounds of questionnaires with more than eight hundred human resource development (HRD) experts. The study identified eleven HRD roles, thirty-five competencies, and seventy-four work outputs.

McLagan's eleven roles for HRD professionals encompass myriad responsibilities (McLagan, 1989, p. 49):

1. *Researcher:* identifies, develops, or tests "new information (theory, research, concepts, technology, models, hardware and so on) and translat[es] the information into implications for improved individual or organizational performance"
2. *Marketer:* markets and contracts "for HRD viewpoints, programs, and services"
3. *Organization Change Agent:* influences and supports "changes in organization behavior"
4. *Needs Analyst:* identifies "ideal and actual performance and performance conditions and determin[es] causes of discrepancies"
5. *Program Designer:* "prepar[es] objectives, defin[es] content, and select[s] and sequenc[es] activities for a specific intervention"
6. *HRD Materials Developer:* produces "written or electronically mediated instructional materials"
7. *Instructor/Facilitator:* "present[s] information, direct[s] structured learning experiences, and manag[es] group discussion and group process"
8. *Individual Career Development Adviser:* helps "individuals to assess personal competencies, values, and goals and to identify, plan, and implement development and career actions"

9. *Administrator:* "provides coordination and support services for the delivery of HRD programs and services"
10. *Evaluator:* identifies "the impact of an intervention on individual or organizational effectiveness"
11. *HRD Manager:* "support[s] and lead[s] a group's work and link[s] that work with the total organization"

The value of McLagan's study, which is soon due to be updated, is that it provides a comprehensive reference point for program planners. It describes in detail the many roles they may play and the competencies they need to function effectively in their roles. Widely accepted and used, the study provides a menu of choices from which aspiring practitioners may select career options for future preparation, and from which experienced practitioners may select new roles or competencies for future development.

In 1986, the first of three related competency studies was published by the International Board of Standards for Training, Performance and Instruction (IBSTPI). All three studies are important for program planners because they are detailed examinations of what instructional designers, instructors, and program administrators should do. The first study, titled *Instructional Design Competencies: The Standards* (Foshay, Silber, and Westgaard, 1986) and based on the work of an expert panel, revealed that instructional designers should distinguish projects that warrant training from those that warrant alternative interventions; assess instructional needs; identify learners' characteristics relevant to the desired outcomes of instruction; analyze the work setting in which learners will apply what they learn; conduct detailed and specific analysis of the job, task, or subject matter for which learners are being trained; prepare performance objectives; establish measurements to assess instructional results; sequence the performance objectives; identify appropriate instructional strategies; design instructional materials; evaluate training; design a system by which to administer training or instruction; plan and monitor instructional projects; communicate effectively; work effectively with others; and promote the use of instructional design. These steps are useful because they clarify what entry-level program planners should be able to do in most jobs as trainers.

A second IBSTPI study focused on the instructor's role. According to *Instructor Competencies* (Stein and Hutchison, 1988), instructors should analyze course materials and learner information, prepare the instructional site so that it will be conducive to learning, establish and maintain credibility, manage the learning environment to ensure psychological and physical support for learners, use communication skills effectively, present information effectively, question learners appropriately, provide learners with clarification or feedback as needed, reinforce and motivate learners, apply instructional methods appropriately, use media effectively, assess learner performance, evaluate instructional delivery, and report evaluation information.

The third study sponsored by IBSTPI is titled *Training Manager Competencies: The Standards* (Hale, 1989). According to that study, training managers should assess organizational, departmental, and program needs; develop plans for the department and programs; link human performance to the effectiveness of the enterprise; apply instructional design and development principles; assure the application of effective training principles; evaluate the instructional design, development, and delivery function; apply the principles of performance management to the manager's own staff; think critically when making decisions and solving problems; assure that actions are consistent with goals and objectives; adapt strategies and solutions in response to change; produce effective and efficient solutions; develop and sustain social relationships; provide leadership; use effective interpersonal communication techniques; and communicate effectively orally and in writing. Most competencies described by this study are directly applicable to the work of experienced program planners in business and educational settings. Of course, some program planners will specialize in only one role or in activities taken from several roles.

The most important recent competency study in the training and development field that is of interest to program planners was published by the Ontario Society for Training and Development (OSTD) (Dixon, Conway, Ashley, and Stewart, 1995). A team led by Valerie Dixon pinpointed five key competency categories. According to the study, training and development professionals should (1) analyze performance needs, (2) design training, (3) instruct/facilitate, (4) evaluate training, and (5) coach the application of training. The researchers further divided each category into thirty-one core competencies. Of note for program planners is the study's emphasis on the importance of ensuring that participants should be held accountable for on-the-job application of what they have learned in training.

Program Planning Roles and Research on Self-Reports

In the authors' 1995 surveys of continuing education directors and HRD professionals, respondents were asked to rate seventeen possible roles for their relative importance to success in their current positions. The roles are listed in Table 4.1, and summaries of the responses are depicted in Figures 4.1 and 4.2.

As the figures show, academically based continuing education professionals ranked their most important roles as manager, promoter, advocate, and professional practitioner, and HRD professionals ranked their most important roles as professional practitioner, trainer, learning specialist, and instructor. Though the

TABLE 4.1. POSSIBLE ROLES OF CONTINUING EDUCATION PROFESSIONALS AND HRD PROFESSIONALS.

Role	Description
Manager	Oversees program planning activities
Promoter	Communicates and markets program planning efforts
Advocate	Champions learning activities in organizations
Professional Practitioner	Focuses on program planning as an occupation or discipline
Consultant	Provides assistance to others in planning, conducting, or evaluating their own planned learning experiences
Spokesperson	Serves as advocate to such stakeholders of planned learning experiences as managers and employees
Negotiator	Finds common ground on which to base program planning efforts
Group Facilitator	Helps groups discover their own ideas
Recruiter	Secures participation in planned learning
OD Specialist	Helps groups to work together more effectively
Coach	Provides support and reinforcement to learners
Arbitrator	Works out conflicts
Instructional Designer	Plans instruction for learners and/or instructors
Learning Specialist	Applies what is known about individual and adult learning to planned learning experiences
Trainer	Helps individuals to achieve competence in the context of their present job or work requirements
Apologist	Serves as spokesperson for others to explain and provide the rationale for what they do
Instructor	Delivers instruction

Source: Cookson and Rothwell, 1995. All rights reserved.

two groups differed slightly in their perspectives about the relative importance of the roles, both groups ranked "apologist" very low and "professional" very high. The importance associated with these roles corresponds approximately to the respondents' perceived importance of activities in the Lifelong Education Program Planning (LEPP) model (see Figures 4.3 and 4.4). The ranking of the program planning roles by continuing education and human resource development professionals provides insight into the nature of education and training program planning. Additional insights are provided by respondents' ratings of the specific activities in which they engage in fulfilling their roles (see Figures 4.3 and 4.4). (Use Appendix One to conduct a self-assessment, if you wish, on competencies in the LEPP model.)

FIGURE 4.1. IMPORTANCE OF PROGRAM PLANNING ROLES AS PERCEIVED BY CONTINUING EDUCATION PROFESSIONALS.

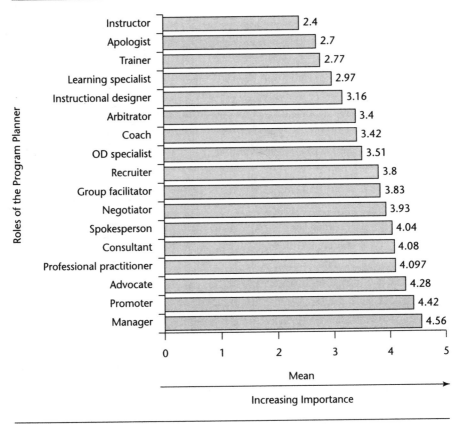

Strategies for Magnifying the Impact of Program Planners

How can program planners magnify their impact at a time when many organizations are restructuring and outsourcing many educational and training activities? The answer to this question is the critical issue of the hour for many program planners—particularly those who function in downsized organizations in which too few people chase too many projects and needs. Of course, magnifying their roles in order to maximize their impact means achieving extraordinary outputs from ordinary (or below ordinary) inputs. It may mean finding ways to work both smarter and harder than before.

FIGURE 4.2. IMPORTANCE OF PROGRAM PLANNING ROLES AS PERCEIVED BY HRD PROFESSIONALS.

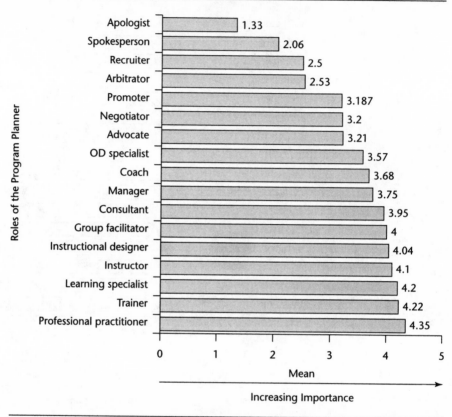

There are several ways in which program planners can magnify their impact. They can (1) increase the number of volunteers who occupy the base of the pyramid of leadership; (2) increase outsourced activities; (3) empower and train learners to identify and carry out their own learning projects by creating so-called learning organizations in which work environments support individual, team, group, and organizational development; or (4) make greater use of technology to provide assistance in program planning.

1. *Increasing the number of volunteers.* This is essentially a collaborative approach. Program planners identify a cadre of individuals who have the interest, ability, and willingness to serve as mentors, sponsors, and helpers to others. That cadre is then trained in program planning and empowered to carry it out on their own.

FIGURE 4.3. IMPORTANCE OF VARIOUS STEPS IN PROGRAM PLANNING FOR CONTINUING EDUCATION PROFESSIONALS.

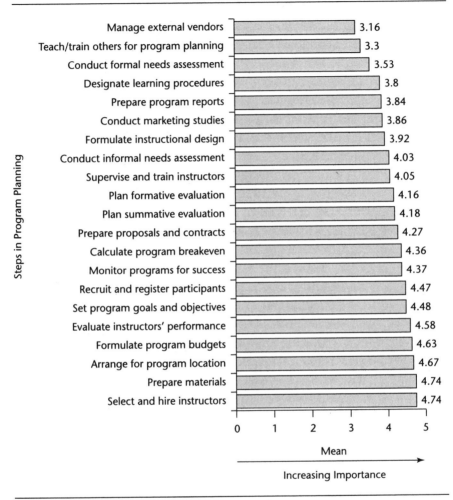

Steps in Program Planning (y-axis)

Step	Mean
Manage external vendors	3.16
Teach/train others for program planning	3.3
Conduct formal needs assessment	3.53
Designate learning procedures	3.8
Prepare program reports	3.84
Conduct marketing studies	3.86
Formulate instructional design	3.92
Conduct informal needs assessment	4.03
Supervise and train instructors	4.05
Plan formative evaluation	4.16
Plan summative evaluation	4.18
Prepare proposals and contracts	4.27
Calculate program breakeven	4.36
Monitor programs for success	4.37
Recruit and register participants	4.47
Set program goals and objectives	4.48
Evaluate instructors' performance	4.58
Formulate program budgets	4.63
Arrange for program location	4.67
Prepare materials	4.74
Select and hire instructors	4.74

Mean

Increasing Importance

One multinational corporation, for example, has trained a group of what they call "black belt quality experts" who train others in the organization on the principles of quality.

Educational institutions are also relying on more part-time instructors and adjunct faculty for continuing education efforts. The work of full-time program planners is being augmented by volunteers and part-time staff members, both in academic continuing education units and in the largest adult education provider in the United States, the U.S. Department of Agriculture's Cooperative Extension

FIGURE 4.4. IMPORTANCE OF VARIOUS STEPS IN PROGRAM PLANNING FOR HRD PROFESSIONALS.

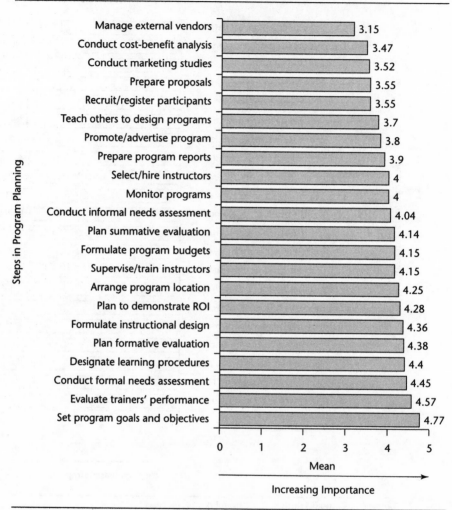

Service. One reason is that relying on part-time staff reduces employee benefit costs. Another reason is that it allows educational institutions to draw on experienced and high-priced talent that may not be immediately available to them from traditional sources—such as the institutions they serve.

2. *Increasing outsourced activities.* Training departments are increasing their reliance on outsourcing by using part-time staff from both inside and outside their organizations and by relying more on external vendors to meet the organization's training needs. Some organizations have gone as far as to outsource the entire training department and rely exclusively on one or more external vendors to design and deliver training and development. Some organizations require that vendors supply training during the process of procuring equipment and services; in other cases they strike up strategic partnerships with academic institutions to establish on-site learning centers.

Key advantages of outsourcing include reduced salary and employee benefit costs to the organization and increased credibility for the external experts. However, external vendors are disadvantageous in that they (1) are unfamiliar with the corporate culture, (2) are usually not held accountable over the long term for the results or effects of their efforts, and (3) can be more expensive to use for prolonged periods than full-time staff.

3. *Empowering and training learners to identify and carry out their own learning projects.* This is a nondirective strategy. Program planners equip the learners to assess their own instructional needs, design and develop their own instruction, deliver (or seek out) their own instruction, and evaluate results (Rothwell, 1996d). It has been shown that adult learners undertake numerous independent learning projects each year to cope with life- or work-related problems (Tough, 1979). This strategy takes maximum advantage of such self-directedness while providing learners with means to improve their ability to identify and meet their learning needs in the future. It also helps transform the work setting into a learning organization (Senge, 1990).

4. *Making use of technology.* Using technology means tapping the power of computers and distance education methods to provide learners with real-time instruction. Instead of relying on traditional group learning experiences such as classroom instruction, program planners rely on technology to offer individualized instruction on demand to learners as they have time available to participate. Examples of such technology may include computer-based or computer-assisted instruction, audio teleconferencing, video teleconferencing, and audiographics. While technology is no panacea, it can magnify the impact of program planning while taking advantage of economies of scale.

Summary

The first part of this chapter reviewed various ways to think of program planners' roles. As noted, *roles* are the parts played by program planners as they carry out their work. Ways to view roles are (1) against the backdrop of the lifelong education field in general, (2) as they are affected by organizational placement, (3) as they are described in various competency studies, and (4) as program planners themselves say they are enacting them.

The second part of the chapter suggested strategies by which program planners can magnify the impact of their role performance. Four strategies were offered: (1) increasing the number of volunteers, (2) increasing outsourced activities, (3) empowering learners to identify and carry out their own learning projects, and (4) using technology to provide assistance in program planning.

Defining the role of the program planner is important because it clarifies what program planners should be held accountable for doing. But roles constitute only part of accountability. Another issue to be considered is the working philosophy of program planning adopted by each planner. That is the topic of the next chapter.

CHAPTER FIVE

ARTICULATING A WORKING PHILOSOPHY OF PROGRAM PLANNING

The story was told of a renowned French author who was passing a construction site when he spotted three workers. He stopped to ask them what they were doing. The first responded, "I'm earning my pay." The second retorted, "I'm laying bricks." The third paused a moment, raised his gaze, and then said majestically, "I am building a cathedral."

On the surface the workers were engaged in the same activity. However, one possessed a keen vision to see beyond immediate tasks to final results. That vision gave him a profound sense of purpose.

By applying the Lifelong Education Program Planning (LEPP) model, program planners will build successful programs. In doing so, they will complete immediate tasks. But to be successful professionally, program planners should reflect on the deeper meaning of what they do, much like the last worker in the anecdote. In that way they can expect to find a sense of self-direction that will help them both to solve everyday problems and to forge a professional identity.

This three-part chapter presents an opportunity to look beyond the immediate. The first part defines the term *working philosophy* and reviews six functions of such a philosophy; the second part helps program planners to develop a working philosophy; and the third part offers two examples of working philosophies.

What Is a Working Philosophy?

Few program planners have articulated their philosophies of education or training. None, however, can escape from acting in line with a philosophical orientation. Everyone possesses a philosophy that guides what they do and how they do it; few have reflected on their philosophy. But what is a *working philosophy* of program planning? And what functions are served by such a philosophy?

Jerold Apps (1973) defined *working philosophy* as a system of beliefs about key issues in program planning and lifelong education. A working philosophy provides program planners with a foundation of principles upon which they can establish goals, identify criteria for excellence, and make decisions. It reflects and is nourished by an individual's general philosophy of life.

A working philosophy enables people to answer three important questions: (1) What is real? (2) How do we know? and (3) What is right? The first question helps people to articulate what they accept as a truthful representation of reality; the second question helps people clarify the underlying basis for their beliefs; and the third question enables a moral compass to point the way to right and wrong.

Although they may not be aware of their working philosophies, program planners never cease to live by them. Although particular beliefs seldom change, the working philosophy as a whole is always evolving. It is continually updated based on new knowledge and experience.

It is our assumption that program planners who engage in this step of formulating and articulating a working philosophy of lifelong education are, thus, better equipped to draw on their own epistemological resources in the critical analysis of their own education and training work. Those who do not engage in such questioning unwittingly leave it to their supervisors and others to define the essential ethical and moral dimensions of their work.

A working philosophy serves six important functions for program planners (Apps, 1973):

1. *It helps them to consider three kinds of questions when making decisions about future programming: what is questions, why questions, and what should be questions. What is* and *why* questions are posed to evaluate current programs. To answer these questions, program planners may turn to the scientific method. But that method can never answer *what should be* questions. The reason: such questions call for an examination of program purposes, learning needs and priorities, and appropriate methods and techniques. They are driven more by assumptions and beliefs than by facts. A working philosophy helps program planners to formulate, identify, and critically examine these assumptions and beliefs.

2. *It provides an independent sense of direction.* Program planners who have never reflected on the values that underlie their decisions and actions are susceptible to following others uncritically. In contrast, those who know what they believe can compare their beliefs to the views of their employer and, when discrepancies exist, can know when it is appropriate to assume leadership and make efforts to influence their employer.

3. *It provides a basis for examining relationships among educational problems.* Program planners who lack a working philosophy will view each problem in isolation. They will be unable to see how the solution to one problem may affect other problems and other solutions in a complex web of interrelationships. A working philosophy provides the basis for seeing interrelationships by providing a central reference point.

4. *It helps program planners to see how their role helps meet the needs of their sponsoring organization or of society in general.* In too many cases program planners are relegated to a marginal role, one not central to the mission of their employer's organization. For instance, top managers in businesses may regard the training department as dispensable, just as administrators in some academic institutions may regard the continuing education function as less important than the teaching function of the academic departments. Program planners are thus perceived by some to offer services that are less valuable than the services offered by others. As a consequence of being acculturated in settings in which they occupy a secondary status, they may see themselves as marginal functionaries. But if they have formed a working philosophy, they know how effective programs can help achieve important organizational or societal objectives. They can then exert positive influence on others to help realize those objectives.

5. *It provides program planners with clues for answering many basic, meaningful questions,* such as

- What is reality?
- How do we know what is real?
- What is of value in society (or in my organization)?
- What is the nature of humankind?
- How is knowledge acquired?
- What is education?
- What is the purpose of education?
- What are lifelong education and program planning?
- What are the purposes of lifelong education and program planning?
- What are the roles of lifelong education and program planning in society or in a sponsoring organization?

6. *It provides a deeper meaning to life.* As program planners look beyond the super-ficial realities that surround program planning activities, they will form behavior patterns that extend to other aspects of their lives. They will no longer be content to live passively, as *objects,* according to the definitions and dictates of others. They will instead become *subjects,* who possess their own definitions and agenda. When it provides the motivation to edify, improve, and serve, a working philosophy enriches the quality of life for program planners, those they serve, and others who interact with them.

Recently Apps (1994) has linked the notion of a working philosophy with ideas on leadership to develop a different approach to practice in adult and continuing education. As leaders in adult and continuing education, program planners can remain open and responsive to change through a new approach to leadership that is all-embracing of ideas and people and that capitalizes on diversity.

Developing a Working Philosophy

To develop a working philosophy, program planners should clarify what they believe and why they believe it. At least five philosophical orientations have been proposed to structure such a working philosophy (Elias and Merriam, 1994): (1) liberal adult education, (2) behaviorist education, (3) progressive adult educa-tion, (4) humanistic education, and (5) radical education. Each of these philo-sophical orientations has influenced program planning. The following paragraphs discuss how these orientations respond to four key questions that should be addressed by a working philosophy (Elias and Merriam, 1994).

1. *What is the overall purpose of lifelong education and program planning?* In short, why is program planning worth doing?
Liberal educators answer that question by focusing on developing the intellec-tual powers of the mind. Program planners who adopt this view seek to make peo-ple *literate* in its broadest sense. In short, they cultivate the intellectual, moral, spiritual, and aesthetic development of program participants.
Behaviorist educators seek to change behavior in ways that will ensure the sur-vival of humanity. Program planners who adopt this view promote behavioral change. They want to affect what people do.
Progressive educators believe that lifelong education and program planning exist to transmit culture and structure, to promote social change, and to supply pro-gram participants with the practical knowledge and problem-solving skills they need. For program planners who adopt this view, training or continuing educa-

tion serves the important purpose of passing down the accumulated wisdom of institutional learning. They seek to reproduce and consolidate rather than radically change corporate or social culture.

Humanistic educators see their purpose as enhancing personal growth and development. Program planners who adopt this view seek individual more than organizational or social empowerment. For these planners, change occurs through individuals more than through institutions or organizations.

Finally, *radical educators* see themselves engaged in a form of guerrilla warfare. Program planners influenced by radical education seek social, political, and economic change in society or in their organization. Lifelong education becomes part of a campaign to install an agenda of change. Toward that end, program planners identify the ideology of an organization or institution, surface facts that differ from the ideology, and use these discrepancies between what is espoused and what is happening to create an impetus for radical change. Programs are merely the means to an end—that is, to radical change for the better.

2. *Who should be the learners?* In the view of *liberal educators,* the learner is a "Renaissance person." Program planners influenced by the philosophy of liberal education believe in encouraging continuous learning. Their aim is to encourage learners to acquire knowledge rather than mere information.

Behaviorist educators see the learner as assuming an active role in the learning process. Program planners influenced by the philosophy of behaviorist education want learners to practice new behaviors and receive feedback on them. They believe that learners are strongly influenced by the environment in which they live and work. If the environment is changed, behaviorists reason, the learners will also be changed.

Progressive educators focus on learner needs, interests, and experiences. Program planners influenced by the philosophy of progressive education regard participants as capable of unlimited development. The role of the learner is to pursue that development.

Humanistic educators believe that learners are, and should be, highly motivated. They believe that learners are self-directed in their outlook and seek to assume responsibility for their own learning. The role of program planners is to encourage that self-direction.

Radical educators see learners and instructors as equal agents in the learning process. There is no status difference between teachers and trainers and those they teach or train. Program planners influenced by the philosophy of radical education direct their attention to learner autonomy. They believe that individuals create history, and change organizational culture, by combining reflection and action.

3. *What should be the role of the program planner?* As Elias and Merriam (1994) point out, the five philosophical orientations differ dramatically in how they answer this question. *Liberal educators* see program planners as experts, as emitters of knowledge; they are authoritative and clearly direct the learning process. *Behaviorists* see program planners as managers and controllers; they predict and direct the learning process by manipulating the environment to create conditions conducive to learning. *Progressive educators* regard program planners as organizers who guide learning; they serve to stimulate learners and to instigate or evaluate the learning process. Because *humanistic educators* regard learners as self-directed, they focus on program planners as facilitators, helpers, companions, and colleagues; they promote but do not direct learning. Finally, *radical educators* see program planners as revolutionaries who suggest but do not direct learning goals. They seek to enhance equality between learners and teachers, trainers, or facilitators. They want to cause change, but they want to do it on the learners' terms.

4. *What key concepts characterize the working philosophy?* Key concepts are central ideas or tenets. Each philosophical framework has its own.

Central to the philosophy of *liberal education* is the fervent belief in learning for its own sake, as a means to its own end. Program planners influenced by this philosophy passionately advocate general education, traditional knowledge, and humanism. In corporate training departments, such planners are "people advocates" who champion the cause of training as a desirable goal in its own right.

Central to the philosophy of *behaviorist education* is competency-based instruction. Program planners influenced by this philosophy clarify outcomes before they undertake the means to achieve them, so they place instructional objectives front and center. They believe in skill training, feedback, and learner reinforcement. Widely influential in corporate training, such planners have won the argument that trainers should always know what results they seek before they undertake anything.

Central to the philosophy of *progressive education* is problem solving, needs assessment, and social responsibility in all its forms. In corporate training, program planners influenced by this philosophy have won the argument that learners should be equipped with the ability to troubleshoot and solve their own problems. They have also been widely influential in making training a means of changing behavior, as indicated by the broad acceptance of programs on diversity, social responsibility, ethics, and avoidance of sexual harassment.

Central to the philosophy of *humanistic education* is learning by experience. Program planners who adopt this view advocate experiential learning. They see many learning experiences occurring in groups or teams, so they foster group learning tasks and group discussions. They favor discovery learning. They have won the argument that corporate trainers should use experiential activities to promote and encourage planned learning.

Central to the philosophy of *radical education* are critical thinking and social action. Program planners influenced by this philosophy favor dialogues, problem posing, and group discussions. By making programs tools for social improvement, radical educators have been broadly influential in transforming training from a tool for worker exploitation (to wring more work out of underpaid labor) to a tool for worker empowerment (to give workers a voice in decisions).

Each of the key questions is central to developing a working philosophy of program planning, while each of the philosophical orientations offers a distinctive view of what program planning is, what program planners should seek to achieve, and why it is worth doing. Program planners are well-advised to reflect on their own views of the four key questions. Answering them is more than an intellectual exercise. Each answer provides an important anchor against the winds of change and the tides of the latest fads. Of course, other questions are also worth considering. Among them are

- What should be the roles of program planners?
- What should be the primary goals and objectives of lifelong education and program planning?
- Who should be regarded as the primary "customers" of program planning? Why?
- Who should be regarded as "participants" and "stakeholders" of program planning? Why?
- What should be the relationship among learners, other stakeholders, and program planners?
- What unique characteristics of adults as learners should be addressed in lifelong education programs?
- Who should be the chief beneficiaries of program planning efforts?
- How much should programs be expected to help individuals advance in their careers? Assume more responsibility in their current work? Meet requirements for occupational or professional entry? Help individuals keep their skills current at a time of continuing change?
- How should participants benefit from program participation? What rewards are realistic and desirable?
- How can program benefits be measured, and how should they be measured?
- What are the most desirable ways to motivate people to learn? How much responsibility does the program planner bear to motivate others to learn?

- What should be the sources of the content?
- How should the learning process be supported? Conducted?
- How should learners learn?
- What should be the role and responsibilities of learners in the learning process? Why do program planners believe so?
- What are the appropriate occasions to use directive, collaborative, and non-directive approaches?
- How should program planning contribute to meeting an organization's strategic objectives? Individual career objectives?

Program planners should reflect on each of these questions as they formulate and articulate their working philosophy of program planning.

Two Examples of Working Philosophies

The first of the following two examples of working philosophies represents the view of a corporate trainer. The second represents the view of a continuing education professional in an academic institution.

A Trainer's Working Philosophy

I believe that the purpose of program planning is to help the business meet its needs. If I can accomplish that, I can help the business stay solvent, thrive amid chaotic conditions, and provide jobs to people who need them to raise their families. I regard that as an important mission, since I think that most people are heavily invested—personally and professionally—in their jobs. If I can help them do their jobs better, then I think everyone benefits from that.

I believe the learners are "employees"—broadly defined. That includes top executives, middle managers, supervisors, hourly workers, salespersons, clerical workers, and the others in our organization. While I admit that customers, suppliers, and distributors are possible "learners," I do not concentrate my efforts on them. I figure that employees can do that if they know what they are doing. Training can help them know what they are doing—and more important, why they are doing what they are doing.

My role is to orchestrate planned learning experiences. My role is not to do the learning for people, entertain them, discipline them, provide them with time off the job with pay, or any one of a thousand other roles that some people would like to give me. I do not believe that my work is so complicated that it should be regarded as mysterious. Program planning is not rocket science. Learners, properly instructed and given the right tools, are quite able to carry it out on their own. Unfortunately, I am not convinced that people are just naturally able to function as self-directed learners. I think they need some help—facilitation, if you want to call it that—to function in that way.

Most important, I do not regard my "customers" as identical to the learners. I think that the organization, broadly viewed, is my true customer. I serve that customer. While I could look at my role in other ways, I work most closely with operating managers to help them equip their employees with what they need to know and do to function competently, even expertly, in their jobs.

A Continuing Education Professional's Working Philosophy

I would like to tell you that the purpose of program planning is to meet noble ends, to benefit society, or to enrich the lives of people. While I think it has the potential to do that, I do not regard those noble ends as the key purpose of the continuing education unit at this institution. Rather, I see my purpose as drumming up cash for a resource-strapped institution that seems to have been forgotten by its governmental sponsors. While that purpose is not noble, it is useful—and leads to the continued existence of an institution that has positively influenced the lives of many people.

I believe the learners are citizens of the community college district. That includes everybody. That means employers, employees, housewives, graduating seniors, dislocated workers, and many others. For the most part, however, I concentrate my attention on learners who have the money to afford the continuing education activities offered by this institution.

My role is to serve as broker of education. I listen to what employers or individuals need and why they need it. I then try to craft a proposal to meet their needs, drawing on the resources of the community college which I serve. My role is not primarily to do company-specific training, though I have provided such oversight in the past. Nor is my role to help people keep their skills current, though I have also provided help to do that. No. My role is to serve as educational services broker, pure and simple.

But I regard that as an important role. I have sometimes said that everybody thinks he or she is an expert on continuing education, just as many people regard themselves as experts on public education. But too often they throw continuing education at a problem that cannot be solved by it. They should pay more attention to what they need, not what they want.

I believe that most adult learners are canny people who try to get the most for their money. They want something immediately useful on their jobs. Increasingly they also want something that can help them remain marketable at a time when jobs are less secure than they once were.

Most important, I focus on maintaining positive, long-term relationships with my clients, whoever they may be. I will do almost anything to maintain that positive relationship. I enjoy what I do, and I feel it is as useful to this institution as any academic department. I am proud to say that due to the efforts of continuing education, many academic departments that do not break even can do so thanks to the considerable outside revenues we generate.

Summary

This chapter defined the term *working philosophy*, reviewed six functions of such a philosophy, discussed how program planners can develop a working philosophy, and provided two examples of working philosophies.

Working philosophy was defined as a system of beliefs about key issues in program planning and lifelong education, as providing program planners with a foundation of principles upon which they can establish goals, identify criteria for excellence, and make decisions. Six important functions of a working philosophy were discussed: (1) it helps to consider *what is* questions, *why* questions, and *what should be* questions; (2) it provides an independent sense of direction; (3) it provides a basis for examining relationships among educational problems; (4) it helps program planners to see how their role helps meet the needs of their sponsoring organization or society in general; (5) it provides program planners with clues to answer many basic, meaningful questions; and (6) it provides a deeper meaning to life.

To develop a working philosophy, program planners should clarify what they believe and why they believe it. The views of five philosophical orientations— liberal adult education, behaviorist education, progressive adult education, humanistic education, and radical education—were discussed in regard to four key questions: (1) What is the purpose of lifelong education and program planning? (2) Who are the learners? (3) What should be the role of the program planners? and (4) What key concepts characterize the working philosophy?

A working philosophy provides a foundation for professional development on which program planners can build. It is the starting point as well for ethical and moral action. Thus, it is fitting that the next chapter focuses on ethical issues in program planning.

CHAPTER SIX

ENACTING A SENSE OF ETHICAL RESPONSIBILITY

Like all professional people, program planners occasionally confront ethical dilemmas. Since ethics has emerged as a key issue in the 1990s, it warrants attention in this book. Furthermore, ethical issues logically follow the expression of a working philosophy of program planning. After all, program planners can often resolve the ethical dilemmas they confront by heeding their working philosophies.

The importance of ethics has been keenly felt in business. Sobering information about managerial ethics was revealed in a study of undergraduate business majors at a large U.S. university. Eighty-eight percent of the student respondents to a survey indicated that they expected to experience ethical pressures in their future careers (Longnecker, McKinney, and Moore, 1989). That is not surprising. More surprising is that 50 percent indicated they would succumb to those pressures. In another study, 76 percent of undergraduate business major respondents to a survey admitted cheating on one or more tests ("Business Students," 1991). That does not bode well for ethical practice in future business organizations. Unfortunately, it is also consistent with reality: 66 percent of companies ranked by *Fortune* on its list of the largest industrial corporations were publicly cited in at least one ethical scandal between 1975 and 1985 (Rosenfeld, 1985).

The need to pay more attention to ethics has also been compellingly voiced in adult education. As Cervero and Wilson (1994, p. 137) write:

Planners are always faced with questions of what to do next and why. This calls for ethical thinking, by which we mean the capacity to think about questions of value, significance, and responsibility when deciding what action to take. We are not suggesting that an ethics of planning practice is necessary because it will produce the right course of action (usually referred to as "the ethical thing to do") to take in a particular situation, for rarely is this the case. Rather, ethics is needed in planning so that planners have a sense of "what for" and not just "how to."

But what are ethics? What common ethical dilemmas confront program planners? How should they resolve those dilemmas? This chapter addresses these questions. It is also the last chapter in Part Two, and the final chapter focused on Quadrant 1 ("Exercising Professional Responsibility") of the Lifelong Education Program Planning (LEPP) model.

What Are Ethics?

Ethics are the moral code that establishes good and bad and that helps individuals, groups, and organizations distinguish right from wrong. *Ethical behavior* is behavior that is acceptable within a particular moral code. What is considered ethical behavior varies among cultures. *Ethical dilemmas* occur when individuals, groups, or organizations are confronted with temptations to depart from ethics—usually for personal or financial gain.

Over the years philosophers have provided at least four different ways to think about ethics. Each way can be helpful to those confronting ethical dilemmas. For lack of better labels we shall call them the utilitarian view, the individualistic view, the protectivist view, and the justice view.

• *The utilitarian view* focuses on the consequences of action. Its central question is *What behavior will lead to the greatest good for the greatest number?* When presented with a need to make a decision, a utilitarian would estimate how the results of each choice, when implemented, would affect other people. The choice leading to the most positive impact for the most people should be chosen.

For example, suppose the top administrators of a community college face the choice of keeping or dropping a job training program that loses money for the school but that everyone agrees succeeds in reducing unemployment in the community. A utilitarian would make the hard choice of keeping the program going despite its costs. After all, the community's good would outweigh the school's losses.

- *The individualistic view* focuses on the self-interest of a decision maker. Its central question is *What behavior will lead to realization of the greatest long-term self-interest for the decision maker?* The operative word here is *long-term.* Providing a client with a training course on Total Quality Management, for instance, may be a response to an immediate client request. But if the program planner has evidence that such a course is unnecessary—or even counterproductive to employee morale—then yielding to the client's short-term request ignores potentially harmful long-term consequences to the client's organization and to the program planner's self-interest. The action would therefore be avoided.

- *The protectivist view* focuses on fundamental human rights. Its central question is *What behavior will be most effective in upholding individual rights to life, liberty, fair treatment, freedom of speech, privacy, due process, freedom of conscience, and other basic rights?* When presented with an apparent ethical dilemma, the protectivist would examine the impact of each possibility on those affected by the decision. Priority would be given to making the decision that was most effective in upholding individual rights.

For example, suppose a corporate training department had funding sufficient to give only one of two courses. One course focuses on business process reengineering, a topic treated as a fad in some quarters. The other course focuses on sexual harassment prevention. In this simplistic scenario, a protectivist would select the latter course because it would be the more likely of the two courses to uphold individual rights.

- *The justice view* aims for objectivity in decision making. Its central question is *What behavior will be the most impartial and objective in its treatment of individuals?* For those espousing this view it is important that rules and policies exist, that they are communicated to others, that they are administered consistently among groups, and that they are not capriciously administered on the basis of such irrelevancies to justice as an individual's race, gender, sexual orientation, color, religion, creed, or national origin.

For example, consider the case of an employer that has thrice requested a proposal for training from a private university's continuing education department but has never funded a proposal. College administrators would be justified in suspecting the employer of taking advantage of the school to provide free consulting advice. Despite that suspicion, however, continuing education professionals would continue to supply proposals to the employer—but would also be likely to confront the employer with the suspicions and/or begin charging for proposal writing services.

The four views are not mutually exclusive. They do, however, provide useful touchstones for ethical decision making. Some situations may warrant one approach over the others.

What Common Ethical Dilemmas Confront Program Planners?

In the authors' 1995 surveys of continuing education professionals and human resource development (HRD) professionals (Cookson and Rothwell, 1995; Rothwell and Cookson, 1995), the respondents were asked several questions about ethics. Figures 6.1 and 6.2 indicate how often continuing education professionals and HRD professionals perceive themselves to be confronting ethical dilemmas. Note that many respondents perceived that they "never" or "seldom" encounter

FIGURE 6.1. CONTINUING EDUCATION PROFESSIONALS' PERCEPTIONS OF HOW FREQUENTLY THEY FACE ETHICAL DILEMMAS.

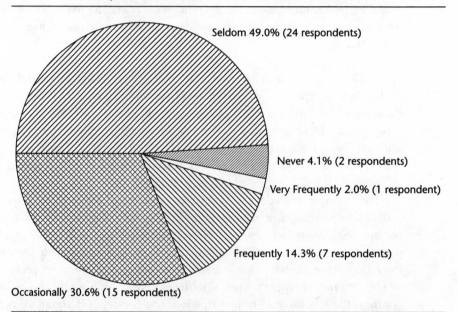

Seldom 49.0% (24 respondents)

Never 4.1% (2 respondents)

Very Frequently 2.0% (1 respondent)

Frequently 14.3% (7 respondents)

Occasionally 30.6% (15 respondents)

$N = 49$; mean = 2.61 (1 = never and 5 = very frequently); standard deviation = 0.86

Source: Cookson and Rothwell, 1995. All rights reserved.

such dilemmas. Although the survey results are not intended to be conclusive or representative, they are revealing.

More interesting results were obtained from additional ethical questions posed by the survey. Applying the critical incident technique (Flanagan, 1954), Cookson and Rothwell (1995) asked the anonymous continuing education respondents to "think of the most difficult ethical dilemma you have ever encountered in your work of planning continuing education." Rothwell and Cookson (1995) also asked the anonymous HRD professionals to "think of the most difficult ethical dilemma you have ever encountered in your work of planning HRD programs." Respondents to both surveys were also asked to answer the following questions about each dilemma they described:

- What happened, and why was it an ethical dilemma? (Do not give names.)
- What did you do in this situation?
- What happened as a result of what you did?
- If you encountered the same situation again, how would you handle it? Why?

FIGURE 6.2. HRD PROFESSIONALS' PERCEPTIONS OF HOW FREQUENTLY THEY FACE ETHICAL DILEMMAS.

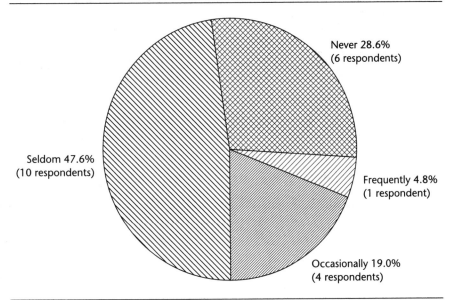

Never 28.6%
(6 respondents)

Seldom 47.6%
(10 respondents)

Frequently 4.8%
(1 respondent)

Occasionally 19.0%
(4 respondents)

$N = 21$; mean = 2.0 (where 1 = never and 5 = very frequently); standard deviation = 0.83

Source: Rothwell and Cookson, 1995.

Although the complete survey results are not reported here, a useful purpose is served by reviewing the real-life ethical dilemmas described by the respondents to both surveys. The lefthand columns of the worksheets that appear in Exhibits 6.1 and 6.2 contain the dilemmas described by the respondents. After you have read the next section of the chapter, review both of the worksheets and describe what *you* would do if *you* were confronted with each situation. You may find it helpful to begin your ethical deliberations by posing the touchstone questions for the utilitarian view (*What behavior will lead to the greatest good for the greatest number?*), the individualistic view (*What behavior will lead to realization of the greatest long-term self-interest for the decision maker?*), the protectivist view (*What behavior will be most effective in upholding individual rights to life, liberty, fair treatment, freedom of speech, privacy, due process, freedom of conscience, and other basic rights?*), and the justice view (*What behavior will be the most impartial and objective in its treatment of individuals?*).

Although analyzing open-ended responses to the survey questions on ethical dilemmas is difficult, content analysis revealed that unethical behavior was more cause for concern than illegal behavior. That is comforting. One ethical dilemma commonly cited by respondents stemmed from efforts to turn institutional initiatives to personal gain; a second stemmed from self-interested efforts to sway institutional actions; a third stemmed from efforts to misrepresent information, program descriptions, or attendance; and a fourth stemmed from unusual or undesirable individual behavior. We shall have more to say about resolving these dilemmas at the end of the next section.

How Should Program Planners Resolve Ethical Dilemmas?

This section examines the questions that can help program planners resolve ethical dilemmas. It then explores several examples that can demonstrate ways of resolving the most common ethical dilemmas that confront program planners.

Questions That Can Help Program Planners Resolve Ethical Dilemmas

Resolving ethical dilemmas can be difficult. When confronting an ethical dilemma, program planners may wish to consider five helpful questions. By answering these questions, they may be able to resolve the dilemma satisfactorily.

1. *Does a law, regulation, policy, or procedure apply to the situation?* If so, what decision will be "legal" or "illegal"? Why?

2. *Is the program planner willing to pay the price for taking the right course of action if it will lead to negative consequences?* For example, whistleblowing on a supervisor who is

embezzling money may lead to termination. While the "right" course of action has negative consequences, it would still be the "right" thing to do—provided that sufficient evidence exists or can be obtained. Conversely, unwillingness to do the right thing due to fear of negative consequences may be unethical in its own right.

3. *Are "right" and "wrong" or "good" and "bad" straightforward in the situation?* If not, what exactly is the source of the confusion? This question calls for additional fact-finding. Often additional facts can make clear what decision or action is most ethical.

4. *Is it ethical to ignore or remain silent about the ethical dilemma?* Some innocent people try to resolve ethical dilemmas by simply ignoring them—or pretending to ignore them. They may also resign their positions so they will not be caught and linked to the crime when a guilty person's transgressions are eventually revealed. In most cases, silence is not the best policy. It is better to seek facts and take action.

5. *How will other people view the program planner's decision or behavior at a later time?* In other words, what decisions or actions would a reasonable person be expected to take under the circumstances? The central issue here is that program planners must be prepared to answer questions about their decisions or actions if they choose for legitimate reasons not to pursue the most obvious and ethical course of action. The general rule is to do only what you would feel comfortable having appear on the front page of tomorrow's newspaper for your friends and family to read about.

While there can be no simple answers to most ethical dilemmas, the best advice is to speak out and take action. That is easy advice to give, but it is often difficult to follow. In any case, program planners' working philosophies should guide them. Program planners should strive to be true to themselves. For additional information about program planning ethics, consult Appendix Two.

Examples of Ways to Resolve the Most Common Ethical Dilemmas

Recall from earlier in this chapter that program planners most often confront four types of ethical dilemmas: (1) efforts to turn institutional initiatives to personal gain; (2) self-interested efforts to sway institutional actions; (3) efforts to misrepresent information, program descriptions, or attendance; and (4) unusual or undesirable individual behavior. It may be helpful to work through four specific critical incidents uncovered by the authors' 1995 surveys of continuing education professionals and HRD professionals. Each incident will be described and then the five questions posed in the previous section will be used to demonstrate ways of successfully resolving ethical dilemmas.

EXHIBIT 6.1. ETHICAL DILEMMAS CONFRONTED
BY CONTINUING EDUCATION PROFESSIONALS.

Directions: Review the actual ethical dilemmas presented in the left column below. For each dilemma, indicate in the right column what you would do to resolve the dilemma—and then explain why you would take that action.

Dilemma	Your Response
I was requested to hire a faculty member who was unfit to teach when more qualified people were available.	
A consultant wanted the university to award continuing education units for her training program and mail the brochures that she would provide.	
I was told to reduce the scope of a program and shift dollars into other programs when the community's need for the program had been demonstrated.	
An outside entrepreneur was using the university as a base for starting his own business under the guise of a university-sponsored program development effort.	
A very capable faculty person was approaching women in class for social occasions.	
We put an instructor into the grant-supported role when an open search should have been conducted.	
A student wanted credit for a mandatory course even though she did not attend it.	
We hire instructors who are also consultants and use our classes as a way to generate more business for themselves. Our position is that any subsequent contract work should be directed to the university, which will then hire the instructor to provide on-site training. However, it is unclear that all consulting work actually flows to the university.	
I allowed a needy student to attend a course for free. We do not give scholarships or free registrations.	
The college encourages nurses, teachers, and other groups to spend much money preparing for advancement by taking courses. However, it is widely known that jobs are not available in this area.	

EXHIBIT 6.1. ETHICAL DILEMMAS CONFRONTED BY CONTINUING EDUCATION PROFESSIONALS, cont'd.

Dilemma	Your Response
On occasion we have corporate sponsors who invade academic freedom or student rights for the sponsors' benefit.	
A person took out advertisements and distributed leaflets saying that a course on financial investment caused her to lose her life's savings. She had been a private client of the instructor for several years prior to taking our course.	
We were directed to eliminate programs that were popular in the community.	
A local company wanted to use the community college as a tool to recruit customers for their own interest.	
Our college is inconsistent because it permits "special arrangements" for students' academic programs. Some requirements have been waived or realigned for some students, but not for others in similar circumstances. That represents an ethical dilemma because policy states that the requirements should be consistent for all students.	
Grant funds are appropriated for people or for programs that are not authorized by the grant requirements.	
Well-to-do customers are overcharged for services.	
Students are placed on a waiting list but are not given accurate information about how long they will have to wait to attend a required course.	
A faculty member tried to find out the pay of another faculty member.	
Local vendors occasionally perceive vocational programming as competition for their businesses.	
I was involved in a situation in which my supervisor was stealing money. Although I did not have all the evidence, I had difficulty deciding whether to report the situation to his supervisor (who was also corrupt, it was later discovered).	
A worthwhile educational program was canceled due to perceived—not real—religious objections.	
Faculty misused dollars and university property.	

Source: Cookson and Rothwell, 1995. All rights reserved.

EXHIBIT 6.2. ETHICAL DILEMMAS CONFRONTED BY HRD PROFESSIONALS.

Directions: Review the actual ethical dilemmas presented in the left column below. For each dilemma, indicate in the right column what you would do to resolve the dilemma—and then explain why you would take that action.

Dilemma	Your Response
I was requested to provide inaccurate information in a program description to improve its marketing.	
Staff of a community college from whom I was subcontracting decided that rather than follow through with the stated program outcomes, they would use my session time to recruit students from our business client.	
The organization's top managers request behavior from employees but do not set a corresponding example. It is a case of "do as I say, not as I do."	
It is necessary to balance serious training activities with entertaining activities to keep the interest of participants. However, "fun" activities can be time-consuming when time is too precious to be wasted.	
I was forced to choose between telling people the "real" message or delivering management's "party line."	
In one case managers were allowed to witness role plays during training. As a result, one participant was fired.	
Participants in training are unwilling to attend compulsory training to comply with requirements of the Environmental Protection Agency or the Occupational Safety and Health Administration. Some have asked to be "signed off" on the training without attending.	

Example 1: A Self-Interested Effort to Sway Institutional Actions

A consultant wanted the university to award continuing education units (CEUs) for her training program and mail the brochures that she would provide.

Three questions appear to be relevant in resolving this dilemma:

1. *Does a law, regulation, policy, or procedure apply to the situation?* One issue here has to do with awarding CEUs. CEUs are not the sole province of the institution; instead, they are subject to external guidelines. So the first issue to resolve is whether the program is eligible for CEU credit under the guidelines of CEU-granting bodies. If so, other questions should be considered. If not, then issuing CEUs would be a clear violation of ethics.

2. *Are "right" and "wrong" or "good" and "bad" straightforward in the situation?* If not, what exactly is the source of the confusion? In this case it would be important to gather more information. Is there something suspicious about the program that may render it otherwise ineligible for CEUs, or is the issue merely the appearance of possible wrongdoing? These questions should be answered.

It is also important, of course, to clarify the institution's policy on this issue. Has it been clearly stated and communicated to the consultant? If so, then disciplinary action is warranted. If not, the best way to begin, if and when the charges are verified, is to inform the consultant to cease efforts to turn institutional initiatives to personal gain.

3. *Is it ethical to ignore or remain silent about the ethical dilemma?* Most program planners would probably consider it unethical to remain silent. At least efforts should be made to substantiate (or refute) the charges made.

Example 2: An Apparent Effort to Turn Institutional Initiatives to Personal Gain

An outside entrepreneur was using the university as a base for starting his own business under the guise of a university-sponsored program development effort.

One question appears to be relevant in resolving this dilemma: *Are "right" and "wrong" or "good" and "bad" straightforward in the situation?* If not, what exactly is the source of the confusion? In this case, as in the previous one, it would be important to gather information before jumping to conclusions. How does the program planner know that the entrepreneur has been doing that? Does the information stem from one source only? Can it be verified?

It is also important, of course, to clarify the institution's policy on the issue. Has it been clearly stated and communicated? If so, disciplinary action may be warranted. If not, the best way to begin, if and when the charges are verified, is to inform the consultant to cease efforts to turn institutional initiatives to personal gain.

Example 3: An Apparent Effort to Misrepresent Information, Program Descriptions, or Attendance

Participants in training are unwilling to attend compulsory training to comply with requirements of the Environmental Protection Agency or the Occupational Safety and Health Administration. Some have asked to be "signed off" on the training without attending.

In this case a relevant question appears to be *Does a law, regulation, policy, or procedure apply to the situation?* The answer seems to be yes, and misrepresentation may have legal if not health-related consequences. The program planner should flatly refuse to misrepresent attendance, and he or she should report to higher authorities the individuals who, jokingly or not, attempted to be "signed off" without attending.

Example 4: Apparent Unusual or Undesirable Individual Behavior

A faculty member tried to find out the pay of another faculty member.

Several questions may help resolve this ethical dilemma. *Does a law, regulation, policy, or procedure apply to the situation? What exactly is the institution's policy on salaries?* If it is a public institution, salaries may be public information; if it is a private institution, the institution may set the policy. If no policy exists, then no ethical dilemma exists.

As these examples show, resolving ethical dilemmas often depends on getting the facts straight first. It is then important to clarify exactly what the ethical issue is. It is then possible to make a decision or determine what action to take.

Summary

This chapter defined *ethics* as the moral code that establishes good and bad and that helps individuals, groups, and organizations to distinguish right from wrong; *ethical behavior* as acceptable behavior within a moral code; and *ethical dilemmas* as occasions when individuals, groups, or organizations are confronted with temptations to depart from ethics for personal or financial gain.

Philosophers have offered four ways to think about ethics. The utilitarian view focuses on the consequences of action; its central question is *What behavior will lead to the greatest good for the greatest number?* The individualistic view focuses on the self-interest of a decision maker; its central question is *What behavior will lead to realization of the greatest long-term self-interest for the decision maker?* The protectivist view focuses on fundamental human rights; its central question is *What behavior will be most effective in upholding individual rights to life, liberty, fair treatment, freedom of speech, privacy, due process, freedom of conscience, and other basic rights?* The justice view aims for objectivity in decision making; its central question is *What behavior will be the most impartial and objective in its treatment of individuals?*

The authors' 1995 surveys of continuing education and HRD professionals shed light on the ethical dilemmas that confronted survey respondents. Although many respondents perceived that they never or seldom encounter ethical dilemmas, content analysis of the surveys' narrative results revealed that unethical behavior more than illegal behavior was cause for concern. The ethical dilemmas commonly cited by respondents stemmed from (1) efforts to turn institutional initiatives to personal gain; (2) self-interested efforts to sway institutional actions; (3) efforts to misrepresent information, program descriptions, or attendance; and (4) unusual or undesirable individual behavior.

When attempting to resolve an ethical dilemma, program planners may wish to pose several important questions: (1) Does a law, regulation, policy, or procedure apply to the situation? If so, what decision or action will be "legal" or "illegal" and why? (2) Are "right" and "wrong" or "good" and "bad" straightforward in the situation? If not, what exactly is the source of the confusion? (3) Is it ethical to ignore or remain silent about the dilemma? (4) If the right course of action may lead to negative consequences, is the program planner willing to accept them and pay the price for taking the right course of action? And (5) If other people hear of the situation at a later time, what actions will they feel should have been taken in the situation? How prepared are program planners to respond to questions about their decisions if they choose not to pursue the most obvious, and ethical, course of action?

This chapter concludes the review of Quadrant 1 of the Lifelong Education Program Planning (LEPP) model. Each subquadrant in Quadrant 1 is important because it provides a basis on which program planners can carry out their responsibilities. Each subquadrant also points the way to dealing with the relevant contexts affecting program planning, the focus of the next part of this book.

PART THREE

ENGAGING RELEVANT CONTEXTS

The Chapters in Part Three focus on Quadrant 2 of the Lifelong Education Program Planning (LEPP) model. This quadrant, like the others, should be approached with flexibility—that is, with a contingency-based attitude. Depending on the situation in which program planners find themselves and on the environments in which they function, activities in the LEPP model may be treated in any sequence.

Chapter Seven guides program planners through the process of appraising the *external environment,* a term meaning the world outside the program planner's sponsoring organization. The chapter describes key sectors of the external environment, introduces open systems theory, and suggests ways that program planners can monitor changes in the external environment. It also describes how program planners say they are monitoring the external environment for changes that affect programs. Chapter Eight is a counterpoint to Chapter Seven. It describes how program planners appraise the *internal environment,* which is the world inside the organization. The chapter also reviews how program planners say they are monitoring the internal environment for changes that affect programs.

Chapter Nine offers suggestions for program planners who are seeking information about their targeted program participants. It describes ways to focus on the characteristics of targeted participants that may affect program planning efforts. The first section of the chapter offers ideas about what to look for; the second section offers some ideas about how to look. Finally, Chapter Ten defines *interests,* *needs,* and *learning needs.* It also summarizes methods for assessing learning needs, and the results of the authors' limited but original research on training needs assessment practices in U.S.-based business organizations.

CHAPTER SEVEN

APPRAISING THE ORGANIZATION'S EXTERNAL ENVIRONMENT

Every program is framed by a specific situation and is profoundly influenced by it. This chapter examines external environmental issues that affect how programs are designed and carried out. It also examines the ways in which external environmental issues affect how program planners enact their roles.

Consider the influence of external environmental change as you read the following vignette:

> Robert Incas is director of human resources for Delicious Cookies. Among other duties, he trains new workers so they will master their work responsibilities as quickly as possible. Because the company is experiencing explosive growth, many employees are hired each month. Robert finds it increasingly difficult to train new workers quickly enough while also meeting his other job responsibilities.
>
> Recently Robert submitted a proposal to top management to promote an employee to coordinate and conduct training for one year. The aim was to relieve Robert temporarily of his training responsibilities so he could devote more time to employee compensation and benefits. The proposal was accepted.
>
> An unexpected increase in the international prices for sugar and coffee, however, jeopardized the company's financial condition. As one response, top managers imposed an immediate freeze on hiring and promoting employees. That action postponed Robert's plan to find a temporary training director.

Despite the freeze, Robert's training duties have not diminished as the company seeks International Standards Organization (ISO) 9000 registration to strengthen its international competitive position. Training must continue even when no new employees are hired. In response to escalating demands, Robert has decided to plan shorter training programs and offer them less frequently.

This vignette illustrates action taken in response to external environmental change. Robert tried to act, but his efforts were stymied by competitive conditions affecting the organization. The vignette dramatizes how important it is for program planners to remain attuned to dynamic external environmental conditions.

Program planners may adopt a variety of approaches to responding to or anticipating external environmental conditions. If they use a directive approach, they will single-handedly conduct an appraisal of the external environment, sometimes known as an *environmental scan*. The results of the environmental scan can then be used to modify programs before, during, or after changes are wrought by the external environment. If program planners use a collaborative approach, they will involve such program stakeholders as managers and learners to carry out joint examinations of the external environment. If they use a nondirective approach, they will train others to examine changing external environmental conditions and to modify their program planning strategies.

This chapter is divided into three parts. The first part defines the term *external environment,* describes open systems theory, and identifies key sectors of the external environment that warrant attention. The second part suggests how program planners can monitor changes in the external environment and adapt programs to those changes. The third part reviews selected results of the authors' surveys of continuing education professionals and human resource development (HRD) professionals; it describes how often the respondents say they are monitoring the external environment for changing conditions and how important they regard such monitoring efforts to be.

What Is the External Environment?

Ludwig von Bertalanffy (1951, 1968) invented the term *general systems theory.* According to von Bertalanffy, any system is composed of two components: the *external environment* and the *internal environment.* The external environment is the world outside the system; the internal environment is the world inside the system. A system derives *inputs* from the environment, changes them through *transformation processes,* and releases them into the environment as *outputs.* An *open system,* on the one hand, is a system that is absolutely dependent upon its external environment. A *closed system*, on the other hand, has no interactions with its external environment because its outputs become inputs in a continuing process. Because few systems can be totally closed, closure can be thought of as a matter of degree (Banathy, 1992, p. 184).

The human body exemplifies an open system. To live, people must obtain at least air, food, and water from the external environment. These elements are inputs. Each input is transformed into materials used by the body. Once the transformation process is complete, by-products of the transformation process are expelled as outputs.

Open systems theory is important because organizations can be viewed as open systems. Such a view permits detailed analysis of issues affecting organizations. In an organizational context, inputs include people, capital, raw materials, and information; transformation processes are the manufacturing or service delivery methods applied by the organization; and outputs include finished goods or services.

To survive, any organization must derive some benefit from its activities. Private sector organizations primarily seek profits or return on equity, while government agencies and nonprofit institutions primarily seek constituent or customer satisfaction.

Key Sectors of the External Environment

Changes that occur in the external environment affect the internal environment. Consequently, changes in the external environment may affect program planning practices that are designed to meet organizational and individual learning needs. For this reason, program planners should be interested in scanning the external environment.

Many issues in the external environment can create pressures for change. However, the most important changes occur in the following sectors:

1. *Social conditions.* These include attitudes toward, for example, the role of business in society, the celebration of diversity, or the importance of work itself that prevail in the society of which the organization is a part.

2. *Economic, market, and competitive conditions.* These reflect the status of the industry and the regional, national, or world economy. Are employment conditions good or bad? Are profits up or down? Why? Are conditions relatively good or bad for one industry—such as retail trade, finance, or manufacturing?

3. *Legal and regulatory conditions.* These include trends in lawsuits, regulations and restrictions on trade, or organizational interactions with the environment. Are laws favorable or unfavorable to growth? Are they affecting profits or customer satisfaction positively or negatively? Why?

4. *Technological conditions.* These include trends in applying know-how to work processes. Are technological conditions affecting an organization's work methods that are key to making products or delivering services? What are those changes? How are they affecting the organization? What changes in work are prompted by technological change?

By monitoring changes in these sectors, program planners are well-positioned to react to—or to anticipate—the learning needs that such changes may create or influence (Jonsen, 1986; Rothwell and Kazanas, 1994a; Schmidt, 1987). To scan the external environment, program planners should pose the following questions about each sector:

1. What is its present status?
2. How is the sector expected to change in the future?
3. Why is the sector changing? What trend or trends are affecting change?
4. How does the sector presently affect program planning practices?
5. How will the sector affect program planning practices in the future if the change continues?
6. How does the sector presently affect the program planner's role?
7. How is a condition likely to affect the program planner's future role?

Monitoring External Environmental Change

Changes in any or all external environmental sectors can affect program planning. How should program planners monitor those changes? They should remain well-informed.

Methods of monitoring environmental change can range from the simple to the sophisticated. Simple methods include reading the newspaper, listening to the radio, watching television, reading professional journals, and networking with well-informed colleagues. By scanning the table of contents of journals related to training and development or related fields, program planners can quickly gain perspective about breaking trends and their implications. More sophisticated monitoring methods include using electronic databases to conduct literature searches, benchmarking with well-known and well-respected organizations, conducting surveys of professional colleagues by mail or over the Internet, participating in professional associations, and meeting with advisory committees.

Professional Associations

Involvement in professional associations is one means by which program planners can gain useful information about breaking trends that affect what they do. To take maximum advantage of professional associations, program planners should attend periodic association meetings, read literature published by the associations, and attend their conferences.

Two advantages can be gained by participating in professional associations. First, program planners can learn what external environmental changes are anticipated by other organizations and what steps those organizations are taking to address those changes. Second, program planners can partner with colleagues in other organizations to attack problems of common concern.

Advisory Committees

Advisory committees also may be useful in monitoring external environmental conditions that could affect program planning practices. Famed anthropologist Margaret Mead once wrote, "Every change should be introduced with the full awareness and participation of those whose daily lives will be affected by the change" (1955, p. 289). For that reason, effective program planning practice should usually incorporate representation by targeted participants and other program stakeholders. To that end, program planners functioning collaboratively may establish advisory committees. Advisory committees can also be used to monitor external environmental change that could affect the programs themselves.

A *program planning advisory committee* is a group assembled to improve programs. Such a committee gives stakeholders ownership in program planning decisions. It also ensures that programs are grounded in the reality and corporate culture of the sponsoring organization. For example, an advisory committee for a proprietary business school could include representation from a university program and from business, government, and nonprofit organizations that hire program graduates. An advisory committee for a corporate training department might include representation from top management, middle management, and supervision as well as hourly employees from different departments. Union representation is also desirable in unionized organizations.

Although an important committee function is to alert program planners to emerging trends, committees may serve other important purposes as well. Indeed, committee members may serve a role in every aspect of the Lifelong Education Program Planning model by helping program planners to work effectively, magnify their roles, articulate a working philosophy of program planning for the organization, enact ethical responsibilities, appraise external environmental conditions that affect programs, appraise internal organizational conditions that affect programs, assess needs and negotiate stakeholders' interests, accommodate adult learners, establish goals and objectives, plan process and outcome evaluation, formulate instructional design, design learning procedures, plan promotion and marketing for programs, plan recruitment and retention strategies, determine financial responsibility, and plan instructor selection, supervision, and training. In fact, one way to open the first meeting of an advisory committee is to ask the members which roles they feel the committee should focus on first, what they should do, and when they feel they should do it. The answers to these questions can clarify the advisory committee's responsibilities effectively and expeditiously.

Knowles (1980, pp. 74–75) pointed out that advisory committees may serve as many as thirteen roles, some of which may overlap with those just listed. They may, for instance, offer advice on instructional needs assessment; share in executing program plans; identify current community and societal problems of concern to program planners; help establish program priorities among competing needs, interests, and problems; and establish policies governing instructional programs within the limits of the committee's delegated authority. They may also help to formulate short-run program goals; interpret past program achievements or future program directions; contribute new ideas to program planning practices; serve as scouts for new instructors, leaders, and resource people; link program planning practices to targeted populations, institutions, community agencies, and possible funding sources; and lend volunteer help, particularly during crisis periods. Finally, they may help in periodic program evaluation and in interpreting the program to the public or to stakeholders.

Program advisory committees may vary in their scope and function (Rothwell and Kazanas, 1993). *Standing program advisory committees* are commissioned for lengthy periods—perhaps as long as the program exists. Members rotate on and off, often on an annual basis. Members may serve one or two years, with membership duration overlapping to ensure retention of experience from previous years' efforts. The chairperson is usually elected by the members, though he or she is sometimes appointed by the organization's board of directors or chief executive officer.

Special purpose program advisory committees are commissioned for temporary periods. They are formed to help program planners grapple with special problems, issues, or programs. For instance, a special purpose advisory committee may be formed to help a downsizing organization address outplacement training. A large research university may establish a special purpose advisory committee to oversee a large-scale, long-term, and complex research project that overlaps disciplines. Members are selected for their expertise with the problem, issue, or program.

Ad hoc program advisory committees are commissioned for one program. For instance, an organization that is planning an extensive business process reengineering (BPR) initiative may form an ad hoc program advisory committee to oversee training associated with BPR. A university may establish an ad hoc program advisory committee to oversee training associated with sexual harassment avoidance training for administrators, faculty, and staff.

When a program advisory committee is formed, program planners should ensure that the members are briefed on their roles and the committee's mission. Members should also be told how much time will be required of them, how long they will serve, when the committee meetings will be held, and what compensation (if any) they will receive for their service. An agenda should be distributed before meetings, and meeting minutes should be distributed soon after each meeting. Refreshments should be provided for meetings lasting longer than a few hours; coffee should be provided if meetings are held early in the day, and meals should be provided for meetings lasting a full day.

According to Knowles (1980), committee members should represent three groups:

1. Those representing different viewpoints within the organization—for instance, it is often wise to empanel the chief critic of the effort.
2. Those representing varied interests or geographic locations—examples might include representatives of business, labor, racial, ethnic, or church groups.
3. Those possessing specialized knowledge needed in program planning—such as librarians, physicians, artists, scientists, audiovisual experts, professional educators, or public relations specialists.

One way that program planners can use program advisory committees to monitor external environmental trends affecting program planning practices is to ask committee members at each meeting to describe what current trends or events are affecting existing programs, how those trends or events are unfolding, and what program planning modifications should be undertaken to react to, or even anticipate, the trends' effects. Other approaches that may yield helpful results include having program advisory committees undertake environmental scanning as an activity in strategic planning and using the results of those scans to double-check how well existing programs are helping the organization meet the challenges confronting it (Rothwell and Kazanas, 1994a). Program planners also may distribute survey questionnaires to advisory committee members and then feed back members' responses in meetings as a basis for making recommendations for program plans.

Actual Monitoring Practices

Writers have long advised program planners to modify their programs based on external environmental conditions in order to better position programs to support organizational strategic plans, competitiveness, and constituent needs (Rothwell and Kazanas, 1988). However, few recent research studies have examined how often program planners actually make efforts to do that—or how important they regard those efforts.

The authors made an effort to do just that in their 1995 surveys of continuing education professionals and HRD professionals. They gave the following instructions to respondents (Cookson and Rothwell, 1995; Rothwell and Cookson, 1995):

> Prior to planning specific programs, the education or training planner can sometimes benefit from making a preliminary overview of various program planning contexts. Some activities related to surveying that context are listed below. For each activity, please place a check ($\checkmark$) to indicate how important you perceive it to be and the extent to which you currently implement it in your practice. Use these scales: for importance: 1 = no importance, 5 = high importance; for frequency: 1 = never, 5 = always.

Academically based continuing education professionals responding to the survey perceived "consider demographic conditions of prospective program audience" to be the most important issue worthy of examination (see Table 7.1). That was followed closely by "consider current and projected economic conditions" and "consider public/institutional policies and regulations." However, the professionals perceived that they most often considered, first, public/institutional policies and regulations, then current and projected economic conditions, and then demographic conditions of prospective program audiences. A possible conclusion to be drawn from these slight differences in results is that program planners may be devoting more time to regulatory compliance than to matching program design to participants' characteristics. They are thus well-advised to revisit how well they are really examining demographic conditions in the program planning process. They should make a deliberate, concerted effort to focus attention on demographic conditions if they genuinely perceive those conditions to be most important.

HRD professionals who responded to the survey, conversely, placed primary importance on scanning the environment to assess future changes that might affect the organization (see Table 7.2). "Consider demographic conditions of prospective program audience" and "help the organization comply with legal or regulatory mandates" ranked second and third. Yet HRD professionals perceived that they most often considered the demographic conditions of prospective program audiences, then focused on complying with legal or regulatory mandates, and then scanned the environment to assess future changes that might affect the organization. A possible conclusion to be drawn from these slight differences in results is that program planners may be devoting more time to matching program design to participants' characteristics than they are to ensuring that programs are kept current. Like their continuing education counterparts, then, HRD professionals may

TABLE 7.1. HOW PROGRAM PLANNERS IN CONTINUING EDUCATION MONITOR THE EXTERNAL ENVIRONMENT.

Specific Activity	How important is this activity?			How often do you do this activity?		
	N =	Mean	Standard Deviation	N =	Mean	Standard Deviation
Consider demographic conditions of prospective program audience	51	4.1	0.85	51	3.62	1.01
Consider current and projected economic conditions	51	4.09	0.83	51	3.74	0.95
Consider public/institutional policies and regulations	51	4.05	0.85	51	3.92	0.84
Scan the environment	51	3.94	0.85	50	3.12	0.85
Survey competitors	50	3.64	0.82	50	3.12	1.00

Source: Cookson and Rothwell, 1995.

be well-advised to revisit the match between what they view as important and what they are doing as they undertake the program planning process.

Summary

This chapter introduced general systems theory, defined the term *external environment* to mean the world outside the system, and pointed out that an *open system* is absolutely dependent on its external environment. It described a system as deriving *inputs* from the external environment, changing them through *transformation processes,* and releasing them into the external environment as *outputs.* Open systems theory is important because organizations can be viewed as open systems. Such a view permits detailed analysis of issues affecting organizations.

The chapter also pinpointed the following sectors as key to examinations of the external environment: (1) social conditions, which include prevailing attitudes in the society of which the organization is part; (2) economic, market, and competitive conditions, which reflect the status of the industry and the regional, national, or world economy; (3) legal and regulatory conditions, which include trends in lawsuits, regulations and restrictions on trade, and organizational interactions with the environment; and (4) technological conditions, which include trends in applying know-how to work processes.

Changes in any or all external environmental sectors can affect program planning. In their 1995 surveys of continuing education professionals and HRD

TABLE 7.2. HOW PROGRAM PLANNERS IN BUSINESS MONITOR THE EXTERNAL ENVIRONMENT.

Specific Activity	How important is this activity?			How often do you do this activity?		
	N =	Mean	Standard Deviation	N =	Mean	Standard Deviation
Scan the environment to assess future changes that might affect the organization	21	4.57	0.67	21	3.857	1.10
Consider demographic conditions of prospective program audience	21	4.285	1.00	21	4.04	1.16
Help the organization comply with legal or regulatory mandates	21	4.14	1.27	21	3.95	1.35
Consider public/institutional policies and regulations	21	4.0	1.22	21	3.71	1.45
Consider current and projected economic/competitive conditions	21	3.8	0.87	21	3.2857	1.27
Survey competitors	21	2.47	0.98	20	2.05	0.99

Source: Rothwell and Cookson, 1995.

professionals, the authors asked program planners to indicate how often they consider external environmental conditions and how important they view such activities to be. Academically based continuing education professionals perceived demographic conditions of the prospective program audience to be the most important issue worthy of examination, but perceived themselves as most often examining public/institutional policies and regulations, current and projected economic conditions, and demographic conditions of prospective program audiences—in that order. HRD professionals, however, placed primary importance on scanning the environment to assess future changes that might affect the organization, but perceived themselves as focusing most often on the demographic conditions of prospective program audiences, compliance with legal or regulatory mandates, and scanning the environment to assess changes—in that order.

But program planners who are keenly aware of changing external conditions are only partially prepared for the challenges that confront them. They also must be aware of how those changing external conditions affect conditions within the organizations they serve. Examining the internal environment is, thus, logically treated in the next chapter.

CHAPTER EIGHT

APPRAISING THE ORGANIZATION'S INTERNAL ENVIRONMENT

The counterbalance to the external environment is the internal environment. Trends and conditions in the external environment are interpreted and acted on internally, and may in turn create or change learning needs. The internal landscape of an organization also has unique features that set the organization apart from others affected by changing external environmental conditions—such as, differences in organizational culture, the values of decision makers, and the collective knowledge of that organization's workforce. Savvy program planners can interpret the reactionary or anticipatory impact of changing external environmental conditions on internal conditions. They also monitor the internal environment itself for issues that could affect program planning practices.

Program planners working in one organization frequently need a way to structure their thinking about the organization. If they function directively, they are often called upon to go beyond merely designing planned learning experiences to clarifying (or even establishing) organizational responses to past, present, or future external environmental changes. That may mean that they must actually establish and communicate organizational policy. While recent research evidence suggests that chief executive officers in at least some organizations think HRD professionals who act as program planners should limit their roles to nothing more than delivering training (Bengtson, 1994), that view runs contrary to the roles of program planners that have been emerging in recent years (Galagan, 1994). Increasingly, the desire is to transform program planners into internal consultants who can offer advice to operating managers on a range of human performance issues that transcend planned learning experiences (Rothwell, 1996a, 1996b). To that end, program planners need a way to structure their thinking about their sponsoring organization.

To complicate matters, program planners who function collaboratively should be prepared to work with program participants, decision makers, and other stakeholders to conduct internal appraisals of the organization. If program planners function nondirectively, they may need to train different stakeholders to conduct their own investigations of the internal environment, and then facilitate the stakeholders' efforts to carry out those investigations.

This three-part chapter represents a counterpoint to the previous chapter and is similarly structured. The first part defines the term *internal environment* and describes elements of the internal environment that can be used to guide an appraisal of that environment; the second part suggests ways that program planners can monitor changes in the internal environment and adapt programs to those changes; and the third part reviews selected results of the authors' surveys of continuing education professionals and human resource development (HRD) professionals to describe how respondents actually monitor the internal environment for changing conditions.

What Is the Internal Environment?

In the simplest sense, of course, the *internal environment* is the world inside an organization. (The organization, itself, may be viewed as a system.) Underlying many organizational theories is the concept that any *system* is both a unitary whole and a dynamic relationship among the whole, its *subsystems*, or interdependent parts, and its *suprasystem*, or the larger entity of which the organization is a part—such as an industry, a nation, or a region. Viewed in this context, the internal environment refers to the many subsystems composing the organizational system. They exist in a dynamic relationship, with each subsystem affecting all others and being affected by all others.

Characteristics of Open Systems

According to Katz and Kahn's (1978) classic description of open systems theory, every organization bears ten key characteristics. They may be used by program planners as a framework for appraising an organization's internal environment.

1. *Importation of energy.* Organizations obtain resources from their external environment to survive and thrive. *Production inputs* consist of materials and energies

that are directly related to transformation processes (that is, production or service-delivery methods); *maintenance inputs* consist of the energies and informational contributions that are necessary to hold people in the system and to persuade them to carry out their activities as members of the system. Raw materials are examples of production inputs; employee retention policies, such as the use of employment contracts, are examples of maintenance inputs.

For program planners who are appraising an organization's importation of energy, the following questions may be worthwhile:

- What are the production and maintenance inputs of the organization as a whole? Of each part of the organization?
- How *are* those inputs changing to respond to external environmental change?
- How *should* those inputs change in the future to respond to external environmental change?
- How *do* present and future changes in inputs affect program planning efforts?
- How *should* present and future changes in inputs affect program planning efforts?

A simple example may serve to illustrate the value of posing these questions. Suppose a continuing education professional is working with a company to install a Total Quality Management (TQM) program. By examining the organization's importation of energy, program planners—either working alone or in collaboration with such stakeholders as managers and program participants—may identify high-priority areas in the organization where the principles of TQM should be targeted first. The way the organization imports energy may provide valuable clues about where initial payoffs from installing a TQM program would likely be greatest.

2. *Throughput.* In the previous chapter throughput was called transformation processes. Organizations are input processors that transform raw inputs into products and services. Consequently, program planners appraising an organization's throughputs may consider such questions as

- What are the throughputs (transformation processes) of the organization? Of each part of the organization?
- How *are* throughputs changing to respond to external environmental change?
- How *should* throughputs change in the future to respond to external environmental change?
- How *do* changes in throughputs currently affect program planning efforts? How *should* changes in throughputs affect future program planning efforts?

3. *Output.* Inputs that are processed by the organization are eventually exported to the environment. The reception of those outputs by the external environment is key to organizational survival and success. Consequently, program planners who are appraising an organization's outputs may pose such questions as

- What are the outputs of the organization? Of each part of the organization?
- How *are* outputs changing in response to external environmental change? How *should* outputs change in the future in response to external environmental change?
- How *do* changes in outputs currently affect program planning efforts? How *should* changes in outputs affect future program planning efforts?

4. *Cycles of events.* The input-throughput-output cycle may be expected to continue as long as the organization works effectively and efficiently. When examining the internal environment, however, program planners may wish to examine those cycles of events—that is, the relationship among inputs, throughputs, and outputs—to detect existing or desirable changes and their impact on present and future programs.

5. *Negative entropy.* The law of entropy suggests that all organization tends to move toward disorganization, chaos, and demise. Steps must be taken to avoid such an eventuality in business or educational organizations. Negative entropy is accomplished by storing surplus or excess energy imported from the environment, such as funds, credit, or other reservoirs of resources collectively called "organizational slack," to be used later if a deficit of energy occurs. When program planners examine an organization's internal environment, they should look for evidence of entropy, negative entropy, and organizational slack. How is the organization preparing itself for handling problems in the future? How do such efforts affect program planning efforts? How should they?

6. *Informational input.* Besides energy, information about the external environment constitutes significant input. Information permits the organization to accommodate external change. Marketing efforts, for instance, should increase and improve the flow of communication between the organization and the environment. Of key importance is how the organization is obtaining information about customer, supplier, and distributor needs and modifying internal inputs, throughputs, and outputs to match those needs. Mismatches here can lead to loss of customers by businesses, loss of constituents by government or nonprofit agencies, or loss of participants by education or training programs. Such losses are possible if organizational products and services do not match customer requirements.

Therefore, when program planners appraise an organization's informational input they may wish to pose the following questions:

- How is the organization obtaining information about customer, supplier, and distributor needs?
- How are decision makers and prospective program participants using that information?
- How should they be using that information to make adaptive—or even proactive—change to meet or exceed customer, supplier, and distributor requirements?
- How are programs supporting—and how should they be supporting—efforts to obtain and use information to meet or exceed customer, supplier, or distributor requirements?

Take the case of an organization that has experienced a dramatic increase in customer complaints. Decision makers are demanding customer service training. By examining informational input, program planners may be able to troubleshoot the source of the complaints and craft an appropriate response. Indeed, simply providing workers with more information about customer perceptions may end up being a more effective way to improve customer satisfaction than training, because this feedback alone may prompt improvements.

7. *Steady state and dynamic homeostasis.* As Katz and Kahn point out, "a steady state is not a motionless or true equilibrium. There is a continuous inflow of energy from the external environment and a continuous export of the products of the system" (1978, p. 26). For program planners who are appraising the steady state and dynamic homeostasis, key questions warranting review may include the following:

- How does the organization maintain stability amid turmoil?
- What functions help to preserve order?
- How are these functions changing to respond to external environmental change?
- How are existing programs helping to preserve order?
- What programmatic changes are necessary to adapt to or anticipate changing external environmental conditions?

8. *Differentiation.* Differentiation occurs when "diffuse global patterns are replaced by more specialized functions" (Katz and Kahn, 1978, p. 29). Evolving organizations become more specialized and differentiated in the outputs they export to the environment. In the realm of business, organizations focus on their

core competencies—that is, what they do especially well—and secure a market niche (Prahalad and Hamel, 1990). For program planners who are appraising an organization's differentiation, valuable questions to consider are:

- What does the organization do best and why?
- How is the organization beginning to focus on specialized customers or needs?
- How are programs changing, or how should programs change, in response?

9. *Integration and coordination.* As differentiation and specialization increase, so does the need to reintegrate diverse organizational activities. Enhanced integration and coordination activities may include control mechanisms, priority setting, rules, meetings, standard operating procedures, and scheduling. For program planners who are appraising integration and coordination, useful questions to ask may include the following:

- Through what methods is the organization unified and coordinated? How are these methods used?
- What role is and should be played by programs at present and in the future as a tool for achieving integration and coordination?

10. *Equifinality.* Equifinality is the tendency of open systems to attain their objectives by various means. Program planners who are appraising equifinality may pose such questions as the following:

- How much variation exists in pursuit of common goals or results in the organization?
- How are those variations manifested?
- What are and what should be the impacts of these variations on program planning practices at present and in the future?

Open systems theory provides useful criteria by which program planners can examine the inner workings of organizational settings. These criteria may provide clues about areas in which planned learning experiences could help the organization address past, present, or future challenges and external environmental changes. They may also yield useful information about issues to address during needs assessment or instructional design.

Organizational Subsystems

A second way that program planners can approach the appraisal of an organization's internal environment is to direct attention to the organization's subsystems. Five such subsystems warrant appraisal: (1) the goals and values subsystem, (2) the technical subsystem, (3) the structural subsystem, (4) the psychosocial subsystem, and (5) the managerial subsystem (Kast and Rosenzweig, 1974).

1. *The goals and values subsystem.* This subsystem focuses on the mission of the organization and of its parts. Goals and values—like mission—are heavily influenced by the external environment. For example, an organizational component may declare its mission to be preparing women to become owners of small businesses; the same program may also increase the visibility, prestige, credibility, legitimacy, and income of the sponsoring organization. Sometimes declared goals and values may contrast with those actually practiced.

Program planners who are conducting an appraisal of an organization's internal environment may ask questions related to the organization's goals and values subsystem, such as the following:

- What is the organization's mission?
- What is the organization's philosophy of service to program participants?
- What is the organization attempting to accomplish? How is success measured?
- What results are sought by the organization over the next year? Five years?

Answers to these and similar questions may affect program efforts—especially when programs are expected to be responsive to and driven by organizational needs.

2. *The technical subsystem.* This subsystem focuses on people using knowledge, techniques, equipment, and facilities. It is comprised of the specialized knowledge and skills an organization requires to transform inputs to outputs. Organizations with efficient technical subsystems are more productive than those that possess less efficient technical subsystems.

Program planners who are appraising an organization's internal environment may focus on the following important questions about the technical subsystem:

- What is the experience level of people working in the organization, and how long have they been doing what they have been doing?
- How does the organization compare to others in the same industry based on costs, profits, and customer satisfaction levels?
- How does the organization compare to best-in-class organizations in the same industry or in other industries?
- How well is the organization making use of state-of-the-art techniques, equipment, and facilities?

- How do the organization's techniques, equipment, and facilities compare to those of competitive organizations?
- How are workers trained on work methods, equipment, and facilities?
- How does the organization's staff training on techniques, equipment, and facilities compare to the training provided by competitive organizations? Best-in-class organizations?

3. *The structural subsystem.* This subsystem focuses on people working together on integrated activities—on how work is performed, including the assignment of work roles and reporting relationships; how tasks are divided among individuals; and how work is coordinated across work units or functions by upper management.

To appraise the organization's structural subsystem, program planners may pose the following important questions:

- What are the formal reporting relationships of the organization as depicted on the organization chart?
- What are individual work duties, tasks, and responsibilities, and how are they communicated? (For instance, are current job descriptions available? Has previous work been done to assess competencies of the workers?)
- How much and what kind of coordination exists among divisions, departments, work units, or teams, and how is that coordination handled by top management? How effective has it been?

4. *The psychosocial subsystem.* This subsystem focuses on people in social relationships. Each organization consists of interacting individuals and groups, "of individual behavior and motivation, status and role relationships, group dynamics, and influence systems. It is also affected by sentiments, values, attitudes, expectations, and aspirations of the people in the organization" (Kast and Rosenzweig, 1974, p. 111).

When appraising an organization's psychosocial subsystem, program planners may pose the following important questions:

- What is the nature of the organizational culture? Has a "culture audit" ever been performed, and with what results?
- How motivated are the workers? What evidence exists to demonstrate level of motivation? What incentives or rewards affect motivation? What other issues may influence it?
- What is the status hierarchy in the organization? What occupations, departments, or work units are considered more prestigious than others? Why? (For instance, in one corporation the last four CEOs were promoted from marketing, so it is considered the most prestigious department.)

- Who are the most influential people in the organization, regardless of their status? What makes them influential?
- Which divisions, departments, work units, or teams are perceived to be "uncooperative" (if any)? Why are they perceived to be that way?
- What attitudes prevail between workers and management in the organization? (Has an "attitude survey" been performed recently? If so, what were the results?)
- What are the aspirations of top management for the organization? What are the aspirations of others in the organization for their respective functions?

In one organization, program planners were called in to install planned on-the-job training. By talking to top managers, middle managers, supervisors, and workers, they learned about the organization's culture. They simply asked each group to "tell us a story about a time when someone had to be trained in this organization. What happened?" From the stories they heard, the program planners detected underlying themes about the corporate culture that made program design more effective by building on past successes and avoiding past failures—and by relating their proposed programs to specific examples from the organization's past.

5. *The managerial subsystem.* This subsystem plans and controls the organization as a whole. Top managers in particular are responsible for coordinating and integrating the four other subsystems to achieve results. Managerial tasks range from long-term, intermediate-term, and short-term and from the externally focused to the internally focused—that is, from the strategic to the coordinative to the operational. Because external and internal environments are constantly in flux, top managers must ensure that the organization's subsystems are adaptive and match the dynamic of the suprasystem.

When appraising the managerial subsystem, then, program planners may pose the following important questions:

- How does top management ensure coordination and integration among the other four subsystems?
- What present and future pressures are affecting coordination and integration?
- How are programs currently contributing to coordination and integration?
- How should programs be contributing to coordination and integration?

By focusing attention on these five subsystems, program planners can gain keen insight into the organization's internal environment. Such a focus can be immensely helpful when program planners are called in from outside to help. It can also be helpful to program planners who are employed full-time by their sponsoring organizations, because it gives them a means by which to frame their assessments of internal environmental issues that may affect program initiatives.

Monitoring the Internal Environment

Numerous internal environmental conditions can affect program planning. As with the external environment, program planners should remain ever-vigilant to changes in those conditions. How should program planners monitor such changes? Methods may include reading organizational publications and strategic plans, attending management or employee meetings, reading annual reports, networking with well-informed colleagues, and interviewing or conversing with individuals throughout the organization. By listening carefully to influential leaders in the industry and in the sponsoring organization, program planners can quickly gain perspective about emergent trends and their implications. More sophisticated monitoring methods include surveying competitors and organizational members, and benchmarking inside and outside sponsoring organizations.

Gaining access to key decision makers is perhaps the most valuable means by which program planners can gain useful information about emergent trends inside an organization. Key decision makers influence the direction of the organization. They are also attuned to what is happening, what should be happening, and what needs to be done to narrow the gap.

Here are two valuable tips for seeing influential people: First, take noticeable action. Do not wait for an invitation; strike out and do something useful. Lead a team in exploring program planning needs. This should lead to a quick success—and that will make access to influential people easier to obtain. Second, find a mentor. Do not wait to be asked. Go as high in the sponsoring organization as possible and seek out the mentor. Declare what you want. Then take steps to demonstrate loyalty to this person. Use this strategy as a means to get in the loop.

Internal advisory committees can also be helpful in appraising conditions inside an organization that can affect program planning efforts. Such committees should include level-spanning and boundary-spanning representatives. Indeed, an excellent appraisal of an organization's internal environment may often result from treating members of a program advisory committee as a focus group.

Actual Monitoring Practices

Few recent research studies have examined how often program planners actually make efforts to monitor internal environmental conditions that influence their organizations, and how often they adapt programs to those changing conditions. The authors made an effort to do just that in their 1995 surveys of continuing education professionals and HRD professionals. Survey respondents were given the following instructions:

Prior to planning specific programs, the education or training planner can sometimes benefit from making a preliminary overview of various program planning contexts. Some activities related to surveying that context are listed below. For each activity, please place a check (√) to indicate how important you perceive it to be and the extent to which you currently implement it in your practice. Use the following scale for *importance:* 1 = no importance, 5 = high importance. Then use the following scale for *frequency:* 1 = never, 5 = always.

The results of these surveys appear in Tables 8.1 and 8.2.

As the survey results indicate, both continuing education professionals and HRD professionals regard monitoring the internal environment as important. However, academically based continuing education professionals ranked the importance of examining conditions internal to the sponsoring organization some-what higher than did HRD professionals, while HRD professionals ranked conducting internal audit/analysis of the sponsoring organization somewhat higher than did academically based continuing educators. Neither respondent group perceived a match between how important they regarded the activity and how often they were doing it. While the reason for this slight mismatch between perceived importance and frequency is not explained by the survey results, it may stem from an inability to find time to carry through on the perceived importance of the activity. Perhaps greater efforts to do so should be made by using the time management methods described in an earlier chapter of this book.

TABLE 8.1. HOW PROGRAM PLANNERS IN CONTINUING EDUCATION MONITOR THE INTERNAL ENVIRONMENT.

Specific Activity	How important is this activity?			How often do you do this activity?		
	N =	Mean	Standard Deviation	N =	Mean	Standard Deviation
Examine conditions internal to sponsoring organization	49	3.55	0.81	49	3.28	0.97
Conduct internal audit/analysis of the sponsoring organization (formal structure, mission statement, strategic plans, policies, goals, objectives, etc.)	51	3.50	0.96	51	3.13	1.18

TABLE 8.2. HOW PROGRAM PLANNERS IN BUSINESS MONITOR THE INTERNAL ENVIRONMENT.

Specific Activity	How important is this activity?			How often do you do this activity?		
	N =	Mean	Standard Deviation	N =	Mean	Standard Deviation
Conduct internal audit/analysis of the sponsoring organization (formal structure, mission statement, strategic plans, policies, goals, objectives, etc.)	21	4.0	0.89	21	3.42	0.97
Examine conditions internal to sponsoring organization	21	2.66	1.15	21	2.57	1.07

Source: Rothwell and Cookson, 1995. All rights reserved.

Summary

As this chapter has shown, trends and conditions in an organization's external environment are interpreted and acted on internally. To be effective, program planners should be able to interpret the reactionary or anticipatory impact of changing external environmental conditions on internal conditions. They should also monitor the internal environment itself for issues that could affect program planning practices.

The first part of this chapter defined the term *internal environment* as the world inside the organization. It also described two groups of elements of the internal environment—characteristics of open systems, and types of subsystems—that can be used to examine internal environmental conditions. The second part of the chapter suggested ways by which program planners can monitor changes in the internal environment and adapt programs to those changes. Finally, the third part reviewed selected results of the authors' surveys of continuing education professionals and HRD professionals to describe how respondents monitor the internal environment for changing conditions.

For the most part, appraisals of the internal environment are carried out on a macro level, that is, they capture the big picture. But more detailed examination of program participants is needed if appraisals are to be put to best use in program planning. For that reason, the next chapter addresses accommodating participant characteristics.

CHAPTER NINE

ACCOMMODATING PARTICIPANT CHARACTERISTICS

If program planners complete the appraisals described in Chapters Seven and Eight, they will know much about the external and internal environments that frame programs. To increase the likelihood of program success, however, they should also learn more about the unique characteristics of the targeted program participants, because those characteristics can dramatically affect the success of planned learning experiences.

This two-part chapter offers suggestions for program planners who seek information about targeted participants. The first part of the chapter offers ideas about *what* to look for; the second part offers ideas about *how* to look.

What Characteristics Are Worthy of Consideration?

What participant characteristics are worthy of consideration as programs are designed? There is no one answer to that question; appropriate answers will vary according to program topic and targeted participants. Many possibilities can be identified. This section will review two ways in which to examine participant characteristics.

Five Key Sets of Participant Characteristics

Five sets of participant characteristics are important when scanning targeted participant groups in organizations or communities:

1. *Physical characteristics.* How healthy are they? How well are they able to withstand the physical, mental, learning, or emotional demands of their work environments? Do they have physical, mental, or learning disabilities that may affect their ability to perform necessary work or community functions? How do their disabilities affect their ability to meet the requirements of a planned learning experience?

Consider a simple example. To offer firefighting instruction, program planners may have to examine the physical stamina of the targeted program participants. After all, climbing ladders and wielding axes to knock down doors can be physically demanding. Indeed, to qualify to attend, participants may have to certify that they can meet the physical challenges posed by the program.

Consider a second example. Adventure learning has become popular in recent years. In adventure learning, participants are subjected to such physically challenging activities as white-water rafting, hang gliding, bungee jumping, logrolling, and mountain climbing. To attend such programs, participants may have to certify that they have the stamina to engage in such activities. (Legal releases may also be needed, even for participants who meet the physical requirements, since adventure learning experiences can be hazardous.)

2. *Backgrounds.* In what education, training, and other experiences have participants already participated? How do their backgrounds, beliefs, and experiences affect what they believe about a program and how they may approach it? The answers to these questions influence the scheduling, speed, sequencing, and selection of planned learning experiences. These issues may also affect decisions about the duration of a planned learning program, the examples to be given, the vocabulary to be used, and the appropriate level of abstraction to be used. Hence, it is important to examine possible participants' schooling, training, and occupational experiences.

3. *Work activities.* What do people in the organization or community do? How do they do it? What impact does what they do and how they do it have on their ability to participate in planned learning experiences? A course on arc welding, for instance, may require participants to meet certain safety prequalifications. Program planners should be aware of what those prequalifications are—and have in place means by which to screen participants based on whether they have met the

requirements. A course on advanced arc welding may also expect all participants to have met the prequalifications of a basic course on the same topic. Program planners can be safe in assuming that all participants have met the requirements if means for screening attendees have been established.

4. *Attitudes.* How do the participants feel about the subject matter of the program? About the organization? About the program planners? About the other stakeholders who may be influencing program planning decisions? What has led to their attitudes, and how might those attitudes affect program plans? Answers to these questions may help program planners define the participant groups they may serve. The answers may also provide valuable clues about participant's motivation levels on various issues.

In an organization that was installing team-based management, participants were emotionally distraught about the way the organization's management had recently handled a forced layoff. Program planners were caught off guard, unaware that they would meet stiff opposition to a team-building program because participants were focused on what Gestalt therapists call "unfinished business." They wanted to vent anger over the handling of the layoff, and that process—while understandable—posed a barrier to program success.

To surface participant attitudes, it may be helpful to question a sample of the targeted participants first, before they attend training, and ask them to identify any special issues that have surfaced in the work environment or occupation that may affect participants' reactions to the program. Program planners may also ask participants about their feelings on the topic at the opening of the program. Of course, it is usually preferable to possess some indication of participant feelings and attitudes before the program is planned rather than to wait until the first session, when midcourse corrections cannot be made easily.

5. *Interests.* What are participants interested in? What accounts for that interest? What do they hope to gain from participating in planned learning experiences, and how realistic are those expectations? How motivated are they to learn?

The worksheet provided in Exhibit 9.1 may be used to consider each of these characteristics as a program is planned. The answers to the key questions should help in tailoring the program to the participants.

Characteristics Based on Adult Learning Principles

Another approach to examining potential program participants is to use the principles of adult learning that have been identified over the years. Each of the

EXHIBIT 9.1. WORKSHEET FOR EXAMINING
CHARACTERISTICS OF TARGETED PROGRAM PARTICIPANTS.

Directions: Note how each characteristic in the left column linked, to corresponding questions in the center column, may affect program planning for a particular targeted participant group.

Characteristics	Questions	Implications
Physical Characteristics	How healthy are targeted participants?	
	How well are targeted participants able to withstand the physical, mental, learning, or emotional demands of their work environments?	
	Do targeted participants possess physical, mental, or learning disabilities that affect their ability to perform necessary work or community functions?	
	How do targeted participants' physical characteristics affect their abilities to meet program requirements?	
Backgrounds	In what education, training, and other experiences have targeted participants already participated?	
	How do targeted participants' backgrounds, beliefs, and other experiences affect what they believe and how they may approach a program?	
Work Activities	What do people in the organization or community do?	
	How do targeted participants go about their work?	
	What impact do the work activities of targeted participants have on their ability to participate in planned learning experiences?	
Attitudes	How do targeted participants feel about the program's subject matter?	
	How do targeted participants feel about their organization?	
	How motivated are targeted participants to learn?	
	How do targeted participants feel about stakeholders who may be influencing program planning decisions?	

EXHIBIT 9.1. WORKSHEET FOR EXAMINING
CHARACTERISTICS OF TARGETED PROGRAM PARTICIPANTS, cont'd.

Characteristics	Questions	Implications
	What has prompted participant attitudes, and how might those attitudes affect program plans?	
Interests	What are targeted participants interested in?	
	What accounts for targeted participants' interest in the program?	
	How realistic are those expectations?	

following twelve principles can become a focal point for considering participants for a specific program (Zemke and Zemke, 1995).

1. *Adults tend to be problem-centered in their outlook.* They want programs that address the immediate problems they are facing in their lives and in their work. For instance, an adult learner who is about to visit Germany may develop an immediate interest in learning the German language and in participating in programs centered on German culture. Likewise, a worker who is about to be sent to Germany to visit a company headquarters—or on an extended work assignment in Germany—may feel the need for instruction about living and working in Germany.

For purposes of program planning, then, targeted participants may be queried about the immediate problems they are facing on their jobs or in their lives that relate to the planned learning program. More specifically, program planners may wish to consider such questions as: What problems are the targeted participants presently facing that relate to their lives and work? How can these problems become a centerpiece for designing and delivering the program? Rather than focusing on conveying information, program planners may build planned instruction around how to deal with the practical problems encountered by the learners.

2. *Adult learners can be motivated by appeals to personal growth or gain.* In other words, immediate application is not the only motivator for adults. They are also motivated by a desire to improve their lives or future prospects. How do learners stand to benefit from instruction? How do they *want* to benefit? Appeals to self-interest will work.

For purposes of program planning, then, the targeted participants may be examined about their interests and desires for personal gain. Program planners may ask: What do learners want to know about a program? Why do they want to know it? How can the information they want be obtained? By answering these questions, program planners can develop keen insights about the targeted participants—and craft planned learning experiences to meet the participants' desires.

For example, consider the case of an organization that is sponsoring outplacement training for recently terminated employees. Participants of this kind are likely to have a need to grieve over job loss. They may also need to take stock of what jobs or occupations they are suited for, polish their job-getting skills, and prepare for a transition to a new work setting.

3. *Motivation to learn can be increased.* By helping learners see how a program can help them, program planners can enhance participants' motivation to learn. Important questions to consider include: What is the participants' present level of motivation to learn in the program? How apparent are the benefits to participants? and What could be done to increase participant motivation?

4. *Preprogram assessment is important.* Effective program planning will thus begin by assessing what program planners already know about the program's subject matter and by determining what they can already do. For example, what is the baseline knowledge and experience of the targeted participants?

Failures in program plans are sometimes attributable to program planners making the wrong assumptions about the participants' level of knowledge or experience. For instance, HRD professionals in one organization offered to supervisors a course in the basics of interviewing. In that organization, however, managers were the only ones permitted to interview job applicants. Supervisors knew little or nothing about the topic—and saw no reason to learn. Hence, to design a successful program, planners should have begun at a fundamental level; they should have focused on why supervisors needed to know about the topic.

5. *Exercises and cases in programs should be realistic and should stem from the experiences and work settings to which program participants can relate.* Activities are more successful to the extent that they are closely tied to the learners' work or life. Program planners should therefore examine the settings in which program participants will apply what they learn.

In one organization, participants in a bank's supervisory development program were shown a videotape on supervision in which the actors and actresses were shown at work in a manufacturing setting. Although many supervisory principles apply as much to the banking industry as to manufacturing, participants could see no similarities whatsoever. They were distracted because the videotape's content did not immediately apply to them. Program planners should be clear about the work settings from which a program's participants come, and based on that understanding they should develop activities, role plays, and simulations that will be appropriate for the settings.

6. *Feedback and recognition should be planned.* Program planners should plan on providing learners with ample opportunity to receive feedback on how well they are learning. To do so, they will need to know more about the targeted participants. What kind of feedback and recognition is likely to be successful with them?

7. *Planned learning experiences should, when possible, account for learning-style differences.* Individuals learn in different ways. What learning styles are evident among a group of targeted participants? How can program planners successfully identify learning-style differences—and build them into the design of their programs? By answering these questions, program planners can begin to adapt to the learning-style differences among their program participants.

8. *Program designs should accommodate adults' continued growth and changing values.* The needs and interests of adults change over their lives. Effective program design adapts to such changes. The question, then, is, What are the participants' values? What do they seek, and why? By conducting values clarification with targeted program participants, program planners can begin to zero in on issues associated with those values that will dovetail with participants' needs. To cite a simple example, one of the authors worked with a firm undergoing a shift in the role of the HRD department. Participants, all HRD professionals, did not value needs assessment because their clients told them what to do. A changing role meant they needed to change their values.

9. *Program plans should include transfer strategies.* How can participants be encouraged to apply on the job what they learned off the job? What transfer strategies may work particularly well with the targeted participants? More than seventy-six effective transfer strategies have been identified (Broad and Newstrom, 1992) including asking participants to bring to a program a work project to be completed on the job; having participants write a letter to a supervisor to pledge on-the-job behavior change resulting from what was learned in off-the-job training; and having participants write a performance contract with the trainer, pledging to change specific on-the-job behaviors after training.

10. *Adults need a safe and comfortable environment in which to learn.* But what is considered safe and comfortable by the participants in one program may be different than what participants in another program consider safe or comfortable. For

instance, "safe" may mean that participants do not feel threatened with physical or mental violence—either in the program or in the environment surrounding it; "comfortable" may have a similar meaning.

An example should serve to illustrate the range of meaning. At one community college, adult learners who attended evening classes were required to walk through a dimly lit parking lot in a crime-ridden city. Although adult learners felt safe while *in* class, some did not feel safe in getting *to* class. To make matters worse, crimes in the school's parking lot had received front-page newspaper coverage.

"Comfortable" can also have a range of meanings—from the types of chairs used to the psychological climate of the setting. In one case, a company brought in a consultant to facilitate sexual harassment avoidance training. The consultant gave the impression to all of the male participants that they were "guilty"—even those who had requested the training. In another case, a company terminated an employee in attendance at training for speaking out about company policies. In neither case could it be said that a comfortable climate had been established.

11. *Facilitation tends to be more effective than lecture with adults.* Adults do not want to hear lecture for hours on end; indeed, the adult attention span averages eight minutes. Generally, facilitation refers to posing questions for group members to answer. The role of the course leader is thus not identical to that of the traditional teacher, who is usually expert in the subject matter. A facilitator works to achieve effective group interaction, thus functioning collaboratively with learners and eventually fostering a climate in which they can learn on their own. Indeed, pure facilitation focuses on group interaction only—with no regard to the topic. The reason is that group interaction *is* the topic.

12. *Activity promotes understanding and retention.* For this reason, it is best to introduce learners to a topic and then give them opportunities to work in small groups on an action-oriented problem situation. Group members should then report about how they dealt with the problem situation, and as noted earlier, the facilitator's role is to foster discussion and information-sharing.

How Should Participant Characteristics Be Examined?

Methods of examining adult characteristics can range from simple to complex. The simplest approach is to *ask representatives of targeted participant groups to describe themselves, their abilities, and their motivations.* Such descriptions, often gathered by interview or survey, can yield valuable insights for use in planning a program. While this approach does serve to build program ownership among the learners, it does not necessarily furnish reliable information about the participants themselves. After all, individuals are not always completely conscious of their strengths and the areas in which they need to improve, or they may lack insight into the need for change.

A second approach is to *ask for information about targeted participants from representatives of groups that deal with them and that are familiar with them.* Examples of such groups might include immediate supervisors, subordinates, customers or clients, suppliers, distributors, and other stakeholders, as well as family members, neighbors, other people in the community, and professional colleagues.

A third approach is to *combine the first and second approaches* just described. The result is a *360-degree assessment* of the targeted participants, so-called because it includes both the targeted group and those that surround it (see Figure 9.1). While conducting a 360-degree assessment can be time-consuming and costly, it should provide valuable information for program design. Typically, 360-degree assessments have been conducted by questionnaire and have focused on individuals, but program planners may also carry out such assessments simply by asking people familiar with the targeted participants about their physical characteristics, backgrounds, work activities, attitudes, and interests. The focus of these efforts is usually on determining the characteristics that are common to a group of targeted participants who will be attending a program.

FIGURE 9.1. 360-DEGREE ASSESSMENT OF TARGETED PROGRAM PARTICIPANTS.

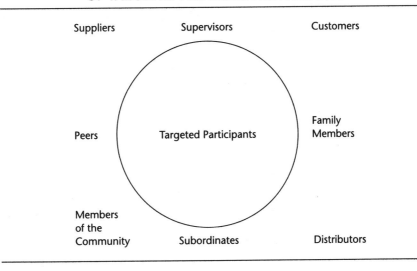

More sophisticated approaches can, of course, be used to examine the targeted participants' characteristics. For instance, program planners who have access to demographic information through personnel file databases may secure detailed statistical information about targeted participants.

Two important points should be kept in mind as this information is collected. First, information about all members of a group need not be true of every individual; and second, although most program planners share strong beliefs about how adults learn and how programs should be designed, their principles are not always true of all individuals.

On the basis of a thoughtful review of targeted participants, program planners are well-positioned to adapt their programs to the needs of targeted participants. At that point they can begin a more in-depth needs assessment, the topic of the next chapter.

Summary

This two-part chapter offered suggestions for program planners who seek information about the targeted participants of their programs. The first part of the chapter offered ideas about what to look for. Two approaches were offered. First, program planners can examine five key participant characteristics: (1) physical characteristics; (2) backgrounds, such as education, training, and other experiences; (3) work activities; (4) attitudes about the subject matter of the program, the organization, the program planners, and other stakeholders who may be influencing program planning decisions; and (5) interests. Second, participants may be examined based on eleven principles of adult learning.

The second part of the chapter offered ideas about how to look for participant characteristics relevant to programs. Methods can range from a simple approach—such as asking representatives of targeted participant groups to describe themselves, their abilities, and their motivations—to a more complex approach—such as asking for information about targeted participants from representatives of groups that deal with and are familiar with them. Examples of such groups might include immediate supervisors, subordinates, customers or clients, suppliers, distributors, or other stakeholders.

Once participant characteristics have been examined, program planners are usually well informed enough about the audience to undertake more detailed investigations of their needs. At that point, they are well positioned to assess participant needs and negotiate stakeholders' interests—the topics reviewed in Chapter Ten.

CHAPTER TEN

ASSESSING NEEDS AND NEGOTIATING STAKEHOLDERS' INTERESTS

As you read the following vignette, consider the issues it raises about assessing needs and negotiating stakeholders' interests.

> Marguerite Diaz, the director of human resources for Rising Star Machinery, walks into the office of the company president. She has been thinking about the major problem confronting the company: quality control has been rejecting a high percentage of machines before shipping.
>
> "Marguerite," begins the president as she enters the office, "we cannot tolerate a high and costly rate of rejection. We have a serious quality problem. I think training will solve the problem. For that reason I would like you to organize a training course on the basics of quality management. Training costs for three hundred workers will be minimal compared to the losses we are experiencing from unshipped machines. Let me know as soon as you start delivering the training."

The vignette dramatizes a common situation: a decision maker jumped to the conclusion that training would solve a problem. He did not analyze the problem sufficiently. Training is only one of many possible solutions to performance problems. It can solve only those problems that stem from individuals' work-related deficiencies of knowledge, skill, or attitude. Human performance problems can

also stem from other deficiencies, and not every problem calls for a specific learning solution (Rothwell, 1996a, 1996b). Since systematic, rigorous training or education is expensive to design, deliver, and evaluate, it usually should be regarded as
the solution of last resort for most human performance problems (Foshay, Silber,
and Westgaard, 1986). But many managers—and some program planners—think
of training or education as a solution of first choice. They are thus prone to making a common mistake. As Geis (1986) explains it, "Give a small boy a hammer,
and he will follow the *Law of the Hammer:* he will discover that a large variety of
things in his environment need hammering—the floor, the dining table, perhaps
even the family cat. . . . Educators and trainers see not only a world filled with
problems, but one with problems that uniquely lend themselves to educational
solutions" (p. 5).

The last three chapters emphasized the importance of analyzing the external environment, the internal environment, and the targeted learners. This chapter focuses on analyzing learners' needs and negotiating the interests of all
stakeholders. The first part of the chapter defines *interests, needs,* and *learning needs;*
the second part summarizes methods by which program planners can assess learning needs; the third part summarizes the results of the authors' original research
on the most commonly used needs assessment methods; and the fourth part offers
advice on negotiating stakeholders' interests.

What Are Interests, Needs, and Learning Needs?

Education and training programs are typically intended to address or respond to
particular conditions of individual course participants or of the organizations to
which they belong. Such conditions may be characterized in terms of interests,
needs, and learning needs. In lifelong education, it seems there is much confusion
surrounding these terms. However, in the planning of effective training and education programs, it is essential that program planners have a clear understanding
of the meaning and significance of these terms.

Interests

Interests are preferences or choices among possibilities. They are synonymous
with *wants.* If a corporate training department distributes a list of courses so that
targeted participants can indicate which courses they want to take, that activity is
an assessment of learning interests or wants rather than learning needs. Although
interests and wants are capable of motivating people to participate in programs,

they are not necessarily linked to the knowledge, skills, and attitudes that are needed for successful work performance or career success.

Needs

A need is a requirement. It is usually understood to be a difference between what is—what people can do or what they know—and what should be—what they must know to perform competently or realize career goals.

Psychologist Abraham Maslow (1970) formulated a well-known theory of needs. He perceived that self-fulfillment was a goal of every healthy person. For Maslow, self-fulfillment meant helping individuals to realize what they are capable of becoming. The need for self-fulfillment represents the pinnacle of human needs that vary from the most basic to the most developed. In general, people cannot satisfy higher-order needs without first satisfying those at lower levels.

Applied to program planning, this principle means that programs cannot satisfy participants' higher-order needs if their lower-level needs have not yet been met. Program planners should pursue opportunities to strengthen and reinforce participant movement toward realization of self-fulfillment.

Learning Needs

A learning need results from a deficiency of knowledge, skill, or attitude. It is thus a specialized need. Learning needs can be classified into five categories:

1. *Unfelt needs.* An unfelt need is a deficiency that is not recognized by those who have the need, such as learners or other stakeholders. Sometimes learners simply do not know that they do not know. To cite an example: a Mexican businesswoman who markets her wares in the United States may need to learn the English language to increase sales, but if she does not recognize the need, it remains unfelt. The aim of the program planner is to create conditions that will enable learners to discover their own needs.

2. *Felt needs.* A felt need is a deficiency that learners recognize in themselves or that stakeholders recognize in learners. Although the need can grow strong enough to stimulate a person to act, until it is expressed, it is maintained as a latent need. An example is the growing sense of unease experienced by telephone company executives in relation to the need to respond to the turbulent market conditions caused by the information-technology revolution. The challenge of the program planner is to enable learners and other stakeholders to express their needs and then

to plan programs with objectives that are directed to meeting those needs. This may be done using such means as interviews, questionnaires, focus groups with representatives of stakeholders, and other participatory approaches. As important as these needs are, program planners should not limit their attention only to felt needs because other types of needs may exist—and may actually be far more important to organizational productivity or to individual career development.

3. *Expressed needs.* A felt need becomes an expressed need when participants and other stakeholders can articulate what they need and why they need it. Program planners should strive to enable participants and other stakeholders to translate their felt needs into expressed needs. One way of doing this is to use organized needs assessment methods. By using such methods, program planners offer participants the opportunity to give voice to their needs. Until that happens, needs remain only unfelt or felt.

4. *Normative needs.* A normative need, writes McMahon (1970), "constitutes a deficiency or a gap between a 'desirable' standard and a standard that really exists. The individual or group that does not reach such a standard may be said to be in need" (pp. 20–21). For example, if team members in a company are expected to produce five hundred widgets daily with only six rejects per million, they have a standard to meet. If the team fails to meet the standard—and the standard has been fairly established—then a normative need exists. The objective of the program planner is to determine whether normative needs have been or will be set relative to specific training or education programs.

5. *Comparative needs.* A comparative need is a difference between two or more similar individuals, groups, or teams. For example, if a new employee is hired and immediately outproduces an experienced worker, questions may be raised about the comparative needs of the experienced worker. A comparative need may also exist if engineers in rural areas do not enjoy the same opportunities to build their professional competencies as engineers in metropolitan areas, or if one work team in an industrial plant consistently outperforms another.

Notions of these different need categories are imperfect, of course. They depend at least to some extent on individual perceptions and value judgments. The weaknesses of the categories suggest that when program planners assess needs, they should take all five categories into account.

Of course program planners bear a responsibility to do far more than merely assess learning needs. They must also negotiate perceptions of learning needs with participants and other key stakeholders. If they collect and then analyze information on their own, they are functioning directively; if they work with such stakeholders as managers and learners, they are functioning collaboratively; and if they function nondirectively, they facilitate the efforts of learners and others to discover their own learning needs. Even when needs are pinpointed and agreed upon, not all needs should be met through a planned learning experience; that was one conclusion reached in the analysis of the vignette at the opening of the chapter. A planned learning experience such as a course is not the only way in which needs can be met.

Assessing Learning Needs

Three methods of assessing learning needs are recommended: performance analysis, task analysis, and needs analysis. Each method is treated here as a process of identifying problem "gaps" to "close."

Performance Analysis

Occasionally called *front-end analysis, performance analysis* distinguishes learning needs from such other needs as management needs or work environment needs. This step is critically important because resources are too scarce to focus learning activities on issues that are not caused by knowledge, skill, or attitude deficiencies. Needs that stem from the work environment rather than from deficiencies of individual knowledge, skill, or attitudes should be met by management action.

Performance analysis diagnoses current conditions. To carry it out, program planners pose questions like the following: (1) Is present performance acceptable or unacceptable? Above, equal to, or below standard? (2) Do differences exist among what performers *do*, that which they *can do*, and that which they *should do*? and (3) Is training or education necessary to resolve the problem?

The most famous performance analysis model was described by Mager and Pipe (1984). Depicted in Figure 10.1, it should be read from the top down. Whether working alone or with others, program planners ask questions about a performance problem to decide on an appropriate solution. Mager and Pipe's model cannot be used proactively, however, in the absence of an existing problem. To avert future performance problems, program planners must rely on other models (see, for instance, Gilley and Coffern, 1993; Rothwell and Sredl, 1992).

A simple example will illustrate how the Mager and Pipe model works. Suppose the operations manager of a small company meets with the director of continuing education of a large community college. The operations manager begins the meeting by declaring, "We need a course on writing for our employees." This

FIGURE 10.1. MAGER AND PIPE'S MODEL OF PERFORMANCE ANALYSIS.

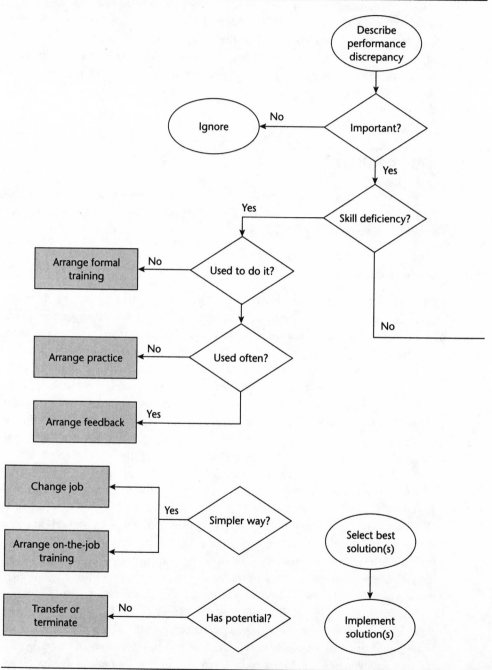

Source: Mager and Pipe, 1984, p. 13. Used by permission of The Center for Effective Performance.

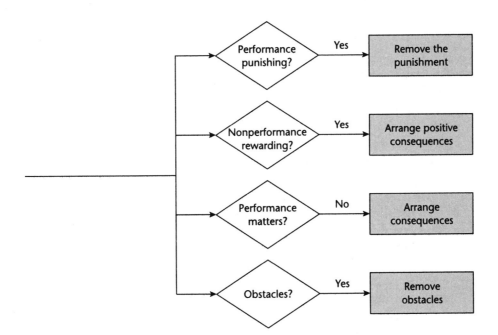

statement indicates that a performance discrepancy exists (see the top "balloon" of the model appearing in Figure 10.1). The operations manager, however, has leaped to a solution—that is, a writing course—without fully examining the problem. That task falls to the director of continuing education. He or she could use the Mager and Pipe model as a guide to troubleshooting the human performance problem. The model would suggest the steps to be taken. The first step would be to learn more about the problem, perhaps by interviewing the employees. A good opening to use might be this: "Tell me more about the problem you see, why it poses a problem for the organization, and the people affected by it." The purpose of this statement is to gather information on the nature of the problem, determine why it is important, and assess possible causes.

Task Analysis

After completing performance analysis and deciding that instruction is an appropriate solution to a problem, program planners conduct task analysis, by working alone or collaboratively with stakeholders, or by facilitating independent stakeholder action. A *task analysis* is a detailed examination of ideal performance (Jonassen, Hannum, and Tessmer, 1989). Its purpose is to tear apart what people do when they perform properly to determine exactly how instruction should be prepared.

When performing task analysis, program planners—working either alone or with others—list all actions taken or tasks carried out by successful performers as they do their work. Each task is in turn further analyzed to determine its related subtasks. The result is a task inventory that describes exactly what people do when they are working competently. Each task is then related to the knowledge, skills, and abilities necessary to carry out that task, which become the foundation for performance objectives on which instruction is built.

Task analysis can be carried out using many approaches. Brief descriptions of ten such approaches follow:

1. *The written questionnaire.* This method yields occupational information. Performers describe their work tasks in their own words—perhaps in terms of the steps required to carry out a work procedure. For instance, they may be instructed as follows: "List the steps in manufacturing a widget in column 1; in column 2, list what people have to do at each step to carry out the tasks."

When used with individuals who are not accustomed to writing, this method can be ineffective. Organizing and analyzing narrative information can also be problematic, because this approach relies heavily on respondents' memories and can therefore lead to incomplete work or task descriptions. However, if several questionnaires are completed by performers doing the same work, the results can be compared, fed back to the performers, and gradually perfected to reflect the full range of tasks performed. The result of this process is a *task inventory*.

2. *The control list.* This method relies on an inventory of tasks prepared previously. Preliminary work is performed to collect and combine task lists from other sources. Such composite lists are called *control lists*. Respondents examine a control list to compare what they do to what similar workers in other settings do. Hence, a task list is assembled based on task similarities. Respondents exercise recognition instead of memory about what they do. While this method does not require as much data collection time as the questionnaire method, the information obtained in this manner is not as useful as alternative approaches in determining task sequences and relationships among tasks because a control list may not contain all of the tasks performed in one setting.

3. *The individual interview.* This method poses standardized questions to job incumbents. Program planners choose exemplary job incumbents to interview about what they do. Task lists are compiled from numerous face-to-face or telephone interviews. This method relies on the respondents' memories and the interviewer's questioning skill. For that reason it is often impractical, excessively expensive, or unnecessarily time-consuming. However, it is a practical method when task analysis focuses on only a few job incumbents or when information cannot be obtained reliably through other methods.

4. *The focus group.* This method is related to the interview method. A focus group consists of a representative or exemplary group of job incumbents and sometimes their immediate supervisors. The goal of a focus group is to collect the same information that would have been conducted in individual interviews but at lower cost and at faster speed. The focus group leader guides a discussion of work activities using a standardized format to preserve consistency. Typical questions may include What work activities do you do? How are those activities carried out? and What work activities give newcomers the most difficulty—and why?

A specialized focus group approach is the DACUM method, an acronym formed from important letters in the phrase **D**eveloping **a C**urricul**um**. A DACUM group consists of eight to twelve job incumbents and their immediate supervisors. They are assembled for one to two days. Participants are asked to list the work activities they carry out on a daily basis. These tasks are then written on sheets of paper and posted on the wall in front of the group. Eventually, the tasks are organized into categories. Participants in the DACUM group are then asked to verify the categories and tasks and arrange them in the order in which they are performed (Norton, 1985). DACUM resembles structured brainstorming, and variations of it can be performed by written survey or on-line.

DACUM is useful because it builds job incumbents' and their supervisors' ownership in the task analysis process. It may thus help reduce disagreements among the incumbents and supervisors about what they should be doing and how they should be doing it. Indeed, a valuable side effect of this method is that it can often uncover inconsistencies among work tasks and procedures themselves, thereby providing a basis for resolving such disagreements before instruction is designed.

5. *The observation interview.* This method combines observation and interview. Program planners observe task performance and question workers about what they do and how they do it. This method is not as dependent upon performer memory as the interview method. There are disadvantages to using the method, however. One disadvantage is that the interviewer may interfere with the typical task activities of the job simply by observing them. Another disadvantage is that the method is time-consuming and labor intensive. For that reason it is not as practical as other methods for collecting large quantities of information.

6. *Worker participation.* This method permits program planners who are conducting task analysis to acquire firsthand experience. They try to do the tasks with the workers. The method is advantageous when the work is simple and easily learned. It is impractical and time-consuming, however, when applied to complicated work. Even when program planners have time to use this method, they may not witness all aspects of the job, gain sufficient exposure to the environment in which the work is performed, or observe changing tasks.

7. *The technical conference.* This method assembles a group of exemplary job incumbents to list work tasks. The experts involved in such a meeting may include supervisors who are experienced in task performance and were promoted for exceptional ability. Their knowledge is valuable. Information gathered using this method may be limited, however, because the experts may no longer perform the tasks and may have lost touch with how they are performed—especially when work methods have changed or are changing rapidly.

8. *The journal.* This method requires participants to maintain a journal, on paper or on-line, of their daily tasks on a predetermined schedule. The tasks may be coded beforehand to facilitate subsequent analysis and classification. Although

journals may indicate how a task is performed, they seldom give clues about how often the tasks are conducted or how critical they are to successful performance. Journals can also be time-consuming to prepare and analyze.

9. *The critical incident method.* This method can be carried out in several ways. One approach is direct observation of tasks that lead to exceptional or unsatisfactory performance. This approach yields clues about critical task components. Critical incidents may also be gathered by questionnaire or by interview. For instance, job incumbents may be asked to think of the most difficult work activity in their jobs. They may then be asked to answer the following questions:

- What happened, and why was it a difficult work activity? (Do not give names.)
- What did you do?
- What happened as a result of what you did?
- If you encountered the same situation again, how would you handle it? Why?

As can be seen from these questions, critical incidents tend to focus on atypical work activities or tasks. Thus, unlike other methods, they are helpful in focusing task analysis on high-stakes activities linked directly to success or failure.

Needs Analysis

Once task analysis has been completed, program planners should collect more detailed information to compare what performers should know or do and what they already know or are doing. Such a comparison can be performed by applying needs analysis methods. Experts occasionally distinguish between needs assessment and needs analysis (Watkins and Kaufman, 1996). Needs analysis is the process of determining, once needs are identified, the size and importance of those needs. In other words, needs assessment discovers what performance gaps exist, while needs analysis determines how important they are and why they exist. The needs analysis process can be carried out in many ways. Table 10.1 summarizes some of the advantages and disadvantages of commonly used needs analysis methods, along with some comments about each method.

In many respects, needs analysis resembles a research project. Both research and needs analysis can involve systematic application of principles of scientific inquiry, measurement, and data analysis. In focusing on the organization as a system, its constituent parts as subsystems, and the environmental context as the suprasystem, program planners also play a role similar to that of the internal consultant. They may find it helpful to use the following ten-step method to guide their actions:

TABLE 10.1. GENERAL METHODS OF ANALYZING LEARNING NEEDS.

Method	Advantages	Disadvantages	Comments
Interview	Reveals feelings, causes, and possible solutions as well as facts.	Takes time. For that reason it reaches few people. The results can be difficult to quantify. Participants in interviews may be uncomfortable with the process.	Conduct a pretest and review interview questions as necessary. Ensure that the interviewer can listen without judging responses.
Questionnaire	May reach many people in a short time. It is relatively inexpensive. It can afford an opportunity for free expression without fear or embarrassment. It generates data easily. If the questionnaire is scaled, data can be easily summarized and reported.	If the questionnaire is scaled, it may afford little opportunity for free expression and unanticipated responses. Questionnaires may be difficult to construct. They may have limited effectiveness in identifying the root causes of problems and the range of possible solutions to them.	Conduct a pretest. Revise questions and questionnaire format as necessary. Offer and give assurance of anonymity and confidentiality. Use questionnaires only if you are prepared to report unfavorable as well as favorable findings and take action on the findings.
Tests	Tests are useful as a diagnostic tool to identify deficiencies of knowledge or skill. They can help narrow down a group of targeted participants, eliminating those who are already proficient. Test results are usually easily compared and reported.	Valid, work—or culture—specific tests are not available for many occupations. Tests that are valid in specific situations may not be valid in all situations. Test results yield clues, not conclusive results. Tests do not produce the best evidence of work performance.	Those who use tests should know what the tests measure—and what they do not measure. They should ensure that test results are worthwhile. They should not use tests to justify difficult or unpopular decisions that should be made by management.

Method	Advantages	Disadvantages	Recommendations
Group Problem Solving	Group interviews are similar to individual interviews. They permit a synthesis of views from multiple viewpoints. They promote understanding, agreement, and possible ownership in the results. This approach may be especially effective in organizations functioning with team-based management.	Group problem solving can be time-consuming and expensive. Supervisors, executives, and other key players may feel too busy to participate. (In down-sized organizations, even participants may feel that way.)	Do not promise or expect immediate results. Begin with recognized problems, such as group concerns. Identify all meaningful problems for the group. Permit the group to make its own analysis and set its own priorities.
Study of Records and Reports	This approach provides excellent clues to performance problems. It provides more objective evidence of problem consequences than do opinions of individuals.	Records and reports rarely reveal the causes of problems or identify possible solutions. They may not provide representative cases. The available information may be outdated or based on special and unusual cases.	Use them to enhance and triangulate other approaches.
Position Analysis and Performance Review	This method can produce specific, precise information about work and performance. It relates problems or needs to real workers.	Conducting analysis in this way can be very time-consuming and expensive. It can be difficult for individuals who are not trained to analyze positions or review performance to use this method. This method may highlight individual but not group needs.	Keep information up-to-date by offering training to those who will analyze positions and review performance. Ensure that analysis focuses on current information and current people.

1. Clarify the model or need.
2. Collect background information.
3. Refine the problem or need.
4. Formulate questions.
5. Construct the study design.
6. Specify how information about problems or needs will be collected.
7. Specify how information about problems or needs will be analyzed.
8. Implement the needs analysis project.
9. Evaluate the results and draw conclusions, noting issues for future investigation.
10. Present the results to stakeholders and establish an action plan for solving problems or meeting needs.

    1. *Clarify the problem or need.* At this stage, program planners conduct performance analysis to distinguish learning needs from management needs. They ask such questions as the following:

- Who or what is the focal point for needs assessment?
- What is known about the problem or need? What is happening, and what should be happening?
- When did the problem or need first become apparent? How has it changed over time, if at all?
- How did the problem or need first become apparent?
- Who is affected by the problem? Where is the problem or need most keenly felt?
- Why is the problem or need important?
- Who are the stakeholders interested in solving the problem or meeting the need? What accounts for their interest at this time?
- How much is the problem or need costing the organization? In what ways is it costing the organization?
- What benefits will result from solving the problem or meeting the need?

By posing these questions, program planners can ensure that they devote attention to problems that can be solved by instruction and not to other problems that can only be solved by management action.

Suppose, for instance, that continuing education professionals are called in by the managers of an industrial plant to develop a planned on-the-job training program. By posing the questions just presented, the continuing education professionals can quickly learn about the issues that have prompted the request. They will thereby be better positioned to craft a proposal that will meet the client's needs. They will also be able to determine whether the problem identified by the client genuinely stems from training needs or from other needs.

2. *Collect background information.* At this point, program planners learn as much as possible about the organization, the stakeholders, the problem, the need, and other issues relevant to the needs assessment effort. For instance, program planners involved in a community development effort would want to know as much as possible about the community. When working with a client who is knowledgeable enough to realize that the needs analysis is warranted, wise program planners will clarify what results the client seeks from the training needs analysis and what business, stakeholder, or client needs prompted the action. If training needs analysis is the focus of the investigation, program planners will gather as much information as possible about the organization, the work, and the workers. For instance, they may want to see job descriptions, job analysis studies, classification descriptions, recent attitude survey results, or other relevant information.

3. *Refine the problem or need.* A needs analysis is difficult to focus initially, since program planners may not know much about the problem or need. But after many questions have been answered and background information has been collected, program planners can focus the needs analysis effort. One approach is to delimit the problem, to focus on one group or one facet of the problem rather than on everything. Industry trainers, for example, would tend to narrow the scope of the needs analysis at this stage. Instead of attempting a *comprehensive training needs assessment,* in which the needs of all job categories, departments, or organizations are simultaneously assessed, they may choose instead to focus initially on one high-priority job category, occupation, department, or area. Likewise, continuing education professionals might narrow the scope of the needs analysis to focus on one community need or occupation rather than on all.

4. *Formulate questions.* At this stage, program planners decide exactly what questions they want the needs analysis to address. These questions should of course provide information about differences between *what is* and *what should be.*

5. *Construct the study design.* At this point, program planners select needs assessment participants (subjects), clarify ways to control or manipulate variables, and clarify how outcomes will later be evaluated. The result of this step is usually a detailed project plan.

6. *Specify how information about problems or needs will be collected.* At this point, program planners determine which data collection methods (such as one or more of those discussed in Table 10.1) will be used and how they will be used.

7. *Specify how information about problems or needs will be analyzed.* This step is dependent, of course, upon the decision made in the previous step. The choice of analytical methods will depend on what data collection methods are used.

8. *Implement the needs analysis project.* At this point program planners actively collect information about the problems or needs. They conduct their mail surveys, interviews, or document examinations, or use other methods. This step is carried out using the plan prepared in step 5.

9. *Evaluate the results, draw conclusions, and note issues for future investigation.* At this point, program planners analyze the results of their data collection efforts, drawing conclusions and interpretations. They may also identify issues that warrant further examination.

10. *Present the results to key stakeholders and establish an action plan for solving problems or meeting needs.* In this final step, program planners present the results of their investigation to stakeholders. In an organization, stakeholders may be prospective participants or operating managers; in a community, they may be community members or leaders. The aim is to present the results of the needs analysis and establish agreement for subsequent steps to be taken, if they are warranted.

Most descriptions of the needs analysis process assume that all or most steps will be conducted by a program planner, which would be the directive approach, according to the Contingency-Based Program Planning model. But needs analysis does not have to be conducted in this way. Indeed, program planners may adopt a collaborative approach, in which they would work on a team, committee, or task force with representatives of key stakeholder groups such as managers and targeted program participants. If the needs analysis process is handled in that way, the program planner's typical role is to brief committee members on the process and assume a leadership role. However, committee members are actively and personally involved in each step.

Alternatively, program planners may only facilitate a process in which a team of key stakeholders—possibly including prospective participants—actively conduct their own training needs analysis. This would be the nondirective approach. One way to carry out this approach is to define in broad and general terms the problem or need warranting investigation. In consultation with key stakeholders, program planners assemble a project team that collectively possesses the knowledge, skills, and abilities necessary to conduct the needs analysis. Program planners brief team members on what they know about the problem or need and on the needs analysis process itself. The team members are then given the task of carrying out all ten steps of the needs analysis project. They select their own leader, and program planners serve as expert resources on needs analysis, as enabling agents for the project, and as team facilitators. Team members plan and execute the needs analysis project.

Commonly Used Needs Assessment Methods

Relatively little research has been conducted on needs assessment practices in U.S. organizations. One result is that program planners are unable to provide decision makers with convincing arguments about the value of needs assessment by pointing to the results of benchmarks elsewhere. Another result is that program planners are unable to compare what they are doing with what others are doing to determine whether their own approaches are exemplary, average, or below average.

The Authors' Studies of Needs Assessment Practices

The authors gave the following instructions to continuing education professionals and human resource development (HRD) professionals in their 1995 survey of program planning practices:

> The process of planning can be broken down into a number of interrelated and often iterative sequences of program planning practices. Below is a list of such practices. For each one, please place a check (√) to indicate how vital it is for effective program planning in general. When you plan programs, how often do you see that such practices are implemented?

The instructions were followed by a list of practices based on the Lifelong Education Program Planning model.

The survey results indicated that the continuing education professionals surveyed considered informal needs assessment slightly more vital to effective program planning than formal needs assessment (see Figure 10.2). *Informal needs assessment* involves simply asking such stakeholders as managers and prospective learners about what they feel they need, and *formal needs assessment* uses a planned, rigorous, and systematic approach. Continuing education respondents also saw informal needs assessment implemented slightly more often than formal needs assessment. In contrast, the HRD professionals surveyed viewed formal needs assessment as somewhat more vital to effective program planning than informal needs assessment, and they saw formal needs assessment implemented as a practice somewhat more often than informal needs assessment (see Figure 10.3). While the differences in mean responses are slight, they may suggest that among the survey respondents targeted results are more important to HRD professionals than to continuing education professionals.

FIGURE 10.2. CONTINUING EDUCATION PROFESSIONALS' PERCEPTIONS OF NEEDS ASSESSMENT PRACTICES.

How vital is the step to effective program planning?

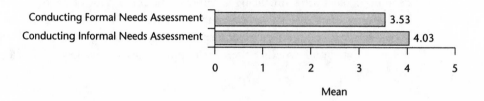

How often do you see this practice implemented?

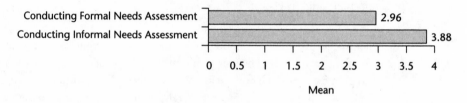

5 = high importance   5 = always

Source: Cookson and Rothwell, 1995.

A Study of Typical Training Needs Assessment Practices

To determine typical training needs assessment (TNA) practices, Rothwell (1995) prepared and mailed a survey to 350 randomly selected HRD professionals in May 1995. The prospective respondents were chosen from the membership directory of the American Society for Training and Development (1994). By August 1995, 41 anonymous surveys were returned. The response rate was thus 11.7 percent, even though a follow-up postcard was mailed. Not all respondents answered every question, so response rates varied by item. HRD professionals from manufacturing organizations accounted for 30 percent of respondents; HRD professionals from organizations employing 2,000 to 4,999 people accounted for another 30 percent. HRD professionals with supervisory responsibility accounted for 54 percent, while those without that responsibility accounted for 46 percent.

FIGURE 10.3. HRD PROFESSIONALS' PERCEPTIONS OF NEEDS ASSESSMENT PRACTICES.

How vital is the step to effective program planning?

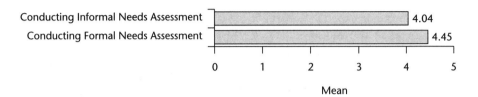

How often do you see this practice implemented?

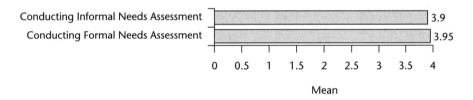

5 = high importance   5 = always

Source: Rothwell and Cookson, 1995.

The survey focused on answering several key questions:

1. How is needs assessment conducted in U.S. organizations?
2. Do program planners who work as HRD professionals conduct needs assessment only when someone asks for training, for entry-level jobs only, or for all jobs in their organizations?
3. How frequently is needs assessment conducted for different job categories?
4. What needs assessment methods are used most frequently?
5. What needs assessment methods are perceived to be most effective?
6. What are the biggest problems or difficulties encountered by HRD professionals when they conduct needs assessment?
7. What are the biggest advantages that HRD professionals perceive to have been gained by conducting needs assessment?

The results of the survey were paradoxical: 48 percent of respondents reported that they conduct TNA only when someone requests a program; 96 percent reported that they conduct TNA for entry-level jobs only; and 51 percent reported that they conduct comprehensive needs assessment for all jobs in their organizations. Respondents also indicated that TNA in their organizations is most commonly performed for technical, clerical, supervisory, professional, middle management, sales, and executive employees, in that order. The methods they reported using most frequently are individual development plans, focus groups, interviews, exit interviews, tests and assessment instruments, surveys, observations, competency assessment studies, document reviews, and DACUM and assessment centers, in that order. And they perceived the most effective methods to be DACUM, interviews, individual development plans, observations, focus groups, competency assessment studies, tests and assessment instruments, document reviews, exit interviews, surveys and assessment centers, in that order. According to the survey respondents, the biggest problems they encounter in conducting TNA involve management. For instance, one respondent indicated that participants in TNA "fear retaliation by senior management." A second cited as a problem "management's [lack of] willingness to deal with" TNA results. A third indicated that a problem in TNA was "getting management and hourly employees to respond." A fourth cited as a problem "getting management to agree to use" TNA. A fifth cited as a problem "perception of senior management that something is a training issue when it is really something else."

Conversely, respondents indicated that the biggest advantage of conducting TNA is that it focuses training on meeting appropriate needs and solving problems. For instance, one respondent said that TNA helps an organization to "avoid expenditures for unnecessary training." A second respondent said that TNA leads to "less resources placed inaccurately." A particularly thoughtful respondent listed three key advantages of TNA: "(1) Focus: employees know what current job competencies are; (2) Specificity: testing is more specific than general; and (3) Unity: processes (i.e., assessment, development, successes) planning all on same system." Another respondent appeared to summarize it all by remarking that TNA encourages "targeted, appropriate training."

While the results of this study are limited by a low response rate—and a respondent group limited to program planners in business, industry, and government—they are revealing about typical TNA methods. To the knowledge of the authors, this study is the only recent attempt to take a snapshot of typical needs assessment practices in U.S.-based organizations.

Negotiating Stakeholders' Interests

Central to effective program planning practice is the ability to negotiate stakeholders' interests. According to Cervero and Wilson (1994), "Power and interests define social contexts in which planners must act. In order to understand what planners are able to do, their actions must be linked to these contexts. Therefore, to make the connection between planner discretion and structural constraint, we argue that negotiation is the central form of action that planners undertake in constructing programs" (p. 29). Negotiating stakeholders' interests is thus central to the role of program planning.

We agree with this assertion. Our view is that program planners should determine how to negotiate stakeholders' interests by first assessing the internal environment in which they, the program planners, find themselves and in which they must function. The resulting approach to negotiating stakeholders' interests may be either directive, collaborative, or nondirective. The directive approach is appropriate when stakeholders do not know where to begin, when they abdicate their desire to participate, or when they prefer program planners who act in this fashion. The collaborative approach is appropriate when stakeholders are willing to take an active role in program planning efforts, when they view such efforts as essential to achieving organizational results, and when they prefer to devote personal time and attention. The nondirective approach is appropriate when stakeholders are well-versed in program planning, when they view program planning as essential and integral to the results they seek, and when they are willing to assume responsibility for making program planning decisions.

We further believe that program planners can best negotiate participants' and other stakeholders' interests by selecting and cultivating the appropriate approach over time. If program planners adopt a directive approach, they will usually be forced to "sell" their ideas, which will make negotiation an exercise in persuasion. If they adopt a collaborative approach, negotiation will occur throughout the program planning process—indeed, it will be inherent in that process. If they adopt a nondirective approach, negotiation will focus more on *process* (how decisions are made) than on *content* (what results are achieved by decisions).

The authors found in the results of their 1995 surveys of continuing education professionals and HRD professionals that these respondent groups attached slightly different weights to the various stakeholder groups they serve (see Figures 10.4 and 10.5). This result may suggest that when conflict arises among stakeholders, program planners weigh some stakeholders' opinions more heavily than others.

Summary

This chapter focused on analyzing learners' needs and negotiating the interests of all stakeholders. The first part of the chapter defined *interests* as preferences or choices among possibilities, and as synonymous with wants; *needs* were defined as requirements, as differences between what is and what should be; and *learning*

FIGURE 10.4. HOW IMPORTANT DO
CONTINUING EDUCATION PROFESSIONALS
CONSIDER THE PARTICIPATION OF VARIOUS STAKEHOLDERS?

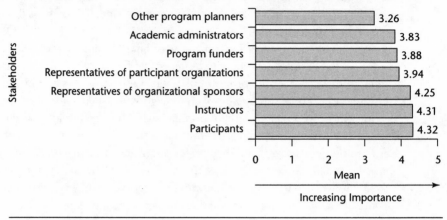

5 = most important

Source: Cookson and Rothwell, 1995.

needs were defined as the result of deficiencies of knowledge, skill, or attitude. The chapter also identified three methods of assessing learning needs: performance analysis, which distinguishes learning needs from others, such as management needs or work environment needs; task analysis, which provides a detailed examination of ideal performance; and needs analysis, which is the process of determining the size and importance of needs once they have been identified.

Ten steps for conducting a needs analysis were identified: (1) clarify the problem or need, (2) collect background information, (3) refine the problem or need, (4) formulate questions, (5) construct the study design, (6) specify how information about problems or needs will be collected, (7) specify how information about needs will be analyzed, (8) implement the needs analysis project, (9) evaluate the results, draw conclusions, and note issues for future investigation; and (10) present the results to key stakeholders and establish an action plan for solving problems or meeting needs.

The chapter pointed out that little is known about typical needs assessment practices in program planning or in training in U.S. organizations. In the authors' 1995 surveys of program planners, they found that continuing education professionals considered informal needs assessment more vital to effective program plan-

FIGURE 10.5. HOW IMPORTANT DO HRD PROFESSIONALS CONSIDER THE PARTICIPATION OF VARIOUS STAKEHOLDERS?

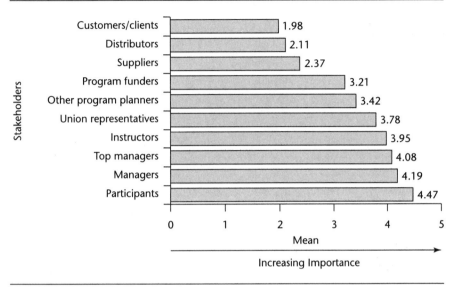

ning than formal needs assessment, while HRD professionals viewed formal needs assessment more vital to effective program planning than informal needs assessment.

This chapter concludes the review of Quandrant 2 of the Lifelong Education Program Planning (LEPP) model. Each subquadrant of Quadrant 2 is important, because it places programs within a context. Each subquadrant also can point the way to program design, which is the focal point for the chapters in Part Four.

PART FOUR

DESIGNING THE PROGRAM

The chapters in Part Four examine Quadrant 3 of the LEPP model and are thus unified in their focus on preparing planned learning experiences. Chapter Eleven describes how to set priorities about needs, formulate program purposes, and establish program goals and objectives. Chapter Twelve defines *evaluation,* explains why it is worthwhile, reviews four approaches to program evaluation, describes measurement issues associated with evaluation, and summarizes research about evaluation practices in U.S.-based organizations. Chapter Thirteen focuses attention on the analysis, design, development, implementation, and evaluation (ADDIE) model and the Action Learning (AL) model in terms of how they may be appropriate for use with the directive, collaborative, and nondirective approaches described in the CBPP model. Chapter Fourteen reviews possible learning formats available to program planners, stakeholders, and learners.

CHAPTER ELEVEN

SETTING GOALS AND OBJECTIVES

Once the decision has been made that a problem or opportunity warrants action in the form of a planned learning experience, program planners are faced with assigning priorities to identified needs. At this point, working alone or with others, program planners formulate the program's purpose, goals, and objectives. This chapter examines how to set priorities about meeting needs, formulate program purposes, and establish program goals and objectives. Taken together, these steps transform learning needs and performance problems or improvement opportunities into program solutions.

Setting Priorities About Meeting Needs

The needs assessment process can produce a bewildering amount of information. Program planners usually find it necessary to set priorities about learning needs to ensure that programs are responsive to stakeholders and that action is directed to meeting only the most important needs. Before assigning priorities to needs, however, criteria for establishing those priorities must be set.

A set of procedures for setting priorities were proposed by Sork (1982). Although suggested fifteen years ago, Sork's procedures are still useful.

1. *Select appropriate criteria.* Sork identified three kinds:

   Criteria related to the importance of meeting a need, including how many people share the need, how important meeting the need is to meeting goals, how immediately the needs are felt, how valuable meeting the needs is perceived to be, and how great the discrepancy is between what is and what should be

   Criteria related to the feasibility of meeting a need, including the educational efficacy of meeting the need, the availability of resources to meet the need, and the commitment of stakeholders to change

   Criteria originating in a particular institution, including the importance associated with meeting the need in one organization and the value that decision makers associate with meeting the need

2. *Assign relative importance to each criterion.* A weighing scheme is required for that purpose. Weighing may stem from organizational, individual, or work-related priorities. Weights may be assigned by program planners, by stakeholders such as managers or learners, or by both groups in partnership.

3. *Apply the criterion to each need.* If priorities are assigned directively, for instance, program planners assign numbers totaling 100. Needs are then prioritized based on the requirement of achieving a score totaling 100. If priorities are assigned collaboratively, program planners work closely with such stakeholders as managers and targeted learners to prioritize which needs to meet and when. If priorities are assigned nondirectively, program planners orchestrate a process by which decision makers identify what needs command highest priority for attention.

4. *Combine individual values to yield a total priority value for each need.*

5. *Arrange needs from highest to lowest total priority value and indicate how priorities will be rated.*

Using this approach, program planners—working alone or with others—can assign relative importance and priorities to needs. Only those needs that garner the most points are considered worthy of corrective action. While not completely objective, this approach is more objective than purely intuitive efforts to assign priorities.

Formulating Program Purposes

Once priorities have been established, needs assessment results must be translated into measurable learning objectives if they are to be useful in program design.

Rarely is it possible, however, to leap directly from needs assessment results into measurable learning objectives that are adequate to guide program design. As an intermediate step, program planners must clarify the program's purpose and instructional goals. Only then can measurable objectives be established.

What Is a Purpose?

A *purpose* is the ultimate reason for designing, developing, and delivering instruction. It answers one simple question: *Why is the program worth doing?* A *purpose statement* is a general expression of the need to be met or the problem to be solved by a program.

Clarifying the purpose of any instructional effort is fundamental to establishing a direction for change. (Programs are change efforts, after all.) Stakeholders often have more than one purpose in mind for a program. They may wish to improve employee morale, improve individual job performance, help individuals improve their career prospects, assist a community in economic development, achieve work unit or team performance improvement, and meet strategic planning objectives for competitive success. While some confusion over purpose is understandable because many stakeholders are involved with each program, too much confusion can make accountability for results difficult to assign. If stakeholders do not know what they want, it is unlikely that they will achieve it. Program planners should work to reduce confusion and thus clarify the direction of change efforts. Establishing purpose is a means to do that.

Two simple examples should serve to illustrate purpose statements. A purpose statement for an organization's orientation program might state that the program is intended to introduce new employees to their benefits, to the organization's work rules, and to the organization's corporate culture. A purpose statement for a community college's paraprofessional program in dental hygiene may indicate that the program is intended to build the competencies necessary for successful employment in the field of dental hygiene. Each purpose statement explains why the program exists.

Ways of Clarifying Program Purposes

The Contingency-Based Program Planning (CBPP) model offers clues to three ways of clarifying program purposes:

1. *The directive approach.* If program planners choose to be directive, they will not seek very much input from stakeholders about the purpose of instruction. Instead, program planners will make a decision, announce it to stakeholders, and

seek to persuade them that it represents a sound course of action. The authors have found that in fast-paced business settings—particularly when dealing with engineers or other technical professionals—the stakeholders actually prefer this approach because it requires less of their time.

For example, program planners were asked to assess the continuing education needs for professional engineers in a multinational corporation. After conducting a needs assessment, they discovered that the engineers had a need for state-of-the-art instruction on design for manufacturability—a topic that was essential to business operations but one that is not a required course in most undergraduate engineering curricula in the United States. The program planners took the initiative to state the program purpose based on that need. They obtained information about the purpose of instruction directly from the engineers and from their managers.

2. *The collaborative approach*. Working with stakeholders in each step of the program planning process, program planners take the lead. They may, for example, suggest a purpose statement and circulate it for comment among stakeholders. Alternatively, they may be assigned to a team, task force, or committee to craft a statement of program purpose, establish program goals and objectives, and design and deliver the program. As disagreements about purpose surface during the program planning process, they are negotiated by representatives of key stakeholder groups working directly with a program planner. The stakeholder representatives, in turn, bear the responsibility to speak for those they represent and to negotiate disagreements about program purpose that may surface later among stakeholder groups.

3. *The nondirective approach*. Program planners take an active role in facilitating decision making among participants or other stakeholders but make no decisions themselves about program purpose, goals, or objectives. Such decisions are made by prospective participants and other stakeholders, perhaps working on a committee or team. Prospective participants can be called into a meeting, presented with the results of needs assessments, and asked to craft a program purpose statement. Program planners facilitate the group's discussion but offer no opinions. Decisions about purpose thus stem directly from participants' or other stakeholders' wishes.

Setting Program Goals

Goals flow from the purpose (Rothwell and Kazanas, 1994a). They clarify in more detail than the purpose what program results are sought. For instance, a program designed to improve customer service (the purpose) may have such goals as building employee appreciation about the importance of customer service, improving employees' courteous treatment of customers, and increasing customer satisfaction. Goals are general in nature and are rarely measurable or timebound. Indeed, it is not clear how goal achievement will be evaluated. Goals represent, however, a starting point for action that can later be transformed into measurable learning objectives.

Program goals can be set in three ways, corresponding to the three ways of establishing program purpose and thus linked to the CBPP model:

1. *The directive approach.* Program planners establish program goals without asking for stakeholder input. This is the swiftest approach.

2. *The collaborative approach.* Program planners work on a team or committee with stakeholders to draft program goals. Not as swift as the directive approach, this approach should produce more ownership among program participants and other stakeholders.

3. *The nondirective approach.* Program planners take no active role in preparing the goals; rather, they direct attention to the dynamics and process in a team, committee, or project group of representative stakeholders assigned to formulate program purpose and goals. This is usually the slowest approach. But what it loses in speed it should gain in increased ownership among stakeholders, who prepare the goals on their own.

Setting Objectives

Objectives flow from goals. They are measurable and timebound.

Results Objectives

Results objectives are different from instructional or program objectives; they focus on the ultimate on-the-job applications or results to be achieved. Sometimes called *performance objectives,* they should be expressed as the measurable work performance results desired from a program or the life changes desired for or by individuals.

Rarely is one planned learning experience sufficient by itself to achieve ambitious results objectives. One reason is that the external environment is fraught with unpredictability. Despite the most carefully constructed plans, organizations can and do fail, even when programs are successful. A second reason is that the internal environment, controlled by management, exerts far more influence over individual and group behavior than one or many instructional programs.

Examples of issues that affect work outcomes, and thus results objectives, include the following:

- The competitive environment
- Changing work methods
- Expectations of program participants
- Laws, rules, and regulations
- Equipment participants use to perform their jobs
- Feedback on performance given to participants
- Rewards and incentives given to participants for their performance and for applying what they learn in programs
- Work inputs (such as raw materials)
- Work processes (methods used)
- Work outputs (such as choosing the best market niche)
- Supervision

Each of these issues may become a starting point for identifying an instructional objective.

With these issues in mind, program planners can distinguish two kinds of results objectives:

1. *General objectives.* Used here as a synonym for *broad social and institutional goals* that achieve the functions of training and education, these objectives correspond to the purposes of the training or education unit or function within an organization. They reflect the relationships among the purposes and general goals of the sponsoring organization and the instructional program. They may be established when the training or educational function is created, or they may revised and updated as stakeholders and program planners conduct strategic planning for planned learning experiences (Rothwell and Kazanas, 1994a).

2. *Program objectives.* These objectives refer to the desired results tied to one program and are oriented to the learning of knowledge, skills, or attitudes. They "provide the platform of specific goals toward which a program should be directed in the period immediately ahead. It is on the basis of the program objectives that decisions will be made as to what particular activities will be scheduled for what groups of participants; they are the concrete guidelines for program development" (Knowles, 1980, p. 121).

For example, suppose a business is working with a community college to establish training to improve the courtesy of employees who speak to customers of the business over the telephone. The *general objective* is to improve employee performance in their dealings with customers over the phone. The *program objective* is stated in measurable and timebound terms. For instance: "The program will result in a 50 percent reduction of customer complaints about employee telephone courtesy over the next year." Of course phone courtesy could be measured in other ways, such as increases in service, or behaviors counted in a random selection of phone calls.

Behavioral Objectives

As instruction is developed, objectives need to become more precise than program objectives; they need to become what are called *behavioral objectives*. Behavioral objectives describe the behaviors that participants should be capable of demonstrating upon program completion. The word *capable* is to be stressed, because many variables affect work performance, and possessing the knowledge to perform (which is provided by planned learning experiences) is not identical to functioning in a work environment that rewards application of knowledge.

Behavioral objectives are useful for eleven major reasons:

1. They describe precisely what learners are expected to know, do, or feel upon program completion.
2. They help establish evaluation criteria to measure and distinguish adequate from inadequate participant performance.
3. They focus participants on desired program results so that participants can in turn organize their own efforts and activities.
4. They reduce participant anxiety and frustration by clarifying desired program outcomes.
5. They permit instructors to identify participants who lack necessary prerequisite abilities.
6. They help participants to determine how well they have achieved mastery of what they learned.
7. They ensure consistency and agreement between what is learned and what is evaluated.
8. They help instructors to appropriately sequence planned learning activities.
9. They supply evidence of systematic planning to support participant learning.
10. They provide a basis for instructor accountability and responsibility.
11. They help other program planners during program design when the tasks of designing and delivering programs are divided between two groups of program planners.

In his classic text, Robert Mager (1975) describes the *what, how,* and *why* of behavioral objectives. He recommends that each behavioral objective be evaluated on the basis of three important questions: (1) Does the objective describe what learners will be able to do when they have achieved the objective? (2) Does the objective describe the important conditions under which learners will be able to demonstrate their ability? and (3) Does the objective explain how learners will be evaluated? Does it describe at least the minimum acceptable, measurable performance? These questions center around the three essential components of any effective behavioral objective:

1. *Behaviors,* or observable products, which represent learner or participant performance upon program completion. They should not be confused with learning activities or instructor performance, nor should they be confused with on-the-job performance change.
2. *Conditions* under which the behavior will be performed. These should include resources, tools, aids, and instruments that must be available to learners so they can perform as desired.
3. *Criteria,* which express the measurable speed, precision, quantity, or quality of a performance or outcome and indicate how well behaviors should be performed, consistent with preestablished criteria or standards.

Program planners should strive to express these essential components when writing behavioral objectives for educational or training programs. If one of these elements is lacking from a particular behavioral objective, it may not be possible to hold learners and program planners accountable for program results, because it may not be clear under what conditions performance is to be realized, how it is to be measured, or what performers are to do.

Consider a simple example: "Given a word processor, the learner should type at least sixty words a minute with three errors or less." The phrase "given a word processor" describes the conditions; the verb "type" describes the behavior; and the measurable criteria are stated by the phrase "sixty words a minute with three errors or less."

In most cases, behavioral objectives describe what learners should *do* upon completion of training. They may be stated in other ways, however. For instance, it is possible to restate the previous example as follows: "Given a word processor, the learner should type at least sixty words a minute with three errors or less *on the job.*" Such an objective focuses the employee's efforts on real-time work improvement rather than off-the-job training. Such a change transforms a behavioral objective into a results objective.

Domains of Human Performance

Behavioral objectives correspond to three domains of human performance: cognitive, affective, and psychomotor (Bloom, 1956). Understanding each domain is helpful in classifying desired program outcomes.

The Cognitive Domain. The cognitive domain "includes those objectives which deal with the recall or recognition of knowledge and the development of intellectual abilities and skills. It is the domain in which most of the work in curriculum development has taken place and where the clearest definitions of objectives are to be found phrased as descriptions of student behavior" (Bloom, 1956, p. 7). The cognitive domain has a number of levels:

- *Knowledge* occupies the lowest level of the cognitive domain. It is defined as remembering previously learned material, including specific facts and complete theories. To achieve knowledge objectives, learners do little more than bring to mind appropriate information. They may or may not understand what they have been taught to do.
- *Comprehension* is defined as the ability to grasp the meaning of material. Such a grasp may be demonstrated by the ability to translate material from one form into another (such as words into numbers), to interpret materials (to explain or summarize), or to estimate future trends (to predict consequences or effects). These learning outcomes go one step beyond simple recall, and represent the lowest level of understanding.
- *Application* is the ability to use learned material in new, concrete situations—for instance, by applying rules, methods, concepts, principles, laws, and theories. Learning outcomes in this area require a higher level of understanding than those that result from comprehension.
- *Analysis* is the ability to break down material into its component parts so that its organizational structure may be understood. Analysis may include identifying parts, analyzing relationships between parts, and recognizing the organizational principles involved. Learning outcomes in this area represent a higher intellectual level than comprehension and application because they require an understanding of both the content and the structural form of the material.
- *Synthesis* is to the ability to put together parts to form a new whole, such as producing a unique communication (a theme or speech), a plan of operations (a research proposal), or a set of abstract relations (a scheme for classifying information). Learning outcomes of this kind stress creative behaviors, with major emphasis on the formulation of new patterns or structures.

- *Evaluation* is the ability to judge the value of such material as statements, novels, poems, or research reports for a given purpose. The judgments are based on definite criteria. These may be internal (organization) or external (relevance to the purpose), and the learners may determine the criteria to be used. Learning outcomes tied to evaluation are the highest outcomes in the cognitive hierarchy because they contain elements of all other categories as well as conscious value judgments based on clearly defined criteria.

The Affective Domain. According to Bloom, the affective domain "includes objectives which describe changes in interest, attitudes, and values, and the development of appreciations and adequate adjustment" (p. 7). Objectives in this domain are growing more important because work is shifting from being physically demanding to being intellectually demanding. How people feel about what they do is more important than it used to be, because they are more likely than before to interact with others on teams to achieve results.

Krathwohl, Bloom, and Masia (1956) identified five levels of the affective domain:

- *Receiving* represents the lowest level of learning outcomes in the affective domain. It refers to the learner's willingness to attend to particular phenomena or stimuli, such as classroom activities, textbooks, or music. From an instructor's standpoint, affective objectives are concerned with getting, holding, and directing learner attention. Learning outcomes in this area range from building awareness that a thing exists to capturing the selective attention of learners.
- *Responding* refers to active participation by learners. At this level, learners attend and react to a phenomenon. Learning outcomes in this area may emphasize acquiescence in responding (reads assigned material), willingness to respond (voluntarily reads beyond assignment), or satisfaction in responding (reads for pleasure or enjoyment). The higher levels of this category include those learning objectives that are commonly classified under "interests"—that is, those that stress seeking out and enjoying particular activities.
- *Valuing* is concerned with the worth or value a learner attaches to a particular object, phenomenon, or behavior. Valuing ranges from simple acceptance of a value (desires to improve group skills) to a more complex level of commitment (assumes responsibility for the effective functioning of a group). Valuing means internalizing a set of values; however, clues to these values are expressed in the learner's overt behavior. Learning outcomes in this area are concerned with behavior that is consistent enough to make the values clearly identifiable. Learning objectives that are commonly classified under attitudes and appreciation would fall into this category.

• *Organization* brings together different values, resolves conflicts between them, and builds an internally consistent value system. Thus the emphasis is on comparing, relating, and synthesizing values. Learning outcomes in this area are concerned with conceptualizing a value (such as recognizing the responsibility of each individual to improve human relations) or with organizing a value system (such as developing a vocational plan that satisfies an individual's need for both economic security and social services). Learning objectives that relate to the development of a philosophy of life would fall into this category.

• *Characterization by a value or value complex* means that learners possess a value system that has developed into a characteristic lifestyle. Their behavior is thus pervasive, consistent, and predictable. Learning outcomes at this level are manifested by typical or characteristic learner behavior. Learning objectives that are concerned with the learner's general patterns of personal, social, and emotional adjustment would be appropriate here.

The Psychomotor Domain. According to Bloom, "a third domain is the manipulative or motor-skill area" (p. 7), which is commonly referred to as the psychomotor domain. Dickinson (1973) identified four major categories of the psychomotor domain, which are particularly important for work and equipment training in industrial settings and vocational instruction in educational settings:

1. *Gross bodily movements.* Learners can move their limbs separately or in combination with other parts of the body. This is the lowest level of the psychomotor domain.
2. *Finely coordinated movements.* Learners can move parts of the body in a pattern coordinated by the eye or ear.
3. *Nonverbal communication.* Learners can communicate using facial expressions, gestures, and body movements.
4. *Speech behaviors.* Learners transmit speech by forming, producing, and projecting sound.

Once behavioral objectives for the training or educational program have been formulated, program planners should develop instructional materials or strategies that can realize the objectives in one or more domains. If the objectives are directed to domains characterized by behaviors that are referred to as internal processes (such as the cognitive or affective domains) it will be necessary to think about what evidence will represent accomplishment. For example, unless the learners demonstrate what they have learned, how will it be known whether they have reached the level of synthesis in the cognitive domain? If objectives are well written and tied to specific behaviors or outcomes, learner expectations will also be clear, and they will be more likely to have achieved desired objectives, and thus to have met learning needs, by the end of the program.

Other steps in the program planning process will underscore the importance of establishing clearly and rigorously defined behavioral objectives based on identified learner needs. Without expressions of objectives, after all, it will be difficult, if not impossible, to evaluate results effectively. Objectives provide the basis for instructor and learner accountability.

Behavioral objectives should be expressed precisely—they should lend themselves to measurement—and each objective should begin with an action verb. The aim is to describe clearly—in precise and measurable terms—what learners should know, do, or feel upon program completion. Precise action verbs should be used that describe performance that can be observed (see Table 11.1). Vague verbs (such as *appreciate* or *understand*) and those that are difficult to assess (such as *pretend*) should be avoided.

Terminal and Subordinate Objectives

Besides the essential components of written statements of objectives, another useful concept is the distinction between subordinate and terminal objectives. *Terminal objectives* describe what learners should be able to do upon program completion; *subordinate* or *enabling objectives* describe corresponding performances that are to be accomplished in the process of achieving terminal objectives. Subordinate or enabling objectives are identified by answering the following questions for each terminal objective: (1) What are the main skills that constitute this performance? (2) Before accomplishing this terminal objective, what must learners do? and (3) What are the significant subskills? By answering these questions, program planners arrive at a second level of objectives. They can then pose the same questions about these subordinate skills to arrive at a third level of objectives. The same questions are posed repeatedly until the subordinate abilities derived correspond to the prerequisites of the planned learning experience—that is, what learners are expected to already know, do, or feel.

Summary

This chapter examined how to set priorities about needs, formulate program purposes, and establish program goals and objectives.

To set priorities about needs, program planners must find a way to make sense of the bewildering amount of information that can result from a needs assessment. One approach suggests that program planners should take the following steps: (1) select appropriate criteria, (2) assign relative importance to each criterion, (3) apply

TABLE 11.1. ACTION VERBS THAT CAN BE USED TO WRITE BEHAVIORAL OBJECTIVES.

Domain	Knowledge/Comprehension		Application		Problem Solving	
	Levels of Learning					
Cognitive	Arrange	Order	Apply	Illustrate	Analyze	Illustrate
	Cite	Outline	Assemble	Infer	Appraise	Infer
	Classify	Recall	Calculate	Interpret	Argue	Inspect
	Convert	Recite	Change	Modify	Arrange	Interpret
	Copy	Record	Choose	Operate	Assemble	Judge
	Define	Relate	Compute	Practice	Assess	Justify
	Describe	Repeat	Defend	Predict	Categorize	Manage
	Discuss	Report	Demonstrate	Prepare	Choose	Modify
	Distinguish	Reproduce	Discover	Produce	Combine	Organize
	Explain	Restate	Draft	Relate	Compare	Plan
	Express	Review	Dramatize	Schedule	Compose	Predict
	Give example	Rewrite	Draw	Select	Conclude	Prepare
	Identify	Specify	Employ	Show	Construct	Propose
	Indicate	Summarize	Estimate	Sketch	Contrast	Question
	Label	Tell	Explain	Use	Convert	Rate
	List	Translate			Create	Recognize
	Locate	Underline			Criticize	Relate
	Match				Debate	Score
	Name				Defend	Select
					Devise	Solve
					Differentiate	Support
					Discriminate	Test
					Distinguish	Value
					Estimate	Write
					Evaluate	
					Examine	
					Experiment	
					Explain	
					Formulate	
Affective	Accept	Locate	Affirm	Perform	Act	Integrate
	Accumulate	Name	Approve	Practice	Adapt	Mediate
	Ask	Point to	Assist	Propose	Change	Organize
	Describe	Respond to	Choose	Select	Defend	Revise
	Follow	Select	Complete	Share	Display	Solve
	Give	Sensitive to	Conform	Study	Influence	Verify
	Identify	Use	Describe	Subscribe to		
			Discuss	Work		
			Follow			
			Initiate			
			Invite			
			Join			
			Justify			
Psychomotor	Complete	Press	Activate	Loosen	Adapt	Fix
	Demonstrate	Pull	Adjust	Manipulate	Combine	Generate
	Distinguish	Push	Assemble	Measure	Compose	Illustrate
	Hear	See	Build	Open	Construct	Modify
	Identify	Select	Construct	Operate	Convert	Organize
	Locate	Set up	Copy	Perform	Create	Plan
	Manipulate	Show	Demonstrate	Remove	Design	Repair
	Move	Sort	Disassemble	Replace	Devise	Service
	Pick up	Specify	Disconnect	Rotate		
	Point to	Touch	Draw	Select		
	Practice	Transport	Duplicate	Set		
			Execute	Slide		
			Load			
			Locate			

the criterion to each need; (4) combine individual values to yield a total priority value for each need, and (5) arrange needs from highest to lowest total priority value and indicate how priorities will be rated.

Rarely is it possible to leap directly from needs assessment results into measurable learning objectives adequate to guide program design. As an intermediate step, program planners must clarify purpose and goals. *Purpose* is the ultimate reason for designing, developing, and delivering instruction. *Goals* flow from purpose. Objectives then flow from goals. Objectives correspond to three domains of human performance: the *cognitive domain*, the *affective domain*, and the *psychomotor domain*.

Objectives, in turn, provide a starting point for clarifying the desired results of programs. They become the foundation for determining program success, which is the topic of the next chapter.

CHAPTER TWELVE

DETERMINING PROGRAM SUCCESS

As you read the following vignette, think about the importance of determining program success through evaluation.

Ishmael Reed, director of the training department for the firm Textronikaca, was called into the office of Adnan Lundgren, the vice president of human resources. Adnan informed Ishmael that half of the training department's personnel would be transferred to other positions over the next month. When a dejected Ishmael asked for an explanation, Adnan said, "You know we are experiencing a crisis in this company. We can no longer justify the high costs of your department."

"But Adnan," Ishmael responded, "how can the training department continue its work with only half the people? The training programs will be demolished! Why, did you know that my department saves the company at least three times what it spends for training programs?"

"How is that so?" Adnan asked Ishmael incredulously.

"That has been the experience of the ten most recent programs," Ishmael answered proudly.

Adnan inquired, "Can you demonstrate those savings?"

"Yes, of course," Ishmael replied. "I can show you the records as proof."

Adnan sighed. "What a pity, Ishmael, that I did not have that information when the board of directors last met. Surely we would not have reassigned training personnel if such evidence of savings existed. Indeed, if we had known that the training department has made such an economic impact on the company, we would probably have hired *more* personnel!"

Ishmael is suffering the consequences of inadequate evaluation practices. The vignette demonstrates what might be called the *Columbus syndrome*. When Columbus set sail from Spain, he had only a vague idea of where he was going; when he arrived, he did not know where he was; and when he returned to Spain, he did not know where he had been. The vignette also illustrates dramatically that evaluation is critical to program survival and success. Unfortunately, too few programs are evaluated adequately. One result is that many worthwhile programs are undervalued or even abolished because insufficient evidence exists to demonstrate their value.

   Although interest in evaluation has been growing in both business and education in response to a clarion call for increased accountability, evaluation efforts are typically hampered by two important problems: (1) stakeholders rarely demand evaluation results until programs are completed or are under way, and (2) few program planners are encouraged by such stakeholders as managers and learners to devote time and effort to evaluation, because many stakeholders prefer instead to see attention devoted to instruction, at least in a program's formative stage.

   This chapter focuses on evaluation. The first part defines evaluation. The second part elaborates on why evaluation is worthwhile. The third part reviews four approaches to program evaluation. Several approaches are described because while each approach is *useful,* none is *definitive.* The best approach depends on stakeholders' needs for information on which to make informed decisions. The fourth part of the chapter describes measurement issues associated with evaluation. And the fifth part summarizes the authors' research about typical training evaluation practices in U.S.–based organizations.

What Is Evaluation?

Evaluation is the process of estimating value. *Program evaluation* is the process of estimating the value of a planned learning experience. Two steps are necessary to carry out program evaluation: describing or comparing results and objectives, and appraising or judging the value of the differences assessed. The essence of evaluation, like the essence of needs assessment, is comparing *what is* and *what should be* and interpreting the results of that comparison. To carry out the process successfully—and avoid the Columbus syndrome—program planners and stakeholders must agree on what they want from a program, why they want it, and how they will measure it.

In a classic treatment of program evaluation, Sara Steele (1970) described five program issues worthy of evaluation:

1. *Quality.* How good was the program? What was the quality of the content, the learning activities, the media, and the instructor's performance? How did people react?
2. *Suitability.* Did the program meet the needs and expectations of the participants? Was it at the appropriate level of difficulty? Did it meet the expectations of the community? Was it within the mission of the programming unit?
3. *Effectiveness.* What did the program accomplish? How well did it accomplish its objectives?
4. *Efficiency.* Were the program accomplishments sufficient for the amount of resources required from the organization and the participants? Was the program the best use of resources?
5. *Importance.* How valuable was the program to those who participated and to society? Was its importance sufficient to warrant the resources that were involved?

For example, take the case in which an organization mounted a large effort to train employees on team-based management. Evaluation focused on the criteria just listed indicated that the program was generally unsuccessful in all five areas. The key reasons: a needs assessment was never conducted, and program and behavioral objectives were never clarified.

An in-depth understanding of evaluation is not possible without distinguishing between *evaluation* and *measurement*. *Measurement* refers to the act of collecting information relative to the dimensions, quantity, or capacity of something. *Evaluation* involves making "judgments about ideas, works, solutions, methods, or materials related to the program" (Laird, 1985, p. 242), often with the aim of determining their value or worth. Evaluating the beauty of the landscape, for example, does not necessitate measurement.

Measurement-based program evaluation offers distinct advantages, however. It reduces the possibility of disagreement among evaluators. It provides concrete feedback about what the program has accomplished, and if used appropriately in connection with training, can provide continuous information about learning progress. And it permits positive comparison between before and after problem states.

Why Is Evaluation Worthwhile?

Evaluating programs is worthwhile for several reasons. First, it leads to program improvements, such as improving "the planning process, structure, decision-making procedures, personnel, physical facilities, finances, recruitment, training, public relations, and administrative management." It also improves the program, "including such aspects as objectives, clientele, methods and techniques, materials, and quality of learning outcomes." Other reasons include that it provides justification for increasing the size of programs, it defends against cutbacks, it raises morale, and it can be used to evaluate personnel (Knowles, 1980, pp. 202–203). Evaluation can also give program planners and stakeholders pride in their accomplishments; it can provide valuable information about programs; it can put continuing emphasis on worthwhile program goals; it can provide learning opportunities and information about the value of programs; and it can serve as the foundation for promotion, marketing, and public relations about the program (Boyle, 1981).

Four Approaches to Program Evaluation

The literature of lifelong education is replete with models of and approaches to evaluation. Four approaches have been particularly influential, however, and are thus worthy of special attention. They are reviewed here as guidance for program planners who are undertaking evaluation, collaborating with stakeholders in conducting program evaluation, or facilitating stakeholder efforts to conduct program evaluation.

Bennett's Evaluation Hierarchy

Claude Bennett's (1976) model was based on his experience in the Cooperative Extension Service, the national system of agricultural extension in the United States. The Cooperative Extension Service is the largest single adult education organization in the world. Although Bennett's model originated in agriculture, it can still serve as a viable approach to evaluating any lifelong educational program.

Bennett's model, which is presented in Table 12.1, is easily applied. It consists of a hierarchical, seven-step "chain of events" (Bennett, 1976, p. 7), proceeding upward from *inputs* to *end results* or resolution of one or more client problems. These steps can be exemplified in terms of the following sets of questions:

1. How many resources, including staff time, were allocated to planning and conducting the program? What were the qualifications of the staff assigned to the program?
2. What was the nature of the specific program being planned?
3. Who were the targeted participants for this program? How many were expected to participate? How continuously, intensively, and frequently did they participate?

4. How interested were the participants in the topic of the program? How accepting were they of the program leaders (presenters)?
5. How well did changes in participant knowledge, attitudes, skills, and aspirations correspond to the changes sought by program planners?
6. What was the nature and direction of changes in practices, technology, or social structure as a result of the changes in participants' knowledge, attitudes, skills, and aspirations?
7. What ultimate outcomes—both expected and unexpected—can be attributed to implementation of this program?

TABLE 12.1. BENNETT'S HIERARCHY OF PROGRAMMING ASPECTS OF EVALUATION.

	Examples	
Level	"Hard" Evidence	"Soft" Evidence
7. End results	Profit-loss statements; life expectancies and pollution indexes	Casual perceptions of quality of health, economy, and environment
6. Practice change	Direct observation of use of recommended farm practices over a series of years	Retrospective reports by farmers of their use of recommended farm practices
5. Knowledge, Attitude, Skills, and Aspiration Change	Changes in scores on validated measures of knowledge, attitudes, skills, and aspirations	Opinions on extent of change in participants' knowledge, attitudes, skills, and aspirations
4. Reactions	Extent to which random sample of viewers can be distracted from watching a demonstration	Views of only those who volunteer to express feelings about demonstration
3. People involvement	Use of social participation scales based on recorded observations of attendance, holding of leadership positions, etc.	Casual observation of attendance and leadership by participants
2. Activities	Prestructured observation of activities and social processes through participant observation, use of videotapes and audiotapes, etc.	Casual observation of attendance and leadership by participants
1. Inputs	Special observation of staff time expenditures, as in time-and-motion study	Staff's subjective reports about time allocation

Source: Bennett, 1976, pp. 4–8. Used by permission.

According to Bennett (1975), the higher the level of the hierarchy tapped by the evaluation, the stronger the evidence of program impact and the greater the difficulty and cost of the evaluation. He also asserts that "hard" evidence, which "reflects precisely true characteristics of individuals, groups, or situations," is more difficult to obtain than "soft" evidence. The hierarchy of events or foci of evaluation, the questions evoked, and the distinction between hard and soft evidence are useful contributions to our understanding of evaluation and suggestive of how evaluation of a specific program might be planned.

Kirkpatrick's Four Categories of Evaluation

Based on his experiences in training adults in business and industry, Donald Kirkpatrick developed his four-level model for evaluating training programs. The four levels concern learner reactions, learning, behavior, and observable results. As Kirkpatrick explains (1995, p. 21):

> The four levels represent a sequence of ways to evaluate programs. Each level is important. As you move from one level to the next, the process becomes more difficult and time-consuming, but it also provides more valuable information. None of the levels should be bypassed simply to get to the level that the trainer considers the most important.

The Kirkpatrick model is the evaluation model most widely used by human resource development (HRD) professionals. The four levels of evaluation are described as follows:

1. *Reaction evaluation.* This type of evaluation focuses on participants' impressions of and attitudes about their learning experiences. An instrument that evaluates participant reactions is normally handed out at the conclusion of a training program or college course. Reaction evaluation can be valuable because it can help instructors to determine the satisfaction level of their students. Participants in lifelong education programs are not likely to learn if they are dissatisfied, and if participation is voluntary, learners are unlikely to sustain their participation. For these reasons, program planners are well advised to seek reaction information both during and after planned learning experiences.

Although reaction evaluation is valuable, it can suffer from limitations that were dramatized by an experiment reported by Lauffer (1977). At a conference of physicians lasting three days, a lecture delivered by a Dr. Fox won widespread acclaim and enthusiastic participant approval. On evaluation forms, participants gave the presentation the highest praise. Among the comments received were the following: "Dr. Fox was marvelous," "I learned more from Dr. Fox than from all of the other presenters combined," and "I wish there were more presenters like Dr. Fox!" But surprisingly, Dr. Fox was an actor and not a physician. His lecture was part of a well-staged experiment to assess the validity of reaction evaluations. He had memorized a lecture that had been calculated to impress an audience but that made no scientific sense. The reaction of the conference participants may be called the *Dr. Fox syndrome*.

Sometimes the positive reactions of conference participants may be a reflection of the Dr. Fox syndrome, the tendency for participants to regard a program as successful merely on the basis of good feelings experienced during the program irrespective of the validity of what is "learned." In spite of this evidence, most program planners make hasty use of reaction evaluation because it is the easiest evaluation method to use. At a time when many training and educational efforts are under increasing pressure to demonstrate their economic value to sponsoring organizations, reaction evaluation remains the most frequently used method. The heart of the problem is that all too often educational and training practitioners construe participant satisfaction as a *prima facie* indicator of program success. By remaining vigilant about the danger of excessive reliance on reaction evaluations, however, wise program planners can seek information beyond mere reactions to include information relating to the other three levels of Kirkpatrick's evaluation model.

2. *Learning evaluation.* This method focuses on how much and how well participants learned from a planned learning experience. Increased knowledge and changed attitudes are typically assessed through paper-and-pencil testing and comparisons of pre- and post-training performance. Improved skills are assessed through tests of actual performance on assigned tasks. Rigorously defined objectives are the foundation for effective learning evaluation, because criterion-referenced tests are concerned with assessing participant ability to perform in line with predetermined objectives.

3. *Behavioral change.* Participants who have achieved the objectives of the planned learning experience will, it is hoped, change their workplace behavior. They will thus demonstrate effective transfer of learning from the instructional to the work environment—assuming that those environments are different. For example, having practiced numerous instrument-guided navigation exercises on the flight simulator, the rookie airline pilot will demonstrate her ability to perform under real-life conditions by completing her first solo night flight.

Evaluating on-the-job behavioral change resulting from planned learning is problematic, however. Many issues affect work performance. Individuals may

effectively master everything they learn and still not change their behavior, through
no fault of their own or of the program. Various approaches are used to assess
on-the-job behavior change, ranging from postprogram questionnaires sent to
participants and others who are familiar with the participants to sophisticated
experimental research designs intended to provide a basis for comparing change
in experimental and control groups.

4. *Results evaluation.* How much has a program influenced the organization's
competitiveness? That is a key question in this type of evaluation. Conducting
results evaluation is notoriously difficult because the relationship between a program and organizational competitiveness is no simple matter to judge. However,
many organizations are attempting to make this assessment (Phillips, 1991, 1994).

A typical approach is to subtract total program costs from total program benefits. Program costs include instructors' wages, participants' wages, the value of
lost production, materials costs, and overhead charges (Head, 1994). Total program benefits are based on expected savings or increased productivity expressed
in quantity, quality, cost, or time.

Stufflebeam's Evaluation Scheme

Daniel Stufflebeam's (1975) model arises from his experience with community education offered to people across the entire life span in public schools. The essence of
his approach is revealed in this passage: "Evaluation is the process of delineating,
obtaining, and applying descriptive and judgmental information . . . concerning
some object's merit; as revealed by its goals, structure, process, and product; and for
some useful purpose such as decision making or accountability" (p. 19).

Stufflebeam (1975) proposes two major purposes of evaluation. The first purpose is *decision making* in order to yield information for program improvement. Evaluation of this kind is referred to as *formative* (or *proactive*) evaluation. It seeks answers
to such questions as: What decisions need to be made? Who has to make them?
When will the decisions be made? In accordance with what criteria (Guba and Lincoln, 1988, p. 14)? The second purpose of evaluation is *accountability,* or justification of the program's value to employers, sponsors, clientele, and society. This
purpose is achieved by gathering information after program completion to describe
and defend what the program has achieved. Evaluation of this kind is called *summative* (or *retroactive*) evaluation. In gathering such information, evaluators seek
descriptive and judgmental information from everyone involved with the program,
as well as from those who influence or who might be influenced by the program.

Program planners usually conduct formative evaluation by assembling a representative group, such as targeted learners and their immediate supervisors, some

time before the instruction is to be delivered on a widespread basis. The group is asked to participate in a practice session. Periodically they are asked to provide feedback about how clearly instruction is presented and how clearly the instructional materials are written. Summative evaluation, conversely, is conducted following widespread training delivery. It summarizes participant reactions, learning, behavior change, and improvements in work results.

The role of the evaluator in Stufflebeam's model encompasses three principal functions: (1) *delineating*, which involves holding as many face-to-face meetings between the evaluator and decision makers as necessary to identify the needed evaluative information; (2) *obtaining*, which involves physically gathering and processing the information; and (3) *applying*, which involves using the information obtained from evaluation to make decisions and establish accountability. This role is jointly shared between program planners and stakeholders.

Stufflebeam does not conceptualize the process of evaluation as a fixed sequence of steps. For both formative and summative evaluation, the basic scheme involves obtaining information for four classes of variables—goals, design, process, and product—each of which corresponds to a different aspect of the program. Table 12.2 illustrates how each use of evaluation addresses each of these variables. The fact that these aspects are stated in general systems terms facilitates the application of this evaluation model to both education and training contexts.

Grotelueschen's Conception of Evaluation

Arden Grotelueschen is a North American specialist in continuing professional education. Based on his experience in evaluating educational programs geared to people in the professions, Grotelueschen (1980) introduced an evaluation scheme composed of three dimensions: evaluation purposes, program elements, and program characteristics.

Grotelueschen believes that evaluation may be used to estimate the value of either past, present, or future programs. Evaluation focused on a program that has been completed is called *summative evaluation* and aims to justify what was done; evaluation focused on a current program is called *formative evaluation* and is conducted to monitor what is happening and encourage improvement; evaluation focused on a program that has yet to be implemented is called *future evaluation* and is intended to make program planning more efficient.

Program elements constitute the features all adult and continuing education programs have in common: adult participants, teachers ("mentors, resource people, or instructors" [Grotelueschen, 1980, p. 83]), subject matter or program topics, and the context or general setting. Together these essential aspects "provide an analytic platform for considering evaluation issues" (p. 84).

TABLE 12.2. HOW STUFFLEBEAM'S TWO USES OF EVALUATION ADDRESS PROGRAM VARIABLES.

Classes of Variables

Uses of Evaluation	Goal-related variables	Design-related variables	Process-related variables	Product variables
Proactive (formative) for decision making	Assesses *needs, problems,* and *opportunities* to assist in forming objectives	Identifies and assesses *alternative plans* that might be chosen to achieve selected objectives	Assesses progress in implementing a chosen design as a means to *process control*	Assesses *attainments* during implementation as a means to *quality control*
Retroactive (summative) for *accountability*	Assists in reporting and defending *chosen objective* against others that might have been chosen	Assists in reporting and defending a *chosen activity plan* against alternatives that might have been chosen	Assists in reporting and defending the *actual process* and interpreting outcomes	Assists in reporting *all outcomes*

Source: Stufflebeam, 1975, p. 7. Used by permission.

Program perspectives refers to the characteristics of the program planning and program conducting processes: goals, designs, implementation, outcomes. *Goals* state the planner's intention and vary in importance according to the evaluation approach; for some approaches, they form the organizing axis for evaluation, for other approaches, they are less important than appraisal of the program's value and importance. Program *design* constitutes the blueprint that links goals to means to ends and presents the rationale for action, although not always explicitly. *Implementation* involves various teaching-learning-administering interactions as goals and design are operationalized. *Outcomes* frequently receive more attention than the other three types of perspectives. Outcomes or results can be classified as either *first-order,* that is, those "that are attained by those instructors, participants, and program administrators who are involved in the program and who share its direct experience" (Grotelueschen, 1980, p. 87), and *second-order,* that is, those that are "once-removed effects of the program and refer to the impact on people or institutions due to their first-order program accomplishments" (Grotelueschen, 1980, p. 87).

Together, evaluation purposes, program elements, and program perspectives comprise a three-fold classificatory scheme to "specify evaluation questions . . . [in education and training] and clarify relationships among those questions" (Grotelueschen, 1980, p. 87). Table 12.3, a depiction of this scheme, presents the objectives for evaluation, the reasons to evaluate, and some questions typically asked for the three kinds of evaluation; Table 12.4 presents specific questions that can be asked about various program elements during formative evaluation to aid in program improvement; Table 12.5 presents questions about the same program elements during summative evaluation to justify a program; and Table 12.6 presents questions that can be asked about those elements during future evaluation to aid in evaluation planning.

Grotelueschen (1980, p. 97) proposed eight steps to serve as guidelines for designing program evaluation:

1. Begin by determining purpose, thus answering the simple question *Why evaluate?*
2. Identify for whom the evaluation is conducted.
3. Focus on the issues. What questions should be answered by the evaluation?
4. Consider what resources are available to carry out the evaluation.
5. Consider what evidence is to be gathered.
6. Determine methods of collecting data.
7. Consider how the evidence should be analyzed.
8. Consider how the findings of the evaluation should be reported.

These eight steps are immensely helpful in conceptualizing a program evaluation. Their simplicity makes the evaluation process easy to describe to stakeholders, as well as making evaluation easy for program planners.

TABLE 12.3. THREE TYPES OF EVALUATION NAMED BY GROTELUESCHEN.

Type	Object of Evaluation	Reasons to Evaluate	Typical Questions
Summative	Past program activities or outcomes	To justify the program or demonstrate accountability	Could it have been more cost-effective?
			Do the elements of the program tend to be more satisfactory than alternative elements?
			Have the program goals been appropriate for the target audience?
			Was the program received by those for whom it was intended and in the intended way?
			Will subsequent programming efforts be better than this one?
Formative	Present efforts	To improve the program	What procedures could be learned to improve instructional delivery?
			How could the content of the program be strengthened?
			How could the planning activities be improved to enhance participation?
Future	A future program	To plan the program	Which agencies are interested in program collaboration?
			Is it probable that the proposed procedures will produce the desired consequences?
			Are program planners overlooking some potential program goals?
			Can the intended outcomes be obtained efficiently?

Source: Adapted from Grotelueschen, 1980, p. 91. Copyright 1980 by the Adult Education Association of the United States and Jossey-Bass Inc., Publishers. Used by permission of Jossey-Bass.

TABLE 12.4. IMPROVEMENT QUESTIONS FOR FORMATIVE EVALUATION.

Program Elements	Program Perspectives			
	Goals	Designs	Implementation	Outcomes
Participants	How could program goals more realistically correspond to learner goals?	Do learners have adequate opportunity to address their practical concerns?	Does the mode of instruction facilitate active learner involvement?	How might greater learner achievement be attained?
Instructors	Would a revision of some of the instructor's goals make them more compatible with one another?	Would the proposed method of instruction be compatible with the learning styles of the target group?	Are instructors capable of using the chosen method of instruction?	What emphasis in technique would increase the likelihood of noncognitive instructional outcomes?
Topics	Are there alternative topics that would better facilitate achieving stated program goals?	Does the explicit ordering of the topics facilitate learning?	Given the topic area, is there a better means for implementing it?	Would it be useful to go into greater topic depth?
Contexts	Does our current knowledge of the context suggest a change of goals?	Is the format of the program consistent with the setting of the instruction?	Does the selection of participants comply with equal opportunity regulations?	How might greater impact on the learners' institutional setting be attained?

Source: Adapted from Grotelueschen, 1980, p. 92. Copyright 1980 by the Adult Education Association of the United States and Jossey-Bass Inc., Publishers. Used by permission of Jossey-Bass.

Recent developments in evaluation have focused on other methods, such as principal evaluation, empowerment evaluation, objectivist evaluation, and evaluation standards (Steele, 1991; Stufflebeam, 1993, 1994).

Measurement Issues Associated with Evaluation

Measurement is usually necessary to conduct evaluation. Numerous methods may be used, including standardized tests, pretests and posttests based on program objectives, performance tests, participant products, records of performance, and instructor evaluations.

If instruction focuses on objectives in the *affective domain,* program planners may wish to measure participant agreement or disagreement using a *Likert scale* (see Exhibit 12.1)—which comprises such response categories as "strongly agree,"

TABLE 12.5. JUSTIFICATION QUESTIONS FOR SUMMATIVE EVALUATION.

| Program Elements | *Program Perspectives* | | | |
	Goals	Designs	Implementation	Outcomes
Participants	Are the educational goals appropriate for these participants?	Is the program emphasis appropriate for the target population?	Was the time allocated to participant discussion sufficient?	Were the attained learner outcomes those most desired by the program sponsor?
Instructors	Are the primary purposes of instruction implicitly incompatible with program purposes?	Did the instructors follow the program design?	Was the method of instruction most suitable for the content being taught?	Were the unintended outcomes of instruction desirable?
Topics	Is this the best topic for achieving program goals?	Are the best topics selected, given the constraints of time and resources?	Was the topic dealt with as intended?	How was this topic useful to program participants?
Contexts	Were the attained goals educationally important?	Does the design optimize available resources?	Was the implementation of this program timely?	Was the impact of outcomes on the agency appropriate?

Source: Adapted from Grotelueschen, 1980, p. 93. Copyright 1980 by the Adult Education Association of the United States and Jossey-Bass Inc., Publishers. Used by permission of Jossey-Bass.

"agree," "disagree," and "strongly disagree"—or a *semantic differential* (see Exhibit 12.2)—which asks respondents to choose between opposite terms, representing polar extremes along a number of dimensions, for example, "enjoyable" or "unenjoyable," "informative" or "uninformative," and "practical" or "impractical" (Babbie, 1995, p. 178). Another way to discover opinions is by using a *pro rata* scale on which participants assign portions of a number to indicate their preferences (see Exhibit 12.3).

If instruction focuses on objectives in the *cognitive domain,* paper-and-pencil tests may be used. Test items can be prepared directly from instructional objectives and before materials are purchased, created, or purchased and modified. Instruction is thus results oriented and designed to be measured through tests.

If instruction focuses on objectives in the *psychomotor domain,* the "I can/cannot" test format can be useful. It affords participants the opportunity to indicate whether they believe they can accomplish the performance objectives. If they cannot, they may need more training, or else the work environment in which they perform may require modifications to support transfer of learning from instructional to work settings. An example of such a test is shown in Exhibit 12.4.

TABLE 12.6. PLANNING QUESTIONS FOR FUTURE EVALUATION.

Program Elements	*Program Perspectives*			
	Goals	Designs	Implementation	Outcomes
Participants	Have expectations been achieved by different potential learners?	Has feedback concerning the design been obtained from potential learners?	Is the sequencing of program components appropriate for the intended learners?	Can the intended learner outcomes be attained?
Instructors	How might an appropriate array of instructional goals be attained?	Have alternative designs of instruction been considered?	Is the proposed method of instruction consistent with the intended goals?	Are the instructor's desired outcomes attainable?
Topics	Is the topic relevant to the proposed goals?	Is the intended scope of topic coverage appropriate?	What is the best method of instruction for this topic?	Will exposure to this topic be beneficial to participants?
Contexts	Are the proposed program goals consistent with the image of the sponsoring agency?	Does the design reflect an awareness of setting differences of program offerings?	Is the pacing of instruction consistent with the philosophy of the program?	What kind of impact will the anticipated goals have on the sponsoring institution?

Source: Adapted from Grotelueschen, 1980.

A variation of this form may use the following open-ended questions:

1. As a result of this program, I plan to make the following changes: . . .
2. As evidence that these changes are producing results, I will be looking for the following indices and/or symptoms of improvement in my organization: . . .
3. To feel completely confident in performing what I have learned, I would like further help in. . . .
4. This program has shown me that I need to learn more about. . . .
5. When I report to my supervisor about this experience, I will ask for help in. . . .
6. The best evidence that I can apply what I have learned is. . . .
7. If someone questions me about doing things differently, I will counter that by. . . .
8. In the future, when my coworkers or colleagues plan to attend this same program, I can help them to optimize their learning by. . . .

A form can also be given to participants at the close of a training session to give them a chance to indicate how much they intend to apply on their jobs what

EXHIBIT 12.1. SAMPLE AGREEMENT/DISAGREEMENT TEST.

HOW DO YOU FEEL ABOUT THE INSTRUCTOR'S ROLE?

Here are several statements. Please show the degree to which you agree or disagree with each statement by placing a check [✓] in one of the columns at the left.

Strongly Agree	Tend to Agree	No Opinion	Tend to Disagree	Strongly Disagree	
_____	_____	_____	_____	_____	1. The instructor should involve participants in course planning.
_____	_____	_____	_____	_____	2. Responsibility for learning should be shared by both instructor and participants.
_____	_____	_____	_____	_____	3. An effective instructor frequently uses visual aids.
_____	_____	_____	_____	_____	4. Lecture is an effective technique when the aim is to convey knowledge.

EXHIBIT 12.2. SAMPLE OF THE SEMANTIC DIFFERENTIAL.

HOW DO YOU FEEL ABOUT VIDEOCONFERENCING?

Here is a list of sets of adjectives that indicate different points of view. Indicate with a check [✓] which point on the continuum between each set of adjectives coincides with your feelings about the technology used in this course.

	+3	+2	+1	+/−	+1	+2	+3	
Good								Bad
Pleasant								Unpleasant
Easy								Difficult
Friendly								Unfriendly
Useful								Useless
Effective								Ineffective
Efficient								Inefficient
Accessible								Inaccessible
Exciting								Dull
Helpful								Unhelpful

EXHIBIT 12.3. SAMPLE OF A *PRO RATA* INSTRUMENT.

Assume that you are using a numerical scale to appraise your employees. You want to indicate the *relative importance* of performance elements. You have exactly 100 points to assign to the elements listed below, and to two other factors if you wish to add elements that are missing. Remember, the numbers you assign must total 100.

Interactions with others	_____
Dependability/Reliability	_____
Obedience	_____
Quality of work	_____
Quantity of work	_____
Personality	_____
Initiative	_____
Total	100

EXHIBIT 12.4. SAMPLE OF A CAN/CANNOT DO FORM.

HOW ARE YOU DOING?

Listed here are the objectives of this training program. Please indicate how well you have mastered each objective by placing an X in the appropriate lefthand column.

I Can	I Cannot	
_____	_____	1. Conduct an analysis of the external environment.
_____	_____	2. Organize and work with an advisory committee.
_____	_____	3. Survey other organizations and individuals likely to compete and/or cooperate with the program planning activities of the organization.

they have learned during a program. A sample of such a form is shown in Exhibit 12.5. Because it is critical to know how much participants actually do transfer what they have learned when they return to the work site, it is advisable to follow up with participants after a certain period following the training program by giving them an opportunity to indicate the frequency with which they apply the competencies they learned (see Exhibit 12.6). Of course, such a measure would have greater value if a baseline were established before training.

Another approach to testing is to substitute specific expressions (such as "each hour," "daily," "weekly," "monthly," or "never") for vague expressions such as "often," "once in a while," and "infrequently." An additional approach avoids predisposing participants toward the desired response by asking open-ended questions, such as the following:

EXHIBIT 12.5. SAMPLE TRAINING FOLLOW-UP INSTRUMENT.

HOW WILL YOU APPLY WHAT YOU HAVE LEARNED?

Now that you have finished this workshop, it is time to think about how you will apply what you have learned. Please give us your best estimate by checking the column at right.

The objectives of the program are listed below. For each of them, indicate your intentions about applying them in your work.	I Plan to Do This				I Do Not Feel I Have Achieved This Objective
	Always	Often	Sometimes	Never	Comments
1. Consider how aspects of my working philosophy of lifelong education relate to my program planning work.					
2. Identify various approaches to responding to ethical dilemmas encountered in my education or training work.					
3. Consider alternative methods for determining needs of a client group.					
4. Consider the possibility of using a variety of methods, techniques, and devices in my programming work.					

EXHIBIT 12.6. SAMPLE TEST OF APPLICATION OF LEARNING.

DID THE TRAINING HELP YOU TO DO YOUR WORK?

Now that you have been back at work for a while after completing the program planning workshop, please take a moment to indicate what you are applying in your work. The program objectives are listed at the left. In the columns at the right, indicate how often you apply each objective and make any comments about how it works out in practice.

Workshop Objectives	How Often Do You Do This?				Comments
	Often	Now and Then	Seldom	Never	
1. Consider how aspects of my working philosophy of lifelong education relate to my program planning work.					
2. Identify various approaches to responding to ethical dilemmas encountered in my education or training work.					
3. Consider alternative methods for determining needs of a client group.					
4. Consider the possibility of using a variety of methods, techniques, and devices in my programming work.					

1. What have you done on the job that you feel especially good about since participating in the course?
2. What has happened on the job as a result of what you learned in the training course?
3. Have you done anything on the job that you wish you had not? In other words, have you done anything that was directly in opposition to what you learned in the training course?
4. What has happened on the job as a result of doing something directly opposed to what you learned in the training course?
5. What new training needs do you feel have become evident since you participated in the training?

Sometimes it is also useful to compare participant and supervisory reports. This might be done by asking the following questions of supervisors:

1. What desirable behavioral changes, if any, have you noticed in the individual who participated in the training?
2. How did you reinforce those behavioral changes?
3. What undesirable behavior changes, if any, have you noticed in the individual who participated in the training?
4. What did you do about those behaviors?

Typical Training Evaluation Practices

Just as few research studies have explored typical training needs assessment practices in the United States (see Chapter Ten), so too have few studies focused on the state of the art of training evaluation. One result is that program planners are unable to provide decision makers with convincing arguments about the value of evaluation by pointing to the results of benchmarks elsewhere. Another result is that program planners are unable to compare what they are doing with what others are doing to determine whether their approaches are exemplary, average, or below average.

The Authors' Studies of Evaluation Practices

The authors gave the following instructions to HRD professionals and continuing education professionals in their 1995 survey of program planning practices:

The process of planning can be broken down into a number of interrelated and often iterative sequences of program planning practices. Below is a list of such practices. For each one, please place a check (√) to indicate how vital it is for effective program planning in general. When you plan programs, how often do you see that such practices are implemented?

The instructions were followed by a list of practices based on the Lifelong Education Program Planning model.

The survey results (see Figure 12.1) indicated that continuing education professionals considered calculating program breakeven to be more vital to effective program planning than calculating cost-benefit. *Breakeven* refers, of course, to the amount of money required of a program so that its revenues equal its expenditures, while *cost-benefit* refers to the comparison of the cost of the instruction to the financial benefits derived from it by solving performance problems or increasing productivity. Continuing education respondents also saw summative (after-instruction) evaluation as slightly more vital to effective program planning than formative (before-instruction) evaluation, and they also believed that summative evaluation is implemented more in practice than formative evaluation.

In contrast, HRD professionals viewed the following evaluation activities as vital to effective program planning (listed in order of importance with most important first): (1) planning formative evaluation, (2) planning summative evaluation, (3) conducting cost-benefit analysis, and (4) calculating breakeven. These results are reinforced by how often the HRD survey respondents indicated they see the same practices implemented (see Figure 12.2). In this survey, then, HRD professionals placed slightly greater emphasis on formative evaluation and cost-benefit analysis than did their continuing education counterparts. This result may simply be an indicator of key differences in the bottom-line measures with which they must comply. Both HRD professionals and academically based continuing education professionals are under pressure to demonstrate business results, but the indicators of such results differ in the two settings.

While indicators of success for business may include specific measures of improved performance linked to reduced costs, increased production or quality, and higher profit margins, such indicators for education may include a growing number and variety of education programs that attract large numbers of participants with high retention rates and generate surplus income that can be transferred to the parent institution.

A Study of Typical Training Evaluation Practices

To investigate typical training evaluation practices, Rothwell prepared and mailed a survey to 350 randomly selected HRD professionals in May 1995 (Rothwell, 1995b). Prospective respondents were chosen from the membership directory of

FIGURE 12.1. CONTINUING EDUCATION PROFESSIONALS' PERCEPTIONS OF EVALUATION PRACTICES.

How vital is the step to effective program planning?

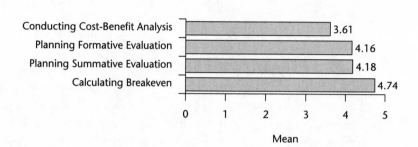

How often do you see this practice implemented?

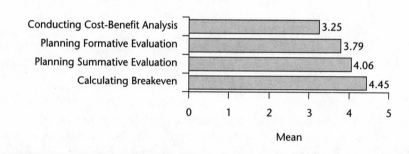

5 = high importance   5 = always

Source: Cookson and Rothwell, 1995.

the American Society for Training and Development (1994). By August 1995, 65 anonymous surveys had been returned. The response rate was thus 18.57 percent, even though a follow-up postcard was mailed. Not all respondents answered every question, so response rates varied by item. No effort was made to follow up with nonrespondents.

Professionals from manufacturing organizations comprised 32 percent of respondents; those from organizations employing 500 to 1999 people accounted for 23 percent; and those who were HRD professionals with supervisory responsibility accounted for 42 percent.

The survey was designed to answer several key questions:

FIGURE 12.2. HRD PROFESSIONALS' PERCEPTIONS OF EVALUATION PRACTICES.

How vital is the step to effective program planning?

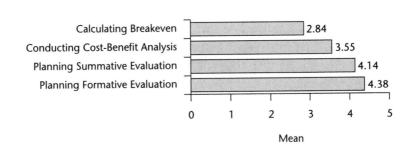

How often do you see this practice implemented?

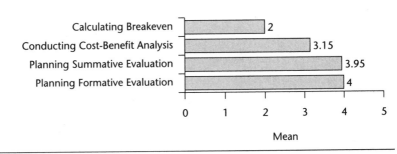

5 = most vital   5 = most often

1. How is training evaluation conducted in the respondents' U.S.–based organizations?
2. Who conducts training evaluation?
3. What percentage of respondents' organizations have established a cost model for training? A benefits model? Computed return-on-investment (ROI)?
4. How often do top managers ask for evidence of the dollar return on training? How often do they ask for that information before training is delivered? After training is delivered?
5. How often do top managers participate personally in conducting cost-benefit analysis of training results?

6. For what job categories is training evaluation most frequently performed in the respondents' organizations? Least frequently performed?

7. What training evaluation methods are most frequently used?

8. What training evaluation methods do respondents perceive to be most effective?

9. What are the biggest problems or difficulties encountered by HRD professionals when they conduct training evaluation?

10. What are the biggest advantages that HRD professionals perceive to have been gained by conducting training evaluation in their organizations?

Of course the study was limited by a low response rate and no follow-up with nonrespondents. Moreover, it did not provide information about program evaluation practices in educational institutions; rather, it focused solely on training/HRD practices in business.

In the respondents' organizations, HRD professionals bear primary responsibility for conducting training evaluation (42 percent), followed by "other" (18.5 percent), informal committees (17.3 percent), "nobody" (9.9 percent), line managers (8.6 percent), and formal committees (3.7 percent). According to 41 percent of the respondents to the survey, "top managers never ask for indications of the dollar return on training." Only 26 percent of the respondents' organizations have established a cost model for training; only 23 percent have established a benefits model for training; and only nine of sixty-five respondents (14 percent) indicated that their organizations computed return-on-investment for training. However, 40 percent indicated that top managers ask for indications of the dollar return on training only *after* it is delivered, and only 19 percent indicated that top managers participate personally in computing cost-benefit analysis of training results.

In the respondents' organizations, training evaluation is most frequently performed for supervisors and technical employees, and least frequently performed for executives (see Table 12.7). The training evaluation methods most frequently used include class evaluations and observations; the training evaluation methods least frequently used are the Delphi Procedure and Nominal Group Technique (see Figure 12.3). The training evaluation methods perceived by respondents to be most effective were observations and work samples; those perceived to be least effective were the Delphi Procedure and Nominal Group Technique (see Figure 12.4).

Survey respondents indicated that making the case to evaluate training and finding the necessary resources to carry it out number among the biggest problems they encounter in conducting training evaluation. One respondent, for instance, wrote that he or she receives "no requests nor emphasis on evaluation. [We] do what has traditionally been done." Another noted that "lack of support, endorsement by senior management" represented a major problem. To some

TABLE 12.7. FREQUENCY OF TRAINING EVALUATION BY JOB CATEGORY.

Job Category	Frequency							Mean	Standard Deviation
	Never	Once Every 6+ Years	Once Every 4–6 Years	Once Every 3–4 Years	Once Every 2–3 Years	Once Every 1–2 Years	Once Every Year		
	1	2	3	4	5	6	7		
Technical Employees	12	2	3	0	4	12	18	4.76	2.46
Supervisors	12	2	4	4	4	5	22	4.68	2.47
Production Employees	12	1	1	2	4	7	16	4.63	2.55
Professional Employees	16	4	3	1	5	8	16	4.19	2.56
Salespersons	13	3	3	2	3	3	13	4.0	2.60
Middle Managers	18	3	1	4	4	9	13	4.0	2.55
Clerical Employees	19	4	2	1	5	7	12	3.76	2.58
Executives	29	2	3	1	2	7	10	3.11	2.57

FIGURE 12.3. TRAINING EVALUATION METHODS USED MOST FREQUENTLY BY HRD PROFESSIONALS.

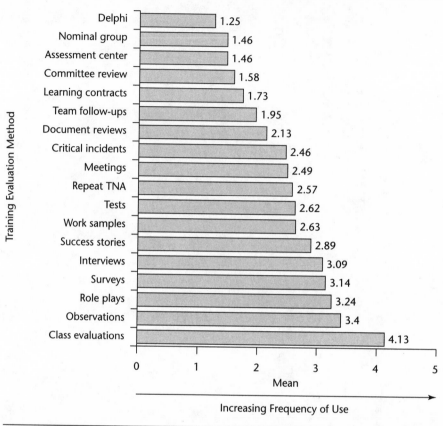

Source: Rothwell, 1995b. All rights reserved.

degree, these problems seem to stem from poor positioning of training departments by company management and a failure by HRD professionals to make a convincing case that what they do is strategically important to meeting pressing organizational needs. Managers tend to see training as a quick fix strategy, one that (in the words of one survey respondent) they "throw at problem situations when employees know how to do the job but are not performing for other reasons. Evaluation is difficult when training is an inappropriate solution." Since few organizations conduct systematic needs assessment before training is designed and delivered to define the problems to be solved by that training, evaluating final results is difficult. In short, if management does not know what results are desired

FIGURE 12.4. TRAINING EVALUATION METHODS CONSIDERED MOST EFFECTIVE BY HRD PROFESSIONALS.

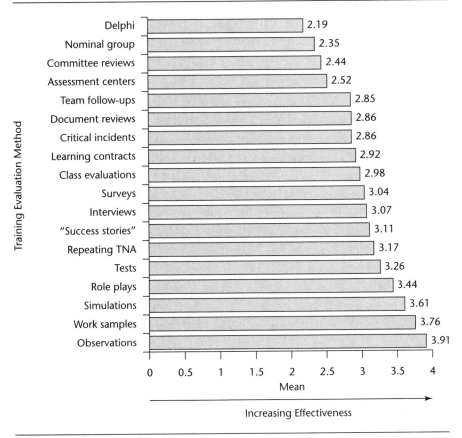

from training—an issue that should be clarified by needs assessment—then evaluating results is more difficult than when desired results are clear, specific, and widely communicated. It could be that requests by management for information about the return on training investments is merely symptomatic of a deeper problem: training has not been properly positioned in the organization to deliver effective business results, so skeptics assail it for proof of tangible economic benefit.

Lack of resources was another problem in conducting evaluation that ranked high among survey respondents. They were succinct in reporting this problem. For example, one respondent wrote: "[I am] not getting cooperation from supervisors and managers. They're too busy." Another wrote that training evaluation efforts are hampered by "lack of resources, needs assessment, and follow-up." A third indicated that a significant problem stemmed from "accepting [the] up-front cost and time associated with systematic evaluation." It should not be too surprising, however, that managers are unwilling to devote time, money, or staff to training evaluation when they do not see useful business reasons for doing it.

The biggest advantages of conducting training evaluation include getting feedback for continuous improvement and evidence of results. As one survey respondent wrote, evaluation "helps us ensure that training is meeting our customers' needs." Another suggested that training evaluation provides "justification for training and identification of areas for improvement in the training program and on the job." These are, of course, significant advantages.

The survey results make for interesting reading, providing a glimpse of real-world practices on an issue of growing importance. Unfortunately, the results of this study do not reveal a high level of sophistication in training evaluation methods. Nor do they demonstrate significant time commitments to training evaluation by program planners working as HRD professionals.

Summary

This chapter focused on evaluation. The first part defined *evaluation* as the process of estimating value, and *program evaluation* as the process of estimating the value of a planned learning experience.

The second part explained that evaluating programs is worthwhile because it improves organizational operations, such as the planning process, decision-making procedures, recruitment and training, public relations, and administrative management. It also improves such program aspects as objectives, selection of methods and materials, and the quality of learning outcomes, and it helps program planners to defend against attack, to justify expansion, to raise morale, and to improve personnel evaluation and promotion and institutional reorganization.

The third part of the chapter reviewed four approaches to program evaluation that have been particularly influential. Bennett's model consists of a chain of seven events to consider when conducting an evaluation. Kirkpatrick's four categories of evaluation are reaction evaluation, learning evaluation, evaluation of on-the-job behavioral change, and outcome evaluation. Stufflebeam's model identifies two purposes of evaluation: to enable decision making for program improvement (formative evaluation) and to enable accountability in order to justify program value (summative evaluation). Grotelueschen proposed eight steps that can serve as guidelines for designing a program evaluation.

The fourth part of the chapter described measurement issues associated with evaluation. And the fifth part summarized the authors' original research about typical training evaluation practices in U.S.-based organizations. The authors found in their 1995 survey of program planning practices that continuing educators considered calculating program breakeven as significantly more vital to effective program planning than calculating cost-benefit, and that HRD professionals viewed the following evaluation activities as vital to effective program planning (listed in order of importance with most important first): (1) planning formative evaluation, (2) planning summative evaluation, (3) conducting cost-benefit analysis, and (4) calculating breakeven. The results of original research by Rothwell answered several key questions. Among the highlights of the survey results was that in the respondents' organizations, trainers bear primary responsibility for conducting training evaluation, and that training evaluation is most frequently performed for supervisors and technical employees and least frequently for executives. The training evaluation methods most frequently used include class evaluations and observations, and the methods least frequently used were the Delphi Procedure and Nominal Group Technique. The methods perceived by respondents to be most effective were observations and work samples; those perceived to be least effective were the Delphi Procedure and Nominal Group Technique.

Once it is clear how program success is to be measured, program planners are able to formulate an instructional design or work with stakeholders in that process. Formulating an instructional design is the topic of the next chapter.

CHAPTER THIRTEEN

FORMULATING THE INSTRUCTIONAL DESIGN

Once program planners have analyzed needs, established objectives, and created a basis for evaluation, they are ready to design planned learning experiences. For most program planners, this step is what they enjoy doing most—and often what they also do best. This chapter builds on the foundation of the preceding steps in the Lifelong Education Program Planning (LEPP) model and reviews important principles of designing instruction.

As discussed in Chapter One, much confusion has long existed about the meaning of the terms *instruction, curriculum,* and *program.* According to the authors, *instruction* focuses on the interaction between a learner and a trainer or educator that is intended to help learners acquire new knowledge, skills, or attitudes, while *curriculum* is the design of instructional and learner interactions and resources intended to accompany those interactions. The broader term *program* refers to a set of organized learning activities systematically designed to achieve planned learning outcomes in a specific period. The development of both instruction and curriculum can be viewed as steps in the program planning process in training and educational settings.

Instruction is the focus of this chapter. While many approaches can serve as the foundation for instructional design (Reigeluth, 1987), this chapter will focus on two key approaches. The first part of the chapter reviews the ADDIE model. ADDIE is an acronym created from the first letters of the words *analysis, design, development, implementation* (or *instruction*), and *evaluation.* The second part of the chapter reviews one approach to the Action Learning (AL) model. ADDIE is perhaps most appropriate when program planners apply a directive approach to program planning, while AL is better suited to the collaborative and nondirective approaches. Program planning trends in both industry-based training and traditional education appear to be shifting away from directive applications represented by the classic ADDIE model and toward more collaborative, team-based, and nondirective approaches (Richey, 1995).

The ADDIE Model

As Carnevale, Gainer, and Villet (1990) wrote, "The systematic dimension of the applied approach has its roots in the seminal work by the United States military on what is called Instructional Systems Design (ISD). Over the years, variations on the ISD theme have evolved. Systematic approaches have many names, but they all include five stages: **a**nalysis of training needs, **d**esign of training curriculum, **d**evelopment of training curriculum, **i**mplementation (delivery), and **e**valuation" (p. 30). ISD has exerted profound influence over instructional design in business and industry. Although more than forty variations of the ISD model have been identified (Andrews and Goodson, 1980), the ADDIE model remains a common denominator that is general enough to have accommodated numerous variations proposed over the years.

Figure 13.1 depicts one way the ADDIE model can be conceptualized. The figure is not intended to be definitive. Rather, it is meant to be representative of many ISD models for planning education and training programs. ADDIE emphasizes instruction as an agent-directed process, done by someone to someone else. Few can doubt that the model, with its strong emphasis on results (outcomes), has exerted immense influence on many educators and human resource development professionals.

FIGURE 13.1. THE ADDIE MODEL.

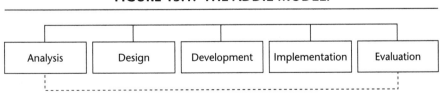

The Analysis Phase

During the analysis phase of the ADDIE model, program planners examine the organizational environment, the prospective participants, and the work or occupational demands and expectations that will affect the eventual application of planned learning. They also distinguish instructional needs from noninstructional needs, thus distinguishing performance gaps that would be appropriately addressed through instruction from gaps more appropriately addressed through management action. Once instructional needs are identified, they are examined in greater depth through needs assessment and analysis.

Figure 13.2 depicts the activities undertaken during the analysis phase, based on a model by Rosenberg (1982). The model illustrates the phase's focus on organizational, learner, and job needs. By analyzing these needs, program planners and others arrive at performance requirements that clarify what should be happening after instruction has occurred. Instructional requirements (depicted as course content in Figure 13.2) flow from performance requirements. Evaluation

FIGURE 13.2. THE ANALYSIS PHASE OF THE ADDIE MODEL.

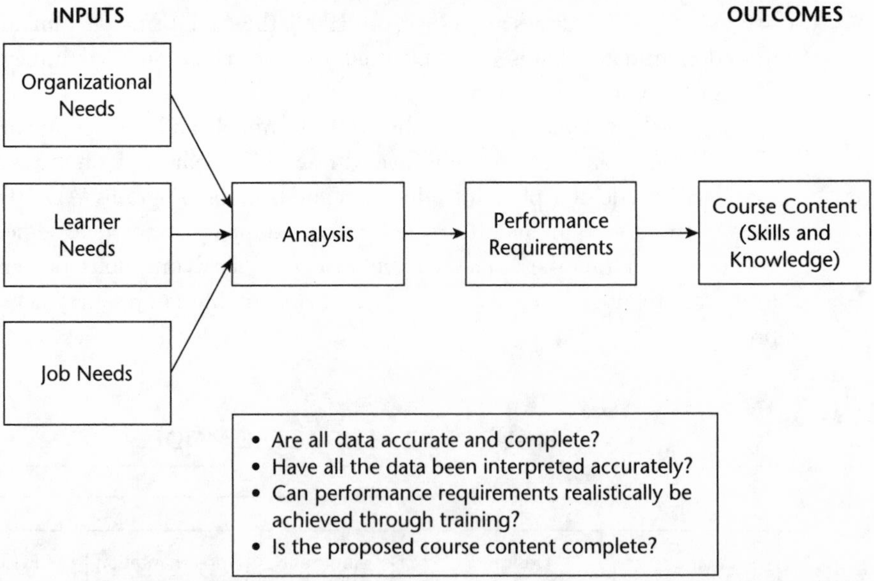
INPUTS
OUTCOMES
Organizational Needs
Learner Needs
Job Needs
Analysis
Performance Requirements
Course Content (Skills and Knowledge)
• Are all data accurate and complete?
• Have all the data been interpreted accurately?
• Can performance requirements realistically be achieved through training?
• Is the proposed course content complete?

Source: Rosenberg, 1982, p. 45. © September 1982, *Training & Development,* American Society for Training and Development. Reprinted with permission. All rights reserved.

criteria for this stage of the ADDIE model are based on the key issues addressed in this phase. In Rosenberg's model, evaluation criteria are posed as questions.

The Design Phase

During the design phase, program planners undertake the task of determining how to meet an instructional need or solve a performance problem. Course content, an input from the analysis phase, becomes the key input that is transformed into objectives and subsequently into test specifications, materials specifications, and instructional strategy. Another input is the instructional design model itself, such as the model by Rosenberg (1982) depicted in Figure 13.3. The model serves as a blueprint for processing the information received and for deriving

FIGURE 13.3. THE DESIGN PHASE OF THE ADDIE MODEL.

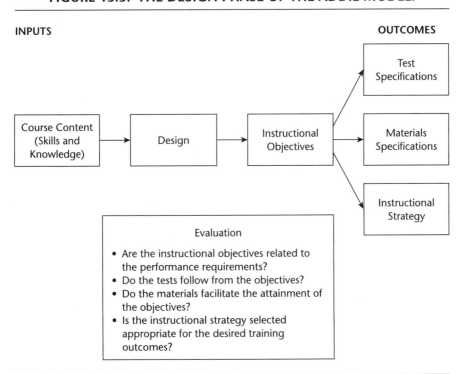

instructional objectives. As in the analysis phase, the evaluation criteria for this phase are posed as questions linked to key issues in the design phase.

The Development Phase

In the development phase, program planners translate instructional design information and ideas about tests, materials, and instructional strategies into instructional materials to be implemented (see the model depicted in Figure 13.4). Tests, media, and instructor and participant materials are initially tried out (that is, subjected to *formative evaluation*) to ensure that they are effective and conform to criteria established in the design phase. They are revised as necessary prior to

FIGURE 13.4. THE DEVELOPMENT PHASE OF THE ADDIE MODEL.

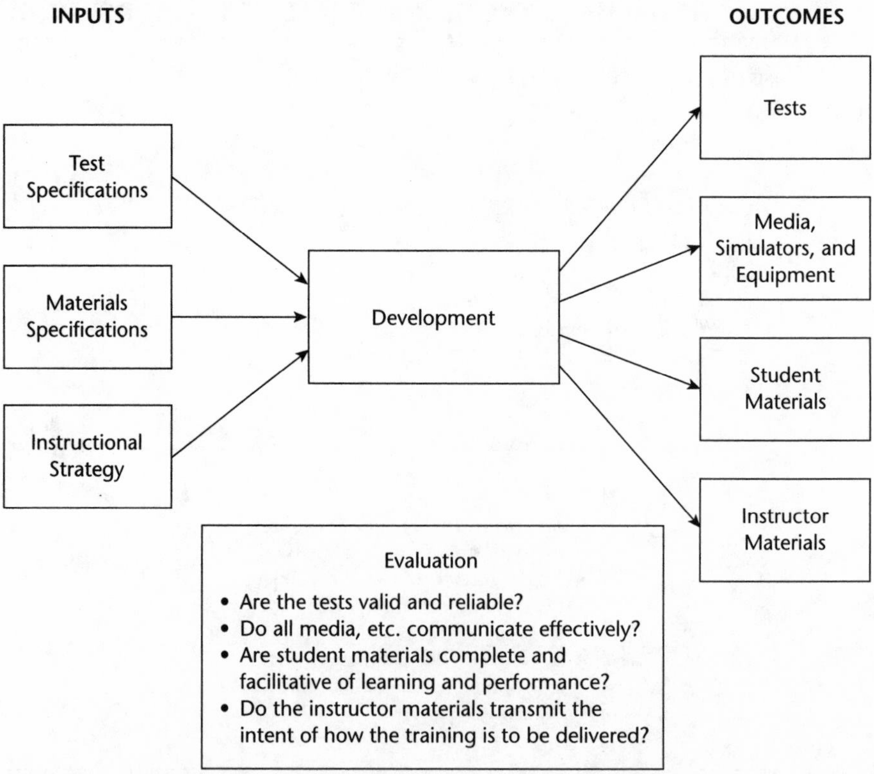

INPUTS   OUTCOMES

- Test Specifications
- Materials Specifications
- Instructional Strategy

→ Development →

- Tests
- Media, Simulators, and Equipment
- Student Materials
- Instructor Materials

Evaluation
- Are the tests valid and reliable?
- Do all media, etc. communicate effectively?
- Are student materials complete and facilitative of learning and performance?
- Do the instructor materials transmit the intent of how the training is to be delivered?

widespread implementation. As for the previous phases, evaluation criteria for the development phase are derived from the essential actions taken in the phase.

The Implementation Phase

The previous phases culminate in implementation. If the previous phases have been completed rigorously, the instructional results should match the instructional objectives. Of course results are affected by variables beyond instructor control, including participants' motivation levels and abilities and the climate of the instructional and work settings. Program planners should remain vigilantly responsive to the need to refine the instruction while it is delivered. During the implementation phase (depicted in Figure 13.5), program planners monitor instructor performance, participant progress, and instructional outcomes so that if difficulties arise, they can be detected and resolved.

FIGURE 13.5. THE IMPLEMENTATION PHASE OF THE ADDIE MODEL.

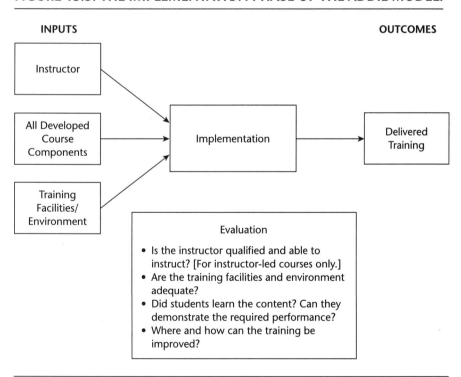

Source: Rosenberg, 1982, p. 49. © September 1982, *Training & Development,* American Society for Training and Development. Reprinted with permission. All rights reserved.

The Evaluation Phase

Evaluation is a thread running throughout all phases of the ADDIE model. It is thus important to regard the evaluation phase in the ADDIE model not as a linear process in which each phase follows the previous phase in order, ending in evaluation, but as a cyclical process in which evaluation is linked to every phase to ensure accountability and quality.

The Action Learning Model

Action learning (AL) was first introduced by Reginald Revans (1971) in a book about management development. The model has since spurred widespread interest and debate (Jones, 1990; Marsick, 1990; Marsick and others, 1992; Marsick and Watkins, 1992; Mumford, 1991; Pedler, 1983; Revans, 1982, 1983; Vince and Martin, 1993; Wallace, 1990; Wortham, 1992). The idea is a simple one, captured succinctly in a few sentences by Garratt (1991, p. 45): "Action Learning is a process for the reform of organizations and the liberation of human vision within organizations. The process is based on taking one or more crucial organizational problems and, in real time, analyzing their dynamics; implementing proposed solutions derived from the constructive criticisms of colleagues; monitoring results; and through being held responsible for these actions, learning from the results so that future problem solving and opportunity taking are improved." This approach is akin to any form of human problem solving.

While in one sense AL is as old as humanity, it is appealing for the 1990s because it is a real-time strategy that lends itself well to applications in team settings. It transforms organizations into learning environments (Senge, 1990), and it transforms the program planner into a learning facilitator (Watkins and Marsick, 1993). It also captures the great power of incidental learning, which is learning that occurs as a by-product of life experience, bending it to planned ends that empower learners.

The basis of AL is a learning spiral, a nine-step model depicted in Figure 13.6.

Step 1: Transitioning from earlier action to learning. Action occurring during life and work gives rise to opportunities for learning, and organizations and individuals develop incrementally through their learning experiences. Such learning can happen in a classroom or, more often, in the work setting. For instance, individuals may be the victims of poor supervision or targets of customer complaints. They may also be motivated to learn by the life or work challenges they face.

FIGURE 13.6. THE LEARNING SPIRAL: AN ACTION LEARNING MODEL.

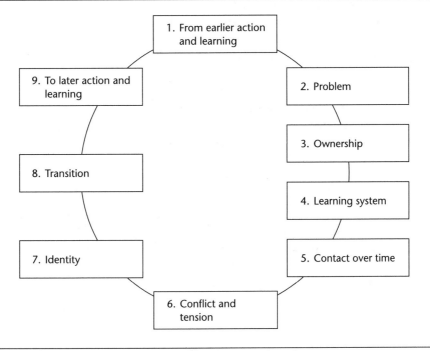

Source: Adapted from Pedler, 1991, p. xxv. Used by permission of Gower.

Step 2: Identifying the problem. Learning does not just happen. It is usually a response to a problem or a crisis occurring in an organization or in an individual's life. This step in the AL model is the identification of a need arising from a problem or crisis, although the need can also stem from a vision, a goal, or an improvement opportunity. The need stimulates ownership of the learning process.

Examples of such needs are easy to find. If error rates on a production line are high and cause concern, there is a problem. If employee turnover exceeds industry norms, a problem exists. If the organization wishes to improve customer service, it has created an opportunity for improvement. All of these situations—and others—can become the basis for AL.

Step 3: Taking ownership of a learning experience. Problems and opportunities prompt planned learning only when people take ownership of them. In this step, stakeholder groups or individuals recognize the need for learning and action, then accept responsibility for taking action. For example, an individual whose employer is transferring her to their German office recognizes the need to learn German and accepts ownership for that effort. Likewise, an organization's decision makers pledge to increase production while decreasing product rejection rates, thus accepting ownership of the effort.

Step 4: Creating a learning system. A learning system is much like an individual support system and is essential for the AL model to be applied successfully. "To tackle problems worthy of the name we need help—allies, comrades, colleagues and resources. Working in a set or small group can provide for mutual empowerment" (Pedler, 1983, p. xxiv).

One approach to establishing a learning system is to form an ad hoc team composed of individuals who share a learning need, individually possess expertise that can contribute to solving the problem, and collectively possess the ability to learn interdependently. For instance, an organization that is formulating a strategic business plan may form a team of the executives. Another example is a group of decision makers who have pledged to establish a new training department. They may create a corporate council, committee, or advisory team to lay the groundwork. That council, committee, or advisory team constitutes a learning system.

Step 5: Establishing contact over time. Members of the learning system need to work together cohesively to tackle a problem, realize a vision, formulate a goal, or meet a need. For this reason, intact or standing teams are better vehicles for implementing the AL model than ad hoc teams that meet only occasionally. However, contact over an extended period of years can still be achieved by an ad hoc team.

Team members work together, with or without a program planner serving as a group facilitator, to carry out most of the steps in the LEPP model. They can thus articulate their own working philosophy to guide the team, establish ethical standards for their relationship, appraise the organization's external and internal environments, accommodate adult learning characteristics, assess their own learning needs and negotiate their own and other stakeholders' interests, set their own planned learning goals and objectives, determine program success by establishing the means to evaluate and measure their planned learning experiences, formulate their own instructional designs, designate appropriate learning procedures to achieve learning objectives, recruit and retain other learners as necessary, promote and market what they do, budget and finance their own planned learning experiences, and select people to coach, advise, instruct, and counsel them. In this way, team members accept responsibility for their own learning. They may also be able to tap into incidental learning opportunities that arise as they perform their work or carry out other tasks. More than eighty-eight such approaches to incidental learning have been identified (Lombardo and Eichinger, 1989).

Step 6: Addressing conflict and tension. Learning is not a painless endeavor. Teams established to carry out action learning may follow all phases of the small group development cycle (Bradford, 1978), and each phase carries its own sources of conflict and tension. *Forming* is the first phase in the small group development cycle. It is during this phase that team members identify the task to be learned or the problem to be solved, and achieve clarity on interpersonal relationships. *Storming,* the second phase, is the phase most fraught with conflict because team members rebel against the task or problem at hand. The third phase is *norming,* during which team members reach agreement on what to do, how to do it, and who should do what. *Performing* is the fourth and final phase, during which team members carry out the task or solve the problem.

Step 7: Developing identity. In this step, team members achieve *group cohesiveness,* best understood as a sense of togetherness. Facilitating group cohesiveness can be an important role for program planners who function as group facilitators. Instrumental to building group cohesiveness is *process consultation,* defined by Schein (1988) as "a set of activities on the part of the consultant that help the client to perceive, understand, and act upon the process events that occur in the client's environment in order to improve the situation as defined by the client" (p. 11). *Processes* are how things happen in a group.

Step 8: Making a transition. During transition, team members consolidate their learning. It is difficult for team members to carry out this step on their own, so program planners functioning as small group facilitators can play an important role. The step involves debriefing at the end of a team learning project—called an *action learning set*—to ensure that team members reach agreement on what they learned, both individually and collectively, during the team experience, and identify problems or needs warranting future investigation.

This step represents a point of departure between an action learning project and other projects. Corporate or university committees, for instance, are team and project-oriented experiences. They are usually formed to address a problem, meet a need, or explore a new initiative. However, rarely is there a formal transition in which team members are debriefed by a facilitator on what they learned and what they feel they may need to learn in the future. Debriefing is called for by the action learning model because it clarifies what has been learned and sets the stage for the final step.

Step 9: Preparing for later action and learning. Learning is not a disconnected process. Past experiences influence learning. In action learning, an effort is made to plan for future learning to meet needs identified during action learning experiences. In this way, one experience leads to another in a continuing cycle of individual, group, and organizational improvement.

Applying the Action Learning Model: An Example

Perhaps the best way to grasp the AL model is to consider an example. Suppose an organization is experiencing explosive growth due to high product demand. Key decision makers decide that production in their manufacturing plant is hampered by a lengthy and poorly organized orientation period. To summarize the problem confronting the organization, one manager said, "We hire people on Friday and shove them onto the production line on Saturday. They are not even told where the restroom is, let alone how to do the job. They are expected to watch an experienced worker perform and absorb what he or she does. That is like expecting someone who watches the sun to learn how to shine." The decision makers have thus transitioned from earlier action and learning (Step 1), identified a problem (Step 2), and taken ownership of it (Step 3).

To address the problem, the decision makers form a team consisting of individuals who have conducted training and who are interested in improving the way the company manages it. Thus, a learning system has been created (Step 4). Team members orient themselves to the problem, establish their own learning objectives for solving it, and set out to investigate current practices (what is happening) and desirable practices (what should be happening). A facilitator helps them work together effectively. By benchmarking on-the-job training practices outside the organization and reading books (such as Rothwell and Kazanas, 1994b), they propose and pilot-test a model of a planned on-the-job training program. During this process they successfully establish contact with each other over time (Step 5), address team conflict and tension (Step 6), and develop a sense of identity (Step 7). Finally, they are debriefed by the facilitator about what they learned (Step 8), and the model is established throughout the organization, preparing the organization for later action and learning (Step 9).

Note that in this example the learners confronted a problem, established their own learning objectives to address it, tapped into external resources, experimented with a solution, were debriefed as they neared problem resolution, and then disbanded once the problem was solved. They functioned in a self-directed way. This is the AL model in action. The same principles may be applied to formulating a vision, establishing a goal, or exploring a new opportunity.

Summary

Once program planners have analyzed needs, established objectives, and created a basis for evaluation, they are ready to design planned learning experiences. The first part of this chapter reviewed the Analysis, Design, Develop, Instruct, and Evaluate (ADDIE) model; the second reviewed one approach to the Action Learning (AL) model. ADDIE, we argue, is appropriate when program planners apply a directive approach to program planning, and AL is better-suited, we believe, to the collaborative and nondirective approaches.

The ADDIE model is a systematic approach to instruction, what some call Instructional Systems Design (ISD). ADDIE views instruction as an agent-directed process that is done by someone to someone else, and emphasizes results (outcomes). Action learning (AL), conversely, is appealing because it is a real-time strategy that lends itself well to applications in team settings. It transforms organizations into learning environments and transforms the program planner's role into that of a learning facilitator who helps groups take action on their own. It also directs the great power of incidental learning to planned ends that empower learners.

The basis of AL is a learning spiral, a nine-step model that begins with transitioning from earlier action and learning and proceeds through identifying a problem, taking ownership for a learning experience, creating a learning system, establishing contact over time, addressing conflict and tension, developing identity, making a transition, and preparing for later action and learning.

Once the instructional design is formulated, it is possible to designate learning procedures—the topic of the next chapter.

CHAPTER FOURTEEN

DESIGNATING LEARNING PROCEDURES

Say the word *program* to educators or trainers and many of them will hear *courses*. So ingrained is the notion that learning occurs in classroom or group settings that many people seem to think that learning can occur only in such situations. That mistake is understandable. Most people have had formal group educational experiences in elementary, secondary, and higher educational institutions. Many others have attended employer-sponsored, group-oriented training programs and occupationally oriented continuing education courses. It is thus natural for them to assume that *program* should be interpreted to mean *course*. However, programs—and learning—may occur outside groups as well as inside them.

This three-part chapter reviews possible learning formats available to program planners, learners, and other stakeholders. How are the terms *method, technique,* and *device* defined? What criteria can help program planners select appropriate learning formats? What learning formats are most commonly used at present? This chapter addresses these important questions. In doing so it emphasizes the importance of designating learning procedures and provides ideas about how to carry out this step of the Lifelong Education Program Planning model.

Defining *Method, Technique,* and *Device*

As trainers and educators become more proficient as planners of lifelong education programs, they will become more sophisticated in their awareness of distinctions among the phenomena to which they seek to respond. They will also become more discriminating with respect to the most appropriate of the wide range of alternative programmatic interventions they can direct toward those phenomena. Trainers and educators who understand the distinctions between the terms *method, technique,* and *device,* for example can draw on conceptual tools that can enhance the precision of their program planning choices.

Method

A *method* is a procedure used in offering a program. Methods reflect the relationship between learners and an organizational sponsor or institutional provider. In a classic treatment, Verner (1964) presents a tripartite classification of methods:

1. *Individual methods* foster relations between a learner and the organizational sponsor through individualized learning experiences. Examples include on-the-job apprenticeship, correspondence courses, and coaching or mentoring by a supervisor or coworker.

2. *Group methods* foster individual learning through group arrangements. When groups are small, individuals benefit from pooling their experiences and insights with those of other participants. When groups are large, small subgroups can sometimes be more difficult to form and hence learning tends to be more individually focused.

   Five group methods are perhaps most familiar to most people:

- *Course.* Learning is organized, directed, and controlled by an instructional agent.
- *Discussion group.* Learning is shared by a group. Participants determine and control content.
- *Workshop or institute.* Learning activities are concentrated within a predetermined period, usually with practical application as an aim.
- *Lecture.* In general, the activity consists of a single instructional session. This method is appropriate for transmitting information, but is usually not appropriate for complex or involved learning tasks because lecture alone does not give learners sufficient opportunity to apply what they learn.
- *Forum or assembly.* This method is composed of open discussion between members of an audience and a speaker.

3. *Community methods* are situated in the community in which the learning is based. Learning stems from the daily problems people experience. Community development is the principal method. Program planners help community members

to reflect on and analyze their own reality and the problems confronting them. On the basis of that analysis, community members select preferred solutions and take collective action.

Technique

Techniques are the forms in which program planners establish relationships between learners and learning tasks. Verner (1964) classified techniques according to the purposes of the learning tasks. Examples of such purposes include acquiring information, building skills, or applying knowledge.

- *Techniques to acquire information* include lectures, or talks, and panels. *Lectures* or *talks* appropriately transmit information for learners to remember over brief time spans. They are less effective for transmitting information to be remembered over long time spans. Lectures of less than thirty minutes are usually more memorable than those exceeding thirty minutes. *Panels* are a series of short lectures by members of a well-informed group. Panels can transmit more diverse viewpoints than can be communicated by one lecturer.
- *Techniques to acquire a skill* require learners to assume active roles. They are therefore given more opportunity to participate than in techniques to acquire information. Examples include process demonstration and role play. In a *process demonstration,* each step in a procedure or process is presented in an isolated but sequential way. In a *role play,* learners act out a vignette dramatically, often to practice interpersonal skills or to solve problems.
- *Techniques to apply knowledge* are necessary when problem solving is emphasized. The classic problem-solving process consists of five steps: (1) identifying the problem, (2) gathering necessary information, (3) identifying possible solutions, (4) evaluating the solutions, and (5) choosing the most appropriate solution. Examples of such techniques include group discussion and buzz group. A *group discussion* permits group members to participate in a problem-solving process usually led by a designated leader. A *buzz group,* composed of six to ten participants, is formed when a larger group divides into smaller groups.

Device

Devices are aids that extend or increase the effectiveness of methods and techniques. Verner (1964) identified four device categories:

- *Illustrative devices* include objects used in connection with a results demonstration, such as a designated test plot where the effects of different planning practices may be observed by local farmers.

- *Extension devices* include radio, television, telephones (audio teleconferencing), or computers (computer-mediated communication).
- *Environmental devices* include the arrangement of chairs and tables in a classroom.
- *Manipulative devices* include tools, equipment, machinery, simulation machines, or computer hardware and software that simulate an environment for learners.

Taken together, methods, techniques, and devices are the processes used to achieve instructional objectives or to help learners pursue their planned learning experiences. The methods, techniques, and devices chosen to support learning experiences and how they are used dramatically affect the success of learning. In the directive approach to program planning, the program planners, of course, decide what methods, techniques, and devices are appropriate and how they will be used. In contrast, in the collaborative approach, program planners work with such stakeholders as learners and managers to decide what methods, techniques, and devices will be used. And in the nondirective approach, learners themselves make the decisions about what methods, techniques, and devices to use and how to use them, although program planners may function as enabling agents and consultants to provide advice on such matters.

Determining Appropriate Learning Formats

Program planners can become better equipped to create enriching experiences for participants by becoming aware of the enormous repertoire of methods, techniques, and devices that can be used to meet instructional objectives. But how should appropriate learning formats be selected? Program planners may find the following twelve questions useful in this process:

1. *What are the major goals of the learning activities?* The behaviors evoked by the methods, techniques, and devices should be in harmony with program goals. For instance, if the goal is to improve courteous treatment of customers, then a role play demonstrating how to be rude to customers would not be appropriate. Well-intentioned but naive program planners may fall victim to using such methods because they believe people can learn from experiencing the opposite of the desired goal. When programs go astray, the problem is often traceable to a learning goal gone astray.

2. *What performance is required to achieve instructional objectives?* The behavior indicated by the instructional objectives should be created by the methods, techniques, and devices that are used. For instance, automotive mechanics who are learning engine repair should have an engine available. Additional aids might

include pictures of engines, tools appropriate for engine repair, and CD-ROMs that provide detailed, labeled schematic drawings of engines.

3. *What instructional resources and materials are available?* The methods, techniques, and devices chosen should match the resources and materials available. If an engine is not available for a course in automotive repair, then conducting such a course may not be advisable.

4. *What are the physical facilities?* The instructional setting creates possibilities—and limitations. For instance, round tables that seat six to seven people are ideal for buzz groups, because they encourage participant interaction in small groups, and auditorium-style seating is ideal for large-group presentations; but placing 30 people in an auditorium that could seat 660—which happened to one of the authors at a conference—impedes the learning process.

5. *What financial resources are available?* The program budget imposes practical constraints on the methods, techniques, and devices that can be selected. Often the willingness of decision makers to supply the necessary financial resources to meet a learning need is a test of commitment. For instance, the chief executive officer who asks for training on quality for all employees but is unwilling to provide the funding to carry it out is not truly committed to the effort.

6. *What instructional expertise is available?* The use of some methods, techniques, and devices requires substantial experience and competence. On occasion, instructors may require training on a format before it can be used. That is often the case when using such emerging technologies as videoconferencing, audiographics, and the World Wide Web or the Internet.

7. *What are the participants' abilities?* Do they possess the prerequisite knowledge and skills to use the methods, techniques, or devices? Not all participants, for example, are willing or able to participate in computer-assisted instruction; they may feel incompetent with it or even fear it.

8. *How much responsibility are participants willing to accept for their own learning?* Do they prefer to accept full responsibility for planning their own learning experiences? Do they prefer to share responsibility? Or do they prefer to relinquish all responsibility for planning because it takes too much time? For instance, in an organization installing team-based management, employees may resist instruction on teams. Reasons might include that they are not rewarded for functioning collectively, that they are unsure what to do or how to function in teams, or that they

are so pressured to produce that no time is readily available to support working together. In this situation, learners are unwilling to take responsibility for their own learning, and a directive approach is likely to be appropriate.

9. *What is the necessary relationship among learning activities?* Some methods, techniques, and devices are incompatible. For instance, if instruction is delivered by audio teleconferencing, unless some other appropriate medium is invoked a demonstration would be difficult, if not impossible.

10. *What participant involvement is necessary or desirable?* Some methods, techniques, and devices are better able to encourage participant involvement than others. For instance, while computer-based training may evoke strong interest among many program planners, it reduces social interaction among participants in their learning. This is a disadvantage because social interaction can make theory more real by helping to relate it to participants' experiences. Some learners also complain that much-touted videoconferencing also tends to reduce participant interaction unless opportunities to communicate are built in through other means, such as hot lines or on-line electronic mail chat rooms.

11. *What are the participants' levels of experience?* Some methods, techniques, and devices build on accumulated participant experience better than others. A key issue to consider, then, is how much participant experience is needed to use a method. For instance, a panel might be quite effective with inexperienced participants, because they are able to hear various viewpoints. But role plays or case studies may not be very effective with the same group, because participants may not have sufficient experience to relate to the situations with which they are presented.

12. *How important is it to use programs to generate new experience?* Some methods, techniques, and devices are more likely than others to generate learner experience and thus reinforce learning. Simulations, for instance, may give participants the benefit of experience without the hazards posed by on-the-job approaches.

Current Most Commonly Used Learning Formats

To assess what learning formats are most commonly used in training and continuing education, the authors posed appropriate questions in their 1995 surveys of continuing education professionals and human resource development (HRD) professionals. Figures 14.1, 14.2, 14.3, and 14.4 convey the respondents' perceptions of how often and how effective those formats are.

FIGURE 14.1. FREQUENCY WITH WHICH VARIOUS FORMATS ARE USED BY CONTINUING EDUCATION PROFESSIONALS.

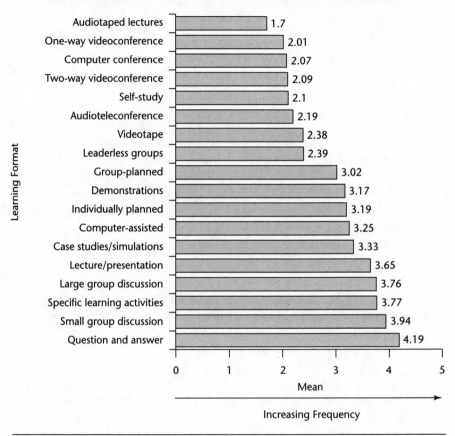

5 = most often

Although the response rates to both surveys were limited, the survey results revealed that respondents perceived question-and-answer and small group discussion formats as both most often used and most effective in their programs, while technology-based formats such as audio lecture and videoconference were perceived by respondents to be both least often used and least effective in their programs. While these results warrant further investigation, they may indicate that learners prefer more individualized methods over technology-based methods. That preference may be understandable in that high touch is preferred to high tech.

FIGURE 14.2. EFFECTIVENESS OF VARIOUS FORMATS AS PERCEIVED BY CONTINUING EDUCATION PROFESSIONALS.

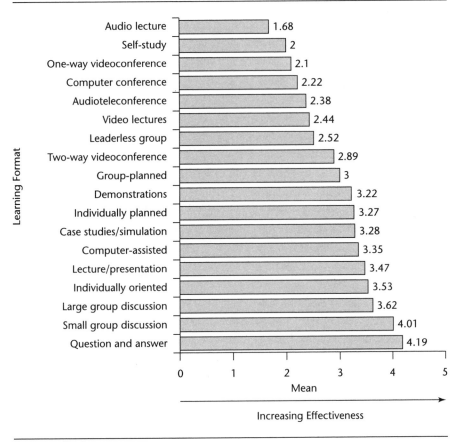

5 = most effective

Summary

This three-part chapter reviewed the various learning formats available to program planners, learners, and other stakeholders. It defined the terms *method, technique,* and *device.* It also provided questions that can help program planners to select appropriate learning formats: (1) What are the major goals of the learning activities? (2) What performance is required to achieve instructional objectives? (3) What instructional resources and materials are available? (4) What are the physical facilities? (5) What financial resources are available? (6) What instructional expertise is

FIGURE 14.3. FREQUENCY WITH WHICH
VARIOUS FORMATS ARE USED BY HRD PROFESSIONALS.

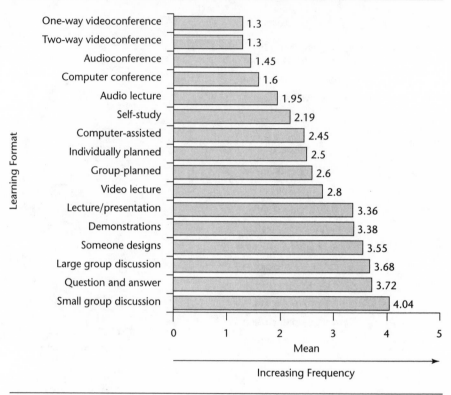

5 = most often

Source: Rothwell and Cookson, 1995. All rights reserved.

available? (7) What are the participants' abilities? (8) How much responsibility are participants willing to accept for their own learning? (9) What is the necessary relationship among learning activities? (10) What participant involvement is necessary or desirable? (11) What are the participants' levels of experience? and (12) How important is it to use programs to generate new experience?

To assess what learning formats are currently used in training and continuing education, the authors surveyed continuing education professionals and HRD professionals about what learning formats they used and which formats they considered most effective. The survey results revealed that respondents perceived question-and-answer and small group discussion as both most often used and most effective in their programs, while technology-based formats such as audio lecture

FIGURE 14.4. EFFECTIVENESS OF VARIOUS FORMATS AS PERCEIVED BY HRD PROFESSIONALS.

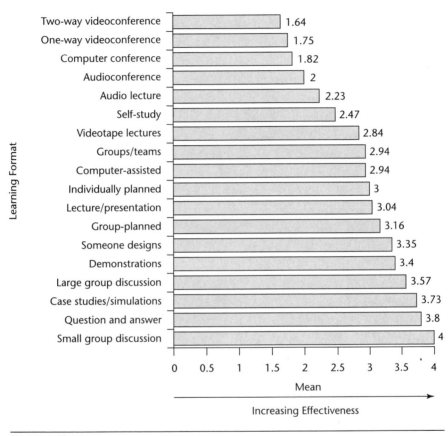

5 = most effective

and videoconference were perceived by respondents to be both least often used and least effective in their programs.

This chapter concludes the review of Quadrant 3 of the Lifelong Education Program Planning (LEPP) model. Each subquadrant of Quadrant 3 is important because it contributes to establishing a solid foundation for effective programs. Each subquadrant can also point the way to administrative aspects that are necessary for effective program management. Hence, administrative aspects are treated in Part Five.

PART FIVE

MANAGING ADMINISTRATIVE ASPECTS

Part Five focuses on Quadrant 4 of the LEPP model. It examines the key administrative aspects of program planning. Chapter Fifteen examines participant recruitment and retention. It addresses three key questions: (1) How can participants be recruited effectively? (2) How can participants be retained in programs successfully? and (3) What practical suggestions can help improve participant recruitment and retention? Chapter Sixteen describes how to promote and market programs. Chapter Seventeen reviews basic budgeting principles, explains how to calculate program costs and benefits, and suggests what to do about program budgeting. Chapter Eighteen offers advice to program planners who select, supervise, evaluate, and develop instructors.

CHAPTER FIFTEEN

RECRUITING AND RETAINING PROGRAM PARTICIPANTS

Recruiting and retaining participants are key responsibilities of all program planners. *Recruitment,* of course, is the process of inducing program participation, often by communicating information about the program to prospective participants. *Retention* means preserving participation. The best-designed and best-delivered program will be unsuccessful if nobody participates—or if participants withdraw before program completion (Cookson, 1989).

Recruitment is most important in voluntary programs. Examples of voluntary programs include conferences organized by college or university continuing education departments, postgraduate courses, and correspondence programs, as well as industry training programs offered on a first-come, first-served basis to an organization's employees. In these situations, a program's continued survival and success depends on participant recruitment and retention.

Recruitment may seem less important in mandatory programs. In these cases participation hinges less on attracting prospective participants and more on convincing decision makers to require attendance. Examples of obligatory programs include safety training (mandated by the U.S. Occupational Safety and Health Administration), hazardous materials training (mandated by the U.S. Environmental Protection Agency), sexual harassment avoidance training (mandated by many employers to reduce the risk of grievances filed with the U.S. Equal Employment Opportunity Commission), new employee orientation for nurses (mandated for hospital accreditation), and continuing professional education for accountants (mandated for renewal of licensure in many states). But even obligatory courses require program planners to apply recruitment and retention principles, since someone must authorize initial and continuing participation. Such efforts are particularly challenging in restructured organizations where reduced staffing prompts stressed out decision makers to seek ways to sidestep off-the-job training so workers can remain on the job and thus remain productive.

How can efforts to recruit program participants be effective? How can participants be retained? This chapter offers guidelines for program planners in answering these questions.

Recruiting Program Participants

Adult learners usually involve themselves in voluntary educational programs only after they see how those programs will help them meet their immediate life or work needs. To make that determination, prospective participants must be aware of programs and form favorable impressions of them. Program planners must therefore be concerned about what program information is communicated and how it is communicated, because what is communicated and how it is communicated will influence participant decision making.

Many program planning models assume there will be participation and therefore devote scant attention to recruitment. One way to think about recruitment is to view it as involving public relations, marketing, and promotion.

Public Relations

Public relations consists of activities undertaken to project a favorable image of planned learning activities in continuing education or training efforts in general. Instead of projecting a favorable image of one program, public relations fosters general awareness of planned learning and purveys positive attitudes toward the program sponsor and the sponsor's services. This image of planned learning and of the sponsor should be visible to actual and prospective learners in everything the organization does.

Broadly construed, public relations precedes and underlies recruitment activities. It is enhanced by what Knowles (1980, p. 66) calls "setting an educative climate for learning," accomplished by providing a policy base, building an advisory committee structure, practicing "a democratic philosophy," and exemplifying, as an organization, a propensity for "change and growth."

Successful public relations strategies identify the public to be served, select the communication channels to reach that public, and convey the message. Effective public relations can predispose target constituencies, including prospective adult learners, to respond to specific programs to be promoted later. Low-cost public relations activities for community-level continuing education organizations include "piggyback ads, marquees, grocery bags, television identification slides, handouts at concerts, license plates on cars, book marks distributed at schools and libraries, feature articles in newspapers, tag lines in bill stuffers, and window displays in area businesses" (Ramsey, 1982, pp. 69–70). Examples of comparable public relations activities for in-house training might include electronic mail bulletin boards, company newsletter articles, speeches made by the chief executive officer, bulletin board posters, lapel pins, ballpoint pens, and training brochures.

Marketing

Marketing is all of the steps in the program planning process that are designed to identify and respond to the needs of targeted learners. It is the total managerial process of mapping the designated population within the sponsor's service area to determine the population's needs and wants and responding to them by developing specialized instructional programs to meet the needs of the prospective adult learner population (Pitt Community College, 1985).

Specific steps to be taken in formulating a marketing strategy include (1) segmenting the market to be served, (2) assessing the needs of targeted learners, (3) setting precise objectives based on the targeted learners' needs, (4) promoting programs to attract the targeted learners, and (5) guiding learners into learning activities. Once the prospective learner population has been mapped, program planners—working alone or with others—choose market segments or issues that warrant priority attention. Recruitment efforts are often directed toward the readily identifiable or priority market segments that are easiest to recruit. Continuing education professionals may, for instance, look to adults with high levels of educational attainment and occupational allegiance and with ready access to discretionary financial resources or time. Human resource development professionals may look to specific groups—such as top managers, engineers, or supervisors—who warrant priority attention due to performance problems, new organizational initiatives, or recently issued government mandates. While conventional marketing strategies may be adequate for these categories of people, conventional methods may prove inadequate for attracting prospective learners belonging to such typically excluded groups as ethnic minority adults, low-income heads-of-household, senior citizens without families, the unemployed, displaced homemakers, immigrants not fluent in English, and undocumented farm laborers.

Even within market segments, not all prospective participants are uniformly disposed to participate in programs. For that reason, program planners who adjust their marketing activities to accommodate diverse motivational orientations are likely to increase the likelihood of participation. Since Houle's (1961) pioneering study more than three decades ago, many people have elaborated on his troika of participant motivational orientations—that is, activity-oriented, goal-oriented, and learning-oriented participants. Few studies, however, have examined the motivational orientations of those who do not choose to participate in planned learning experiences. Not surprisingly, then, the motivational orientations of nonparticipants are seldom considered during market segmentation.

Recognizing this omission, Houle (1985) modified his original scheme to conceptualize six categories of adults to whom programs are offered: the oblivious, the uninvolved, the resistant, the focused, the eclectic, and the comprehensive. Resistant people commonly cite seven excuses for not participating in planned learning:

1. Factors beyond the individual's control impede participation.
2. The planned learning experience is offered too late.
3. The individual is fearful of the learning processes.
4. The individual is fearful of the results.
5. The individual perceives the experience to be designed for other people.
6. The individual feels that the time is not right.
7. The individual has previously had bad experiences with planned learning.

Focused people, however, experience the following motivations: (1) the desire to know, (2) the desire to achieve a personal goal, (3) the desire to achieve a social goal, (4) the desire to achieve a religious goal, (5) the desire to enjoy learning as an activity, (6) the desire to escape, (7) the need to respond to a requirement, or (8) the need to respond to social pressure.

By segmenting the market not only by specific categories of prospective participants but also by learners' motivational orientations, program planners may increase the likelihood of attracting participants from any or all categories. A practical approach to doing that is to double-check the marketing plan to ensure that the marketing strategy offers appeals to most or all of these groups.

Promotion

Promotion is a subset of marketing. If viewed from the standpoint of diffusion theory (Rogers, 1962), which explains the process whereby innovations are adopted within a population, promotion enables program planners to guide prospective participants through the stages of awareness, interest, positive evaluation, and trial.

To be effective, promotion must meet six criteria (Strother and Klus, 1982):

1. Communication about the program must reach the targeted group.
2. It must get the group's attention.

3. Group members must understand the message.
4. The message must appeal to their needs.
5. The message must persuade them that this way is the preferred way to satisfy their needs.
6. The promotion efforts must be cost-effective.

Planning promotional strategies involves a two-step process (Strother and Klus, 1982): identifying the channels of communication and designing the communications. The choice of channels may vary according to targeted learners. Appropriate promotional channels for many adults will include direct mailing and use of such media as newspapers, radio, and television. For reaching excluded groups effectively, less conventional approaches have proven effective, such as single-page leaflets, illustrated beer mats in taverns and clubs, publicity in centers for the unemployed, displays in supermarkets and shopping malls, signs on buses or mobile homes, adult counseling services in community centers and public libraries, and door-to-door contacts. Using less conventional channels demonstrates a commitment by program planners to attract typically excluded groups by capitalizing on specific social linkages or social support mechanisms through the organizations with which such adults affiliate.

Retaining Participants

Once people have decided to participate, program planners should consider means by which to build their motivation to continue (Boshier, 1985, 1990). Retaining participants demonstrates a program's ability to meet participants' needs and meet the challenges posed by their lives and work. Retention also reflects a participant's positive behavioral response to the program, to the organizational sponsor, and to the learning experience itself, in combination with the learner's motivational orientation and different aspects of the learner's life external to the program.

Although individual characteristics and life issues affect retention, program planners are limited in what they can do to influence those issues. Obviously they can exert more influence over program and organizational features. Figure 15.1 depicts one way to think about the organizational attributes that encourage participant retention. As the model illustrates, four key attributes impact retention. Consideration of each attribute can lead to modifications in education and training programs designed to increase the organization's capacity to motivate learners to continue their participation.

FIGURE 15.1. KEY ORGANIZATIONAL
ATTRIBUTES THAT AFFECT PROGRAM RETENTION.

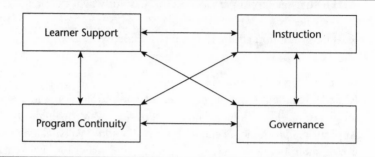

• *Learner support factors* affect individual participation. Even from the time learners decide to participate until the time they actually enter a program, they must come to perceive the sponsoring organization as supportive of their needs and interests. To be successful in retaining participants, programs must be tailored to meet participants' learning needs, provide guidance to relate the program to an individual's life situation, provide access to financial resources when necessary, and provide ways to interpret the experience to employers or others, and they must be offered at convenient times and locations.

• *Instructional factors* are associated with how learning is formatted and delivered. These factors are often more important than any other factors. To be successful in retaining participants, programs should link program objectives and behavioral objectives; provide participants with learning tasks that are moderately difficult and challenging; allow participants to recognize how the learning tasks relate to their individual needs, interests, problems, or aspirations; afford participants opportunities to experience success in mastering new knowledge and skills; and give participants a favorable view of the way instruction is delivered. Participants should also perceive instructors to be competent and supportive.

Instructional factors also include the group learning experience (Jensen, 1964). The shared perceptions of group members influence individual perceptions. Indicators of successful programs thus include the achievement of the group as a whole, the sense of group cohesiveness, the degree to which all group members take an active part in the learning process, the positive evaluation of the shared experience, and the learning success of individual group members. These elements may also affect participant retention.

- *Governance factors* refer to the ways in which decisions about the training or education program are made and by whom. If program planners function directively, they will make most (or all) of the decisions. As a consequence, learners and other stakeholders may feel little or no ownership in the program. If program planners function collaboratively, they will work on all or most steps of program planning with prospective participants and other representative stakeholders. If they function nondirectively, they will give the prospective participants and other stakeholders complete ownership of the planning process and product, and simply facilitate group decision making about planned learning experiences. When stakeholders ask for their opinions, program planners functioning nondirectively will offer their opinions in a straightforward way and explain the reasons behind their opinions. Program planners thus become consultants to stakeholders.

Program governance is a particularly important organizational attribute because it affects how much ownership participants and other stakeholders feel about the program. If program planners function directively, they call on the organizational command structure to promote the program or resort to persuasive "hard sell" tactics. If they function collaboratively, programs will probably enjoy the ownership of the learners who helped create them while the program planner plays a coordinating and facilitative role. If program planners function nondirectively, programs are the product of learner and other stakeholder action—and should therefore enjoy their complete and unqualified support.

- *Program continuity factors* involve the *retention capacity* that is transferable from one program to another. Such factors are manifest when programs collectively constitute a meaningful set—as is the case when many courses comprise a baccalaureate of liberal studies, a distance education diploma, or job certification—and the retention capacity for the whole may exceed the retention capacity of the respective parts if they were offered alone. Other continuity factors are exemplified by formative evaluation devices, such as self-addressed postcards or questionnaires that encourage feedback to instructors and others in the organization about the need for corrective action when participants encounter difficulty that, without resolution, may lead to discontinuation.

These four sets of organizational factors provide a useful way to frame issues linked to participant retention in programs. All things being equal, programs that are skewed positively on all four criteria should exhibit higher retention rates than programs that are not skewed positively.

Suggestions for Improving Recruitment and Retention

Program planners can take proactive steps to improve recruitment of participants if they follow four suggestions (Cookson, 1989, pp. 108–109):

1. Conduct effective public relations to inform and favorably impress relevant groups (including prospective participants and other stakeholders) about the value of programs.
2. Develop sound marketing strategies that include mapping the designated population of prospective adult students, identifying specific market segments, and assessing the learning needs, intentions, beliefs, and attitudes of prospective participants and other key stakeholders.
3. Promote the program by advertising program availability and participation benefits through all communication channels appropriate to the targeted participants.
4. Guide learners into the learning activities by communicating the correspondence between the behavioral objectives and the program objectives through preenrollment information and orientation sessions, appropriate admissions and registration procedures, and access to counseling and advising.

Program planners can take proactive steps to improve retention of participants if they follow four general guidelines:

1. Maintain a range of high-quality and accessible participant support services, counseling services to advise students about programs, convenient registration and admissions procedures, financial assistance when appropriate, peer support groups, and continual interpretation of the learning activities to others who are important to the learners.
2. Offer high-quality instruction by providing effective and satisfying individual learning experiences and positive group experiences.
3. Engage participants in program governance by applying methods to increase learner participation in planning and demonstrating the responsiveness of the program to participant and other stakeholder feedback and evaluation.
4. Establish continuity by linking programs to previously available and succeeding programs, by packaging programs to cultivate long-term loyalty to the institutional sponsor, and by establishing rituals and symbols that contribute to forming shared meaning and connectedness among participants, program faculty and staff, and other key stakeholders. Examples might include graduation ceremonies or celebrations, gifts for participation or sponsorship, and other rites of passage or celebration.

Summary

This chapter offered program planners guidelines for effective recruitment and retention efforts. *Recruitment* was defined as the process of inducing program participation, and *retention* was defined as preserving participation. Even the best-designed and best-delivered program will be unsuccessful if nobody participates—or if participants withdraw before program completion.

Key to recruitment is integrating public relations, marketing, and promotion efforts. *Public relations* consists of activities undertaken to project a favorable image of planned learning activities or training efforts in general. *Marketing* is all of the steps in the program planning process that are designed to identify and respond to the needs of targeted learners. *Promotion* is a subset of marketing that guides prospective participants through the stages of awareness, interest, positive evaluation, and trial.

Retention of participants demonstrates a program's ability to meet participants' needs and to help them meet the challenges posed by their lives and work. Retention also reflects a participant's positive behavioral response to the program, to the organizational sponsor, and to the learning experience itself, in combination with the learner's motivational orientation and different aspects of the learners' life external to the program.

However, recruiting and retaining program participants are greatly influenced by how well programs are promoted and marketed. It is fitting, then, that promoting and marketing programs are reviewed at greater length in Chapter Sixteen.

CHAPTER SIXTEEN

PROMOTING AND MARKETING PROGRAMS

Most program planners make an effort to identify and meet participants' learning needs, but not all program planners take active steps to cultivate the markets for their programs or to demonstrate to participants or to sponsoring organizations the financial or nonfinancial value of their efforts. While interest in these issues has been increasing in today's cost-conscious corporations and universities, common practices may still lag behind published admonitions.

Although program marketing and promotion were briefly reviewed in the previous chapter as they pertain to participant recruitment and retention, this chapter focuses on the broader issues of identifying and segmenting the markets to be served. It describes how to conduct a marketing survey and how to use the survey results to improve program promotion and marketing.

Conducting a Market Survey

A market survey is a broad examination of the clientele and stakeholders to be served by program planning efforts. A market survey is carried out in seven steps (Griffith, 1989):

1. The individual or group conducting the survey classifies the organization according to its marketing activities.

2. The individual or group conducts a marketing audit.
3. The individual or group classifies the demand.
4. The market is defined and segmented.
5. Programs are reconceptualized based on the market.
6. Programs are planned from a marketing perspective.
7. Programs are promoted based on survey results.

Step 1: Classifying Organizations

What is the organization's orientation to marketing? All organizations can be classified into one of four categories (Kotler, 1975). Program planners are well-advised to familiarize themselves with the marketing orientation of the organization in which they function.

1. *Unresponsive organizations.* These organizations do nothing to measure participant or stakeholder needs, perceptions, preferences, or satisfaction. They merely offer programs. They offer programs out of custom or management preference, thus treading a perilous path in today's cost-conscious work environment. One example is a university perceived by local employers as "just sitting there and waiting for employers to ask for help."

2. *Casually responsive organizations.* These organizations take steps to learn about stakeholder and participant needs, perceptions, and preferences. They offer planned learning experiences designed to meet the explicit needs and interests of vocal groups that press their demands. However, they are risk-aversive. They rarely offer innovative services or take steps to anticipate participants' or other stakeholders' needs.

3. *Responsive organizations.* These organizations show substantial interest in discovering—even anticipating—the needs of participants and other stakeholders. They make use of systematic procedures to collect and analyze data when planning programs, conducting regular needs assessment designed to discover needs and market existing services.

4. *Fully responsive organizations.* These organizations conduct formal audits at regular intervals to discover and anticipate participants' and other stakeholders' needs, perceptions, preferences, and satisfactions. They also encourage active learner and other stakeholder participation on advisory councils or training committees.

Step 2: Conducting a Marketing Audit

A marketing audit is an independent examination of the marketing effort (Kotler, 1975). An initial step in reaching full responsiveness, a marketing audit examines how often and how well marketing principles are applied. It aids program planners and others in determining how programs could be more effectively marketed.

Three forms of evaluation are used in carrying out a marketing audit:

1. *Evaluation of the marketing context.* Typical questions posed by this evaluation include the following:

- What are the markets for the programs offered? To what individuals are programs directed? To which societal sectors or organizational parts are the programs directed?
- Who are the participants in the programs offered? What are their characteristics?
- Who are the other stakeholders? In other words, whose support and backing are necessary for programs to be successful?
- Who are the competitors?
- What aspects of the external environment affect program design and delivery, and how?
- What aspects of the internal environment affect program effectiveness, and how?

2. *Evaluating the marketing system within programming.* The objects of this form of evaluation are objectives, implementation methods, and related issues. Typical questions posed by this form of evaluation include How much attention is consciously devoted to marketing during program planning? and How well has a marketing system been established to select and implement objectives and strategies?

3. *Evaluating the marketing system within the organization.* The objects of this form of evaluation are the organization's major areas of marketing activity. Examples of such areas include the organization's products and services, process of setting prices, process of distribution, personal contacts, advertising, publicity, and product or service promotion practices. Typical questions posed by this form of evaluation include the following:

1. How are program services presented?
2. How competitive are the prices for the services?
3. How satisfied are participants and stakeholders with the ways programs are currently distributed?

4. How effective are personal contacts made by training and education personnel with the market's target population or specific market segments?
5. How are programs advertised and promoted? How effective are these activities?

Step 3: Classifying Demand

Demand is reflected by the number of persons willing to participate or support a program. Kotler (1975) offers three useful categories that can be used to consider demand. All three categories can be applied to program planning to permit program planners to classify the current demand for their products and services.

1. *Underdemand.* This category can be further divided into three subcategories: *negative demand,* which indicates that all or most important market segments are disinterested or indifferent to an offering; *latent demand,* which indicates that segments of the market exist that have a demand yet to be met; and *faltering demand,* which indicates that interest is waning and greater declines are anticipated.

2. *Adequate demand.* This category can be divided into two subcategories: *irregular demand* is characterized by temporary and volatile changes, and *full demand* indicates that the level and duration of the demand equals the desired level and duration.

3. *Overdemand.* This category can be divided into two subcategories. *Excessive demand* indicates that product or service demand exceeds the level that the organization feels capable of supplying or motivated to supply. An example is a large corporation committed to training twenty thousand people worldwide on quality principles within a few months. *Unhealthy demand* is linked to undesirable qualities associated with a response. An example might be a request for a continuing education course on how to place bets on the Internet.

Once demand has been mapped, program planners may consider how well-equipped and committed the organization is to respond to that demand.

Step 4: Defining and Segmenting the Market

Defining and segmenting are essential steps in examining a market. Program planners may define or specify the market to which each program is directed. The public—either inside or outside an organizational setting—can then be divided into three groups (Kotler, 1975):

1. *The current market:* those who are already interested in the product or service.
2. *The potential market:* those who may eventually develop an interest in the product or service.
3. *The nonmarket:* those who will never develop interest.

Once the markets have been identified, program planners can subdivide them to craft effective marketing strategies for each group. Kotler (1975) offers three strategies based on market segmentation:

1. *The undifferentiated market.* The organization elects to treat the entire market as if it were homogeneous, focusing on what all members have in common. The market is not segmented into distinctive groups.
2. *The concentrated market.* The organization decides to divide the market into significant segments and dedicate their efforts to only one segment.
3. *The differentiated market.* Decision makers choose to direct their attention to two or more market segments at once. A marketing strategy is then formulated for each market segment.

How will the organization identify what products to make or what services to offer to meet the needs of people in its chosen markets? That is the central question to be addressed in this step. When defining the needs to which the organization will respond, program planners typically confront three problems. First, there is no definitive definition of *need* to permit distinctions between need and *desire* or *lack.* Second, people do not reflect much on their needs. Hence, they have difficulty clearly articulating them—or perhaps do not care to share them openly. For that reason it is difficult to pinpoint needs. Third, even when needs are identified, the process of assigning them relative importance can pose practical dilemmas. For these reasons, assessing learning needs calls for planned rather than unplanned approaches.

Step 5: Reconceptualizing Programs

Once the previous steps have been completed for a continuing education or training function, program planners can contribute to successful marketing by simply reconfiguring how they think about what they do. In other words, program planners should adopt a new, more entrepreneurial mind-set.

Three useful ways have been suggested for program planners to consider what they do, by categorizing their activities, products, and services (Kotler, 1975). The first way is to examine their *tangible product*—the physical entity or service offered to the public. This may be a planned learning experience, such as a training course.

The second way is to examine their *core product*—the essential value or benefit that a participant recognizes in the product or service. For a program, this may be the participants' perception that they will come away from a course with a specific solution or course of action to deal with a work-related problem. The third way is to examine their *augmented product*—the total costs and benefits that participants experience and receive. For a program, this may include not only the actual learning experience but also the benefit of being temporarily away from the work setting and meeting new people. It also may include changes participants make on the jobs that increase productivity.

Program planners are accustomed to emphasizing their tangible products while deemphasizing the core and augmented products. Nevertheless, if program planners choose to emphasize these other products, the perceived value of what they do could be enhanced in the minds of participants and other stakeholders.

Step 6: Planning Programs from a Marketing Perspective

A marketing perspective can be an important foundation for program planning. In suggesting how program planners can adopt and use that perspective more effectively, Griffith (1989) offered eleven points based on elements of Houle's (1972) framework of educational program decision making:

1. *Selection of resources.* Consider the symbolic value as well as the functional value.
2. *Selection of leaders.* Communicate the quality of leaders to enhance and build interest in programs.
3. *Description of the format.* Pique participant satisfaction and interest by issuing advance announcements about the format and methods to be used in a planned learning experience.
4. *Social reinforcement.* Consider the social aspects of programs, since some participants view those aspects as important.
5. *Roles and relations.* Inform participants ahead of time about the probable nature of the learning group.
6. *Explanation of the design.* Inform prospective participants about what they will be expected to do during a program.
7. *Recruitment of the suitable audience.* Communicate the assumptions and expectations of the leader in advance. Building an appropriate orientation to learning is part of planning effective programs, not tangential to it.
8. *Lifestyle considerations.* Make an effort to ensure that program plans correspond to participants' lifestyles.
9. *Financial considerations.* Consider the prospective participants' financial resources, since they will impose a constraint on how much participants are willing to pay.

10. *Information for supportive publics.* Interpret the program to third-party stakeholders who may influence participation. Show how it benefits them, the sponsoring organization, or the community.

11. *Research on successful strategies.* Conduct research to create new knowledge about
specific market segments and develop appropriate marketing strategies for them.

Step 7: Promoting Programs

A publicity plan is necessary to promote a training or education program. Five
major steps should be taken when crafting such a plan (Kotler and Fox, 1985, pp.
295–316): (1) set objectives for publicity, (2) determine the budget for publicity, (3)
determine the message, (4) select the media, and (5) evaluate the effectiveness of
the publicity. These steps are depicted schematically in Figure 16.1.

FIGURE 16.1. STEPS IN CRAFTING AN ADVERTISING PLAN.

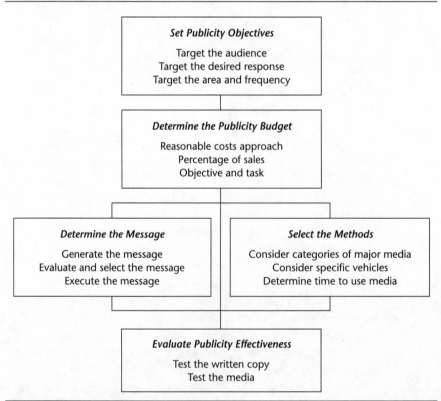

Source: Kotler and Fox, *Strategic Marketing for Educational Institutions,* 1985, p. 297. Adapted by
permission of Prentice-Hall, Inc., Upper Saddle River, NJ.

Setting objectives for publicity means targeting the audience, determining the desired response, and selecting the area and frequency for publicity. The audience should of course be related to the intended program participants or those who can make decisions about attendance. The program planner should be clear about the desired response. Is it merely to make people aware of a program, or is it to give them the information they need in order to recognize that they should sign up?

In *determining the budget,* the program planner should seek the best value for the money expended while achieving the established publicity objectives. One way to budget is to provide a percentage of receipts or profits from previous programs.

Determining the message and *selecting the methods* go together. Both the message and the methods should be clearly linked to the desired results. Building on the ideas of Gardner (1979), Exhibit 16.1 presents a list of media that may be used to publicize programs. It also indicates when using each medium would be appropriate. Again elaborating on the ideas of Gardner (1979), Table 16.1 offers some useful guidelines for preparing program publicity for each medium. These guidelines emphasize just how different these media can be.

Finally, *evaluating the effectiveness of publicity* means determining how well it works. That can be done by testing the written copy on focus groups or on selected members of the targeted audience. The overall value of the publicity effort is of course evaluated by how many people actually enroll in a program and pay for it.

Summary

This chapter focused on the broad issues of identifying and segmenting the markets to be served. Essential to this process is a *market survey,* defined as a broad examination of the clientele and stakeholders to be served by program planning efforts. A market survey is carried out in seven steps: (1) classifying the organization according to its marketing activities, (2) conducting a marketing audit, (3) classifying the demand, (4) defining and segmenting the market, (5) reconceptualizing the programs offered to the market, (6) planning programs from a marketing perspective, and (7) promoting the programs.

Effective marketing is transformed into programs by effective budgeting and financing. The best programs cannot be designed and delivered unless financial plans are created. It is thus appropriate that budgeting and financing programs are treated in the next chapter.

EXHIBIT 16.1. WHEN TO USE DIFFERENT MEDIA.

Use newspapers to:
1. Reach the population within a given geographical area.
2. Obtain immediate results.
3. Provide prospective participants with written reference material.

Use radio to:
1. Disseminate a brief and changing message.
2. Direct your message to specific segments of the market.
3. Repeat the message.
4. Convey a simple message that does not require detailed instructions to evoke action.

Use television to:
1. Reach a general audience.
2. Convey a show-and-tell message.
3. Advertise continuing education programs varied enough to justify the large expense.
4. Convey a message to which a written message is not essential.

Use direct mail to:
1. Convey a message to identified segments of market.
2. Disseminate information to all homes within a given geographical area.
3. Trigger an immediate response on the part of prospective program participants.
4. Convey a personal message.

Use fixed and mobile signs to:
1. Repeat your message.
2. Convey a sense of program continuity.
3. Disseminate a brief institutional message.

Use specialty items to:
1. Recognize constituents or participants.
2. Conduct special promotion campaigns.
3. Convey a simple message over time.
4. Create a sense of good will toward specific programs and the sponsoring organization.

Use internal publicity to:
1. Encourage workers and their supervisors to promote the education or training program.
2. Involve coworkers in the training or education program.

Use the Internet to:
1. Disseminate large amounts of information concerning specific programs and the sponsoring organization to a wide audience.
2. Provide continuously updated information to current and prospective program participants.
3. Reach specific segments of the market.
4. Override the barriers of time and distance that might exist between the program and its prospective participants.

Use voice mail to:
1. Provide continuously updated information to current and prospective program participants.
2. Reach specific segments of the market.
3. Convey information that is readily accessible to anyone with access to a telephone.
4. Convey a sense of personal support and nurturance.
5. Override the barriers of time and distance that might exist between the program and its prospective participants.

Source: Adapted from Gardner, 1979.

TABLE 16.1. GUIDELINES FOR PREPARATION OF MESSAGES ABOUT PROGRAMS USING DIFFERENT MEDIA.

Type of Media	Material Needed Before Implementing the Advertising
Newspaper	1. An advertisement that presents the symbolic as well as practical benefits of participation in the program. 2. A brief, catchy title. 3. Illustrations and graphics that complement the message.
Radio	1. An announcement that emphasizes the symbolic as well as practical benefits of participation in the program. 2. Simple but concrete words. 3. Repetition of key points to strengthen recall. 4. Clear instructions about what action prospective participants should take.
Television	1. Information that adheres basically to the guidelines for radio announcements. 2. Graphics and color that enhance the visual message. 3. No "talking heads." Emphasis on action wherever possible.
Direct Mail	1. Written material that adheres basically to the guidelines for radio announcements. 2. Graphics and color that simplify and emphasize various parts of the message. 3. Presentation of multiple reasons why prospective participants should enroll in the program.
Telephone	1. 800 numbers supplying program information that encourage inquiries from prospective participants. 2. Voice-mail systems that facilitate both automated distribution of information and individualized messages (through use of a menu of topics and options). 3. Telephone attendants who provide a human dimension to serious inquiries. 4. The options for prospective participants to request further informative materials (such as information packets delivered by mail).
Internet	1. Web pages that promote both particular programs and their sponsoring organizations. 2. Information that adheres to the guidelines for both radio and television announcements. 3. Graphics, color, sound, and videoclips that enhance and support the message. 4. The option for prospective participants to register their personal address and to request further contact and communication.
Sign Boards and Mobile Advertising	1. Graphics and typesize that correspond to the size of the board. 2. A common or unifying theme that can be repeated in various locations. 3. A limited number of words (fewer than ten as a general rule).
Specialty Items	1. Specialty items that are useful. 2. Colorful specialty items, where appropriate. 3. Clarity about the relationship between the specialty item and the program or services being offered. 4. An explanation about the link between the specialty item and the program or service in as few words as possible.

Source: Adapted from Gardner, 1979.

CHAPTER SEVENTEEN

BUDGETING AND
FINANCING PROGRAMS

This three-part chapter presents an overview of program budgeting and financing. The first part reviews basic budgeting principles; the second part describes how to calculate program costs and benefits, especially in business-based training and development settings; and the third part focuses on the unique features of budgets in higher and continuing education.

Basic Principles of Budgeting and Financing

A *budget* is a financial plan that estimates the income and expenses for a defined period, such as a fiscal year, calendar year, or academic year. It translates operational action plans into financial plans. A budget is a useful communication tool between those who take action and those who authorize expenditures, and it also provides a basis for accountability by providing a standard against which to compare performance.

A key question in budgeting is *Will the unit that plans programs prepare its own budget, or will its budget be part of another budget?* Some units prepare their own budgets. Some are part of a human resources, manufacturing, or operating budget. Some budgets, of course, are tied to a project, as is the case for programs conducted as part of external consulting or outsourcing arrangements.

There are several different approaches to budgeting, and several different sources of funding for budgets.

Budgeting Approaches

If a training or human resource development (HRD) department has its own budget, on what is it based? One approach to establishing a budget is to base it on employee head count or percentage of payroll. In this approach, each employee or group of employees is allocated a fixed annual sum for training. For example, Motorola sets aside a fixed percent of annual payroll for employee training, and requires forty hours of training for everyone from janitors to the chief executive officer. Another example is the United Auto Workers union, which has reached a collective bargaining agreement with Detroit automakers in which five cents of every employee payroll dollar earned is contributed by the companies to individualized employee training accounts.

A second approach to budgeting is to estimate an activity level, such as the number of people estimated to receive training during the budget period. Many organizations that reimburse all or part of employee tuition and fees for external courses, public seminars, or professional conferences use this approach, estimating activity levels from previous years and adding funds as necessary to take into account inflation or increased headcount.

A third approach is to budget based on historical precedent. A training director or continuing education director simply examines expenditures from the previous year and adds or subtracts funds based on revised activity estimates and inflation. While far from thorough, this approach can occasionally be performed in a few minutes on an electronic spreadsheet or on specialized budgeting software.

A fourth approach is to prepare a training budget for each training project or for each department, function, or plant site and then accumulate them into a master budget. That approach is workable in small organizations, but it has drawbacks in large, geographically diversified organizations in which budget estimates can be complicated by differing training or education policies, values, or finances and exchange rates among nations or work sites.

While other approaches to budgeting are possible, none is foolproof. Budgeting may be inadequate if events unfold in ways not envisioned by the budgeters. Examples of such surprises might include mergers, forced layoffs, new programs demanded on the spur of the moment by a chief executive officer, the establishment of a new facility, or the appointment of a new executive who is a special friend or foe of training. The important point to understand is that effective budgeting is rarely possible in the absence of an organizational strategic business plan, a training or HRD department strategic plan, needs assessment results, and the willingness of stakeholders to follow through on the information provided by these sources.

Sources of Budget Funding

Program planners will usually encounter six major funding sources. A thorough understanding of these sources is important for successful budgeting.

1. *A subsidy of a sponsoring organization.* When funds originate from an organizational sponsor, they are part of an internal budget. Such a budget is usually assigned to the unit responsible for continuing education, training, or HRD. Sometimes the unit is part of another department and does not have its own budget, as is often the case when the training director reports to the human resources or manufacturing manager.

2. *Fees paid by participants.* Program planners will occasionally collect participant fees sufficient to cover their expenses and earn a profit. Some units collect fees from the participants' organizations. When services are provided internally, many units collect fees that are transferred internally from the units receiving the services. Such funds are called *chargebacks* or *internal reimbursements.*

3. *Auxiliary businesses and sales.* Some training or continuing education units are successful in marketing to other organizations the services or products they prepared for internal use. They serve other audiences and receive funding from the corresponding sales. For instance, courses, study materials, and books developed for one group may be sold externally to others. Additionally, program planners may work externally, offering consulting services or delivering classroom training in other organizations, thereby generating additional revenue for their employing organization.

4. *Donations and contracts.* Government agencies, nonprofit associations, labor unions, and foundations are often disposed to underwrite or contract for training and education programs geared to their employees or members. In fact, some companies' HRD departments have transformed themselves into consulting firms that receive sizable sums from their external operations—on occasion exceeding the profit margin of their sponsoring organization. An example of such a training department is found in the manufacturing firm Fluor Daniel. Some college or university continuing education departments have also arranged to serve as the outsourcing agents for in-house company training departments. This arrangement

is typically contractual and renewed annually. Such relationships exist between, for example, the University of Vermont and a Vermont-based plant of International Business Machines, between Corning and the College of the Finger Lakes, and between the Forum Corporation and Dupont.

5. *Local, state, or federal funding.* As an economic development tool, some local, regional, and national governments will fund, partially fund, or guarantee funding for training or educational expenses of an employer to create or preserve jobs in the jurisdiction. Similar funding may be available to assist specialized groups afflicted with unique adversity—such as unemployed workers, welfare recipients, displaced homemakers, teen mothers, or technologically displaced employees. Sometimes governments contract with educational institutions to provide specialized training and education services; sometimes the funding is also available to training vendors operating for profit. The level of governmental funding varies, of course, by locale.

6. *Miscellaneous income.* This includes in-kind contributions offered by organizations in exchange for training or educational services, such as offering meeting rooms on company premises at no charge, contributing the time of instructors, providing audiovisual or manufacturing equipment, providing refreshments or meals, or photocopying course materials.

If training or education units are flexible in how they operate, they can take full advantage of all funding sources. They can maximize their operations, too, by holding down operational expenses. One way to hold down expenses is to rely on contingent instructors or other service providers so as to restrict permanently assigned training or continuing education staff to a cadre of highly skilled professional program planners. In this way, resources can match demand, and the organization can benefit by holding down compensation and benefits expenses, holding down the size of a bureaucracy that can retard entrepreneurship, and drawing on specialized expertise as necessary to meet unique program demands. Of course, this approach may imply that program planners have to establish a talent pool representing specialized expertise from inside and outside the organization that can be drawn on quickly when need requires.

Calculating Program Costs and Benefits

Estimating the costs and related benefits of training and educational expenditures has emerged as a major issue of this decade. A recent publication lists hundreds of literature citations on this subject (American Society for Training and Development, 1994b), reflecting keen interest in determining the return on training or educational investments. Understanding cost-benefit analysis and return on investment (ROI) is critically important to success in budgeting for program planners in today's increasingly cost-sensitive business and education environments.

Determining costs and benefits is a three-step process: (1) determining what a performance problem is costing the organization, (2) determining what a training program intended to solve the problem will cost the organization, and (3) determining the difference between the problem's cost and the program's cost. By subtracting program cost from problem cost, program planners can derive an estimated program benefit. Taken a step further, the ratio of program benefit to program cost amounts to training's ROI.

Calculating Costs of Performance Problems

Calculating the costs associated with a performance problem or deficiency is a four-step process (Laird, 1985): (1) identify the performance unit or discrepancy; (2) determine the cost per unit; (3) count or calculate the number of defective units or the impact of dissatisfied customers, usually for a year; and (4) multiply the cost per unit of product or service by the number of defective units or estimated lost sales to determine the annual cost of the performance problem.

Consider a simple example. Workers in a large construction firm are making mistakes in following blueprints. Fifteen percent of the workers' time is lost in correcting otherwise unnecessary errors. The payroll for all the construction workers amounts to $25,000 per week. The three supervisors are dedicating 25 percent of their time to conducting work inspections, giving new orders, and overseeing follow-ups.

For simplicity's sake the analysis will not include the value of lost time in committing errors or the cost of additional materials. It will focus only on payroll costs of the workers and their supervisors. From the annual payroll of $1,250,000 for workers, in a year comprised of fifty weeks, $187,500 is wasted by having to repeat the work. The annual cost from the total salaries of the three supervisors is $180,000, and they are devoting an estimated $45,000 of their time to fixing unnecessary errors.

The unit cost is calculated by adding the $187,500 to the $45,000 to reach a sum of $232,500. That is what the performance deficiency is costing the construction firm.

Not all performance problems are as easily calculated as this example. However, nearly all performance problems can be analyzed according to their cost in time, and time can be translated into payroll costs. Payroll information is usually available for making the calculations. It is also possible to estimate the monetary value of materials expended in defective performance.

Many performance indicators can reflect the presence or absence of optimal performance, including the following (Powers, 1992, pp. 20–21):

- Units of work per hour
- Units of work per worker
- Number of sales
- Monetary value per sale
- Ratio of sales to calls
- Percentage of production or sales quota achieved
- Total monetary value of sales
- Number of grievances
- Percentage of grievances decided
- Percentage of grievance decisions sustained
- Percentage of counseling problems solved
- Total minutes of tardiness
- Total days of absenteeism
- Number of absenteeism incidents
- Scrap rates

- Rejects
- Back orders filled
- Monetary value for back orders filled
- Tasks completed
- Percentage of tasks completed properly
- Budgets submitted
- Budgets achieved within X percent of forecast
- Employee turnover
- Inventory turnover
- Machine downtime
- Number of disabling accidents
- Cost of accidents
- Letters and reports completed
- Percentage of letters and reports that get the desired results

The cost of defective performance can be calculated by using many of the indicators just listed. But not all performance problems involve tangible costs. Think, for example, about the damages to the work climate caused by supervisors who operate on the basis of inflexible rules, with closed minds, and out of croneyism or nepotism. Program planners can provide whatever evidence they may have to support their view of the intangible costs resulting from performance problems. Such evidence may be gathered from exit interview questionnaires completed by departing (and perhaps disgruntled) workers, from employee attitude survey results, from customer satisfaction surveys, from employee performance appraisals, and from complaint letters sent by the organization's suppliers, distributors, or customers. Once the costs of defective performance have been calculated, program planners can then proceed to the next step: calculating training program costs.

Calculating Training Program Costs

Recall that training or education represents only one possible solution to performance problems. Training is not appropriate if the performance problem stems from a cause other than an individual deficiency of knowledge, skill, or attitude (Mager and Pipe, 1984; Rothwell, 1996a). If performance analysis was properly handled, program planners have already determined that training is the appropriate solution to a performance problem.

In that case, program planners should estimate what the training program will cost (Head, 1994). Such an estimate usually focuses on two cost categories: support and production. *Support costs* include personnel, equipment, special materials, travel and per diem, and costs of upgrading personnel to apply state-of-the-art instructional technologies (Warren, 1979). *Production costs* are divided into two subcategories: costs of personnel time and costs of materials. *Costs of personnel time* include the value of investments to determine the problem's cause, select appropriate solutions, and prepare instruction. *Costs of materials* include the value of investments to design, pilot, evaluate, and revise training.

To underscore the central importance of performance analysis, Laird (1985) estimates the time spent planning training at 5 percent, analyzing work tasks at 30 percent, developing instructional objectives at 5 percent, evaluating training at 10 percent, validating tests based on training at 10 percent, developing instructional materials at 15 percent, piloting instructional programs at 10 percent, revising instructional programs at 10 percent, and implementing instructional programs at 5 percent. While these percentages are general enough to be useful, program planners may change their estimates based on experience, differences in the media chosen (computer-based training can require 350 hours of development for each hour of deliverable instruction), and instructional requirements.

Several worksheets are provided for use in calculating program costs. They may be used as follows: Exhibit 17.1, to estimate training production costs; Exhibit 17.2, to estimate time commitments for training that need to be budgeted in order to estimate realistic production costs; Exhibit 17.3, to estimate the costs of conducting training; and Exhibit 17.4, to calculate program evaluation costs. The totals from each worksheet may then be inserted in the formula presented in Exhibit 17.5 to arrive at estimated total program or training costs.

Calculating Benefits

Having estimated the costs of training and of performance problems, program planners can calculate the benefits. If the cost of the performance problem exceeds the cost of the program, then the remainder is the benefit. If, however, the program cost exceeds that of the performance problem, then no investment should be made. To determine the ROI, simply divide the training cost into the remainder.

EXHIBIT 17.1. WORKSHEET FOR
COMPUTING TRAINING PRODUCTION COSTS.

Item	Formula	Total
Staff Costs:		
Salaries: Analysis Design Development Implementation Evaluation	Number of people × average salary × hours devoted to the project	_____
Fees: External vendors	Total fees and expenses paid out	_____
Travel:	Total from travel reports	_____
	Total from other travel-related expenses	_____
Overhead:	Use standard organization estimates	_____
Materials:		
Film	Costs if purchased: number of people × average salary × hours devoted to project production if produced internally	_____
Videotape	Costs if purchased: number of people × average salary × hours devoted to project production if produced internally	_____
Videodiscs	Costs if purchased: number of people × average salary × hours devoted to project production if produced internally	_____
Audiotapes	Costs if purchased: number of people × average salary × hours devoted to project production if produced internally	_____
35 mm slides	Costs if purchased: number of people × average salary × hours devoted to project production if produced internally	_____
Overhead transparencies	Costs if purchased: number of people × average salary × hours devoted to project production if produced internally	_____
Manuals and materials	Costs if purchased: number of people × average salary × hours devoted to project production if produced internally	_____
Announcements		_____
Special equipment		_____
	Total cost:	_____

Source: Adapted from Laird, 1985, pp. 233–234. © 1985 by Addison-Wesley Publishing Company, Inc. Reprinted by permission of Addison-Wesley Longman, Inc.

EXHIBIT 17.2. WORKSHEET FOR
ESTIMATING TRAINING TIME COMMITMENTS.

Format	Figure this many hours of production for each hour of presentation:
Technical course	5 to 15
Self-contained course for hand-off to other instructors	50 to 100
Computer-assisted instruction	Up to 350

Course Duration	For each class hour, budget the following estimated preparation hours:
5 days or less	3 hours of preparation for each 1 hour of instruction
Between 5 and 10 days	2.5 hours of preparation for each 1 hour of instruction
Over 10 days	2 hours of preparation for each 1 hour of instruction

Source: Adapted from Laird, 1985, p. 235. © 1985 by Addison-Wesley Publishing Company, Inc. Reprinted by permission of Addison-Wesley Longman, Inc.

Budgets in Continuing and Higher Education

Budgets for continuing education in higher education institutions are almost always partially or completely self-financed by fees. In these settings, budget preparation is essential to planning, controlling, and communicating programs. This section reviews five steps in calculating costs and setting fees in these settings.

1. *Designating the budget objective.* The budget objective is the activity for which a budget is needed. Without such planning, it will not be possible to answer such questions as (1) What fee should be collected from each participant? (2) How much money needs to be raised by fee collection? (3) How much can be paid for the physical facilities? and (4) How much can instructors be paid?

2. *Calculating the variable, fixed, semifixed, and sunk costs.* Variable costs fluctuate according to the number of participants. Such costs include books, other study materials, computer usage fees, lodging expenses, refreshments and meal expenses. Consider, for instance, a one-day course on small electrical generating plants (Matkin, 1985). Producing one set of instructional materials would cost $24, refreshments for the opening session would cost $6 per person, and coffee or juice during breaks would cost another $6 per person. Therefore, every participant represents $36 in variable costs. If thirty people register, the variable costs would

EXHIBIT 17.3. WORKSHEET FOR ESTIMATING TRAINING DELIVERY COSTS.

Participant costs:	Total
Number of participants (by pay group) × average salary × training hours	_____
Number of participants × hourly fringe benefit charges × hours	_____
Travel costs: total from expense reports, or average cost × number of participants	_____
Per day: total from expense reports, or average allowance × the number of participants × number of days	_____
Participant materials: cost of each unit × number of participants	_____
Participant replacement costs: number of hours × average salary	_____
Lost production: value of each unit × number of lost units, or value of each unit × reduced production	_____

Instructor costs:	Total
Number of instructors × number of hours × average salary	_____
Travel costs: expense reports × number of instructors	_____
Per diem: total from expense reports, or average allowance × number of instructors × number of days	_____

Special equipment or services:	Total
Rental or purchase of equipment	_____

Source: Adapted from Laird, 1985, p. 236. © 1985 by Addison-Wesley Publishing Company, Inc. Reprinted by permission of Addison-Wesley Longman, Inc.

amount to $1,080. If fifty people register, the printer will collect only $18 per set of instructional materials, thus lowering the variable costs per person by $300.

Fixed costs do not vary by the volume of the activity. Examples include rental charges for the physical facility, audiovisual expenses, promotion and marketing expenses, salaries for instructors, and other personnel and travel expenses. Following the previous example, meeting room rental costs $240, visual aids cost $360, the instructors cost $3,600, and travel and per diem costs amount to $600. The total fixed costs thus represent $4,800. Sometimes fixed costs are only "fixed" to a limited extent. For example, if attendance exceeds fifty people, the meeting room cost could double to $480. Such costs, then, are fixed only over a limited range.

Semifixed costs vary by volume but as volume increases, such costs decrease to a lesser proportion. Some examples would include the cost of materials or of refreshments. The charge per unit decreases with greater quantities.

EXHIBIT 17.4. WORKSHEET FOR
ESTIMATING TRAINING EVALUATION COSTS.

Item	Formula	Total
Salaries:		
Analysis	Number of hours × average salary	_____
Design	Number of hours × average salary	_____
Development	Number of hours × average salary	_____
Implementation	Number of hours × average salary	_____
Evaluation	Number of hours × average salary	_____
Materials:		
Printing	Actual costs	_____
Mailing	Units × two-way postage	_____
Total Costs:		_____

Source: Adapted from Laird, 1985, p. 237. © 1985 by Addison-Wesley Publishing Company, Inc. Reprinted by permission of Addison-Wesley Longman, Inc.

Sunk costs are costs that, once incurred, cannot be rescinded. One example would include individually imprinted participant certificates. The cost has been incurred once the certificates are printed—even if the participants do not attend. Advertising in trade journals or printing and mailing program brochures are other examples. Once the advertising has been carried out, media representatives expect payment—even if the program is subsequently canceled for lack of interest.

3. *Calculating direct and indirect costs. Direct costs* can be conveniently attributed to the program activity that corresponds to the cost object, "the target of cost analysis" (Matkin, 1985, p. 38). *Indirect costs,* conversely, cannot be directly and easily associated with a program activity. Sometimes called *overhead,* indirect costs include classroom, management, and general expenses associated with the functioning of the continuing education unit and the sponsoring organization. Additional examples include administrative salaries, costs of electricity and telephone, rental of administrative space, expenses of equipment such as photocopying machines and computers, and office supplies.

4. *Calculating unit cost.* The unit cost is calculated by dividing the sum of all costs by the number of anticipated program participants. The resulting cost constitutes the fee to be charged participants. If additional financial support is

**EXHIBIT 17.5. WORKSHEET FOR
CALCULATING ESTIMATED TOTAL TRAINING COSTS.**

Cost items	Dollars	Cost per participant: divide $ by number of participants	Cost per hour: divide $ by number of hours	Cost per participant-hour: divide $ by (number of participants × number of hours)
Production costs:				
Staff	_____	_____	_____	_____
Material	_____	_____	_____	_____
Course conduct costs:				
Participant	_____	_____	_____	_____
Instructor	_____	_____	_____	_____
Equipment/services	_____	_____	_____	_____
Evaluation costs:				
Salaries	_____	_____	_____	_____
Materials	_____	_____	_____	_____
Travel	_____	_____	_____	_____
Totals:				

Source: Adapted from Laird, 1985, pp. 237–238. © 1985 by Addison-Wesley Publishing Company, Inc. Reprinted by permission of Addison-Wesley Longman, Inc.

available, and all other factors are held constant, the participant fee may be reduced.

5. *Calculating the break-even point between costs and revenues.* After carrying out the four previous steps, program planners are now able to calculate total income, total costs, and the difference between these two sums (called the *margin*). The break-even point between expenses and income reflects the number of participants who must register and attend in order to match total program costs.

Summary

This three-part chapter presented an overview of program budgeting and financing. The first part reviewed basic budgeting principles, the second part described how to calculate program costs and benefits, and the third part focused on budgets in higher and continuing education.

A *budget*, as defined in the chapter, is a financial plan that estimates the income and expenses for a defined period, such as a fiscal or academic year. It translates operational action plans into financial terms. A key question in budgeting is *Will the unit that plans programs prepare its own budget, or will its budget be part of another unit?*

There are several different approaches to budgeting, and several different sources of funding, including establishing the budget based on employee headcount or percentage of payroll; estimating an activity level, such as number of people to receive training during the budget period; budgeting from historical precedent; and preparing a training budget for each training project or for each department, function, or plant site and then accumulating them into a master budget.

Program planners will usually encounter six major funding sources: (1) a subsidy of a sponsoring organization; (2) fees paid by participants; (3) auxiliary businesses and sales; (4) donations and contracts; (5) local, state, or federal funding; and (6) miscellaneous income, such as in-kind contributions offered by organizations in exchange for training or educational services.

Estimating the costs and related benefits of training and educational expenditures has emerged as a major issue of this decade. Determining costs and benefits involves three steps: (1) determining what a performance problem is costing the organization; (2) determining what a training program intended to solve the problem will cost the organization; and (3) determining the difference between the problem's cost and the program's cost. By subtracting program cost from problem cost, program planners can derive an estimated program benefit.

Budgets for continuing education in higher education are almost always partially or completely self-financed by fee-generated income. In these settings, budget preparation is essential to planning, controlling, and communicating programs.

Once budgets have been established and programs have been effectively promoted, program planners face the important tasks of selecting, supervising, evaluating, and developing instructors. These tasks are the focus of Chapter Eighteen.

CHAPTER EIGHTEEN

SELECTING, SUPERVISING, EVALUATING, AND DEVELOPING INSTRUCTORS

Most people have found themselves in learning situations in which the instructors did not perform adequately. The reasons may not have been apparent. Perhaps the instructors were ill-prepared; perhaps they did not grasp the topic; or perhaps they were simply unable to energize the group. Whatever the cause, the result was an unfortunate experience. The participants endured it, but were relieved when it was finally over.

Too many participants in training and continuing education programs have had such experiences. Of course, as the Contingency-Based Program Planning model indicates, participants themselves can design and carry out planned learning experiences, either as individual learning projects or as group experiences. In these cases, no instructor is necessary. Participants bear full responsibility for ensuring that learning activities are engaging, useful, and goal-directed.

Planned learning experiences that are instructor-dependent, however, call for wise decisions about what instructors to select, and how to supervise, evaluate, and develop them. This final chapter briefly reviews these topics. It shows that the Lifelong Education Program Planning (LEPP) model, while intended to serve as a guide for planning comprehensive programs, may also show program planners how to construct questions and activities to guide instructor selection, supervision, evaluation, and development.

In Chapter Four, the authors suggested that program planners might want to use the Competency Self-Assessment Form found in Appendix One to assess their own competencies based on the LEPP model. The instrument can be adapted for other uses, however. For instance, it can become a starting point for selecting effective instructors for an education or training program, for monitoring and evaluating effective performance of current instructors, and for identifying areas for instructors' professional development.

Selecting Instructors

How should instructors be selected? Answering this question is not always as simple as it might appear. Obvious but unreliable criteria are easy to find. They may include subject-matter expertise, years of experience, number of articles written, years of formal schooling, desire to appear on the program, reactions of participants in previous presentations, experience in giving speeches, and participation in other programs. If these criteria are unreliable, then what criteria can be used to select instructors? One approach is to follow a simple five-step process.

Step 1: Identify Criteria from the LEPP Model

Begin identifying what criteria must be met by an instructor by extrapolating from the LEPP model. Use the assessment instrument provided in Appendix One as a starting point. Confer with key stakeholder groups in the organization about which competencies listed in the instrument are needed by an instructor in a given program situation, setting, or participant group. An instructor may not need every ability listed in the assessment instrument. In any case, some competencies may be more critical than others.

One way to begin is to pose a question such as the following: *What competencies listed on the instrument are most critical to successful instructor performance in this organization or in the situation and setting of the particular program?* Appropriate individuals to respond to that question may include full-time program planners employed by the organization, exemplary instructors with proven track records, and such key stakeholders as managers and targeted or past program participants. A focus group setting, in which representatives of stakeholder groups are called together to review the instrument and identify the most important competencies needed by an instructor applicant, may be an appropriate place to pose the question. Exhibit 18.1 provides a simple worksheet that can be used to guide a focus group in this process. The result of this process should be a refined list of competencies suitable for selecting an instructor for a unique setting, situation, or program participant group.

EXHIBIT 18.1. WORKSHEET FOR
IDENTIFYING CRITICAL INSTRUCTOR COMPETENCIES.

Directions: Use this worksheet with the Program Planning for Lifelong Education Competency Self-Assessment Form. Assemble a group of key stakeholders in the instructor selection process, which may include individuals responsible for selecting instructors, exemplary instructors who have worked in the organization, line managers, participants, and others who have a stake in the quality of instructors who are selected. Assemble participants for a one-hour focus group meeting. Ask participants to review the self-assessment form and identify the five to seven essential competencies for instructors in the organization. On the worksheet below, they should identify the essential competencies in the left column and explain their reasons in the right column.

Essential competencies for instructors	Explain why you believe they are essential competencies

Step 2: Create a Profile of an Ideal Job Candidate

Your success in selecting instructors will be only as good as your picture of the ideal job candidate. Exactly what kind of person do you want, based on the criteria identified in the previous step? In other words, what kind of background, education, experience, and other characteristics are likely to be linked to success in the competencies identified?

To answer these questions, program planners should work with key stakeholders to create a *profile* (that is, a detailed description) of an ideal job candidate who has previously demonstrated success in every key competency area. Suppose, for instance, that one essential competency is the ability to involve target participants in program design. Program planners and stakeholders may therefore indicate in the instructor profile that an ideal job applicant will have had experience in involving target participants in program design.

A good approach to developing a profile of an ideal job applicant begins with preparing a job description, which usually lists what the instructor is expected to do. Each activity area listed in the description can then be linked to a competency in the LEPP model, and in turn to the education, experience, and other information that an individual would possess if he or she were able to demonstrate that competency. In short, the profile of an ideal job applicant can be prepared directly from a job description but it lists the characteristics of the person who is best

EXHIBIT 18.2. WORKSHEET FOR
PREPARING A PROFILE OF AN IDEAL JOB CANDIDATE.

Directions: Use this worksheet when preparing a profile of an ideal job candidate for instructor. Assemble a group of five to seven key stakeholders for one hour. Ask them to review the job description, list the work activities to be performed in the left column below, then indicate in the right column what education, experience, or other characteristics an individual should possess to perform the activity. There are no right or wrong answers. The aim of this activity is to clarify exactly what education, experience, or other characteristics should be possessed by an individual to carry out the work activities of an instructor most effectively.

What are the work activities of an instructor in the organization (from a job description)?	For each work activity, what education, experience, or other characteristics should be possessed by an ideal job applicant for instructor?

equipped to perform the activities or to demonstrate the competencies listed on the job description. The worksheet that appears in Exhibit 18.2 can be used to guide the preparation of a profile of an ideal job applicant.

Step 3: Assign Weights to the Profile of an Ideal Job Candidate

Some instructor competencies are more important than others for success in a given situation or setting or with a given program participant group. When selecting instructors, program planners and other interested parties should be clear about which competencies are most important. One way to achieve that clarity is to assign weights to the different characteristics of an ideal job candidate.

Suppose, for instance, that an instructor will facilitate a senior executive group in establishing an organization's strategic business plan. For that reason, an essential competency is the ability to identify a variety of issues and conditions external to the organization. The ideal job applicant is therefore described as someone who has previously led senior executive groups in establishing strategic business plans, and as someone who can bring to a group information about changing external environmental trends that are affecting the workplace and workforce. If

EXHIBIT 18.3. WORKSHEET FOR
WEIGHTING INSTRUCTOR CRITERIA.

Directions: Use this worksheet when weighting the criteria associated with the profile of an ideal job candidate for instructor. Assemble a group of five to seven key stakeholders for one hour. Ask them to review the profile of an ideal instructor candidate listed in the left column below. Then ask the group members to assign points in the right column to each characteristic to show how important it is to success as an instructor. Explain that the weighting scheme will later be used to score applicants against the criteria. Emphasize to the group members that there are no right or wrong answers. The aim of this activity is to clarify the importance of different criteria for instructors in the organization.

What education, experience, or other characteristics should be possessed by an ideal job applicant for an instructor?	How important is each characteristic? (Assign a point value where total points equal 100.)
Total	100

these are two of five characteristics listed in the job profile, then each characteristic can be weighted at 20 points, for a total of 100 points. That means that 40 of 100 points in decisions about ranking applicants will focus on these two areas. The worksheet that appears in Exhibit 18.3 can be used to weight instructor criteria.

Step 4: Prepare Selection Protocol

A *selection protocol* is the approach used to select an individual for a position. The selection process should be carried out consistently for all applicants so that some individuals do not gain unfair advantages over others. For instance, if one applicant is given a ten-minute interview and a second is given a two-day interview process, the selection protocol may have given an unfair advantage to the second applicant simply on the basis of time allocation. To maintain consistency among all applicants, the protocol should be planned. An agenda should be established and followed with all applicants.

A second goal of an effective selection protocol is to gather sufficient information about applicants so that they can be rated relative to the criteria and weightings established for the position. The selection protocol should thus help stakeholders to answer one question: How qualified is the individual for the position, given the competencies and weightings associated with it?

Selection protocols may be handled in many ways. For instance, one possible starting point is to ask each applicant to complete a self-assessment to indicate how competent he or she feels in each essential competency area. Applicants can also be asked to supply evidence of that competence.

Competence can be documented in various ways. One way is to ask applicants for oral evidence through interview questions. For instance, if an instructor must show competence in setting goals and objectives, an appropriate interview question might take this form: "Tell me about a time when you were called upon to set goals and objectives for instruction. What did you do and how did you do it?" Such a question reduces the chance that applicants will be tempted to tell the interviewer what the interviewer wants to hear. A story must be told, and the question assumes experience in performing an activity deemed essential to job success. The same approach can be used to assess competence in other key areas of instructor performance.

Other approaches may be used in the selection process to gather evidence of instructor competence. For instance, applicants may be asked during the interview process to conduct an on-site group session, to supply interviewers with a videotape demonstrating their ability to speak to groups, or to supply references from previous employers, clients, or participants who can speak to the applicant's ability to perform. Applicants may also be asked to demonstrate their abilities by providing such documentary evidence as previously developed lesson plans, reaction evaluation forms, or results from previous groups.

Step 5: Reach a Decision

Once instructor applicants have been interviewed, a decision must be reached. Using the evidence supplied by each applicant, program planners and other interested stakeholders should score the applicants based on the evidence they supplied. The applicants can then be ranked based on that evidence according to the weights associated with each competency area. The result should thus be more objective than might otherwise be the case.

Supervising, Evaluating, and Developing Instructors

Just as the LEPP model and the assessment instrument in Appendix One can be used as a starting point for selecting instructors, so can they serve as a starting point for supervising, evaluating, and developing instructors. For simplicity's sake, we only summarize the model's implications for each issue.

Supervising Instructors

The LEPP model provides a common language by which program planners and instructors can communicate about instructor performance. By referring to specific competencies identified in the model, program planners with supervisory responsibility can discuss program preparations with instructors. Such discussions usually center on the unique features of a program, the participant group, or the setting or situation. The LEPP model may thus be adapted to contingencies.

Program planners may also wish to apply the LEPP model by directly observing instructor delivery in group settings. For each competency listed in the assessment instrument in Appendix One, instructors may demonstrate a particular behavior or behaviors. The program planner thus observes the instructor's application of the competencies identified by the model, and this observation provides the basis for individualized feedback to improve performance. According to research conducted by Rothwell (1996b), lack of feedback is the single most common cause of performance problems—and improved feedback is the most promising approach to improving individual performance.

Consider a simple example. Suppose a program planner is observing an instructor who is delivering a course entitled "The Basics of Supervision." One competency listed in the instrument in Appendix One is *formulating objectives*, which means the ability to identify, select, and write various types of objectives to use in program planning. Various behaviors may be demonstrated by instructors who are competent in that area. They may, for instance, clearly describe the program objectives to participants at the outset of the group experience. They may also explain why achieving the program objectives is important to participants. By creating a list of behaviors linked to each competency area of the instrument (Exhibit 18.4 provides a worksheet that may be used for that purpose), program planners may provide a basis for observing how often and how well instructors display these key behaviors in a group setting, which in turn can provide the basis for giving timely concrete feedback to instructors about how well they are performing.

How can behaviors be linked to the competencies listed in the instrument? Program planners can call together a focus group of program planners, exemplary instructors, their immediate supervisors, and representatives of such key stakeholder groups as managers and participants and ask them to list and rank the most important behaviors linked to each essential competency of the LEPP model. A key advantage of doing this is that the resulting behaviors will be tied directly to the setting, situations, participants, and programs of one organizational culture rather than being so generic that they are not applicable.

EXHIBIT 18.4. WORKSHEET FOR
LINKING BEHAVIORS TO INSTRUCTOR COMPETENCIES.

Directions: Use this worksheet when generating behaviors for each essential competency identified for instructors in an organization. Assemble a group of five to seven key stakeholders for one hour. Ask them to review the essential competencies identified for instructors in Exhibit 18.1. Write those competencies in the left column below. Then ask the participants to write behaviors associated with each competency in the right column. A behavior is something that can be observed. For instance, for "setting goals and objectives," a behavior might be "the instructor describes the program goals and objectives at the outset of instruction." Any number of behaviors may be identified for a competency. The purpose of this activity is to identify the most important behaviors that are associated with success as an instructor in an organization. Emphasize to the group members that there are no right or wrong answers.

What are the essential competencies of an instructor in the organization?	What measurable, observable behaviors are linked to each competency? (List as many behaviors as necessary for each competency.)

Evaluating Instructors

The LEPP model can be adapted to instructor evaluation by asking stakeholders and participants how often and how well an instructor has functioned according to competencies listed in the model and the behaviors linked to those competencies. While all competencies may not be appropriate to all situations, continued references to them will build instructor accountability—and begin to raise valuable questions about the relative responsibilities of participants and stakeholders in each area. In follow-up interviews with program planners who function as supervisors, instructors may also use the LEPP model to discuss goals and strategies for personal and program improvement.

The assessment instrument that appears in Appendix One may also be adapted to the special evaluation needs of a particular setting, situation, or participant group. A new instrument can be developed that lists the essential competencies and associated behaviors for instructor success. The instrument can be used as a basis for continuing instructor performance appraisals, thus linking appraisal directly to the essential competencies and behaviors associated with instructor success.

Developing Instructors

Both instructors and program planners deserve to be kept up-to-date through planned learning experiences. Just as the LEPP model can be used to suggest areas for developing program planners, it can be adapted to suggest areas for developing instructors. To be used in that way, readers may revise the instrument that appears in Appendix One to develop an instrument to assess instructor competencies.

To make that revision, retain the listing of competencies in the left column of the instrument but revise the rating scheme. Add two columns on the right. Above the first column ask this question: *How well does this individual currently demonstrate this competency?* Above the second column ask this question: *How much should this individual develop this competency in the future?* Revise the rating scales. Above the first column describe the scales as follows: DK–Unsure how well this individual currently demonstrates this competency; LO–The individual's current competence related to the listed area is especially low; MD–The individual's current competence related to the listed area is in the middle; and HI–The individual's current competence related to the listed area is high. Above the second column describe the scales as follows: DK–Unsure how much this individual should develop this competency in the future; LO–The individual's need to develop competence related to the listed area is especially low; MD–The individual's need to develop competence related to the listed area is about in the middle; and HI–The individual's need to develop competence related to the listed area is high. Ask the individual, his or her immediate supervisors, program participants, managers, and other stakeholders to rate the individual on the instrument. Then pinpoint and rank the areas in which improvement is needed. This should serve as an excellent approach to identifying gaps between current and desired instructor competence.

Once the gaps have been identified and ranked, brainstorm approaches to filling the gaps in order to meet the individual's need for development. Compare the individual's self-ratings to those of others who rated the individual. This approach may stimulate individual efforts to improve competence.

Summary

This chapter showed how program planners may draw on the LEPP model to construct questions and activities to guide instructor selection, supervision, evaluation, and development. The assessment instrument provided in Appendix One can be adapted as a tool for selecting effective instructors for an education or training program, for monitoring and evaluating effective performance of current instructors, and for identifying areas for instructor professional development. The chapter provided guidance in using the instrument for these purposes.

Chapter Eighteen concludes the review of Quadrant 4 of the Lifelong Education Program Planning (LEPP) model. Each subquadrant of Quadrant 4 is important because it provides administrative support essential to effective program planning.

AFTERWORD

W hat are the most effective ways that program planners may apply the Lifelong Education Program Planning (LEPP) and Contingency-Based Program Planning models (CBPP) that have served as the centerpieces of this book? What words of inspiration do the authors have to offer program planners?

The authors agree with Rita Richey's (1995) observation that "today, the [program planning] field is alive with intellectual activity that is generating diversity not only in theory, but also in the practical applications of these new theories" (p. 96). No longer is it appropriate to apply one approach to every situation and every setting. Increasingly, program planners must adapt their approaches creatively to the situations and settings in which they find themselves. They must depart from any semblance of rigidity in what they do during program planning, in how they do it, and in when they do what they do. These are the central messages of the book.

Summary of the LEPP and CBPP Models

The book has provided a practical guide for achieving these purposes. The LEPP model, described in Chapter One and elaborated on throughout the book, orients program planners to the lifelong education program planning process. Providing guidance but not prescriptions about what should be done, the model comprehensively summarizes the complexity of program planning activities. No single point of entry or fixed sequence exists in the LEPP model. The planning process has multiple entry points and may follow divergent sequences. Program planners are thus free to begin and end the program planning process wherever they wish and as circumstances require. The model is thus intended to be *contingency-based*—that is, applied according to the needs and exigencies of situations, participants, and settings.

As discussed in Chapter One, the four quadrants and sixteen subquadrants of the LEPP model illustrate areas in which program planners need to be competent. Each of the quadrants is related to all of the other quadrants.

To demonstrate competence in Quadrant 1, "Exercising Professional Responsibility," program planners must work effectively by exercising time management and project management skills; they must magnify their roles by finding ways to do more with less and by seizing the initiative to ensure that programs support their sponsoring organizations, program participants, and other stakeholders; they must articulate a working philosophy by expressing what they believe in and why, thus providing an anchor for holding fast amid the ebbs and tides of organizational events; and they must enact a sense of ethical responsibility by recognizing the moral dimensions of program planning.

To demonstrate competence in Quadrant 2, "Engaging Relevant Contexts," program planners must take into account the environmental conditions that affect their work. They must appraise external conditions by identifying and monitoring trends and adapting planned learning experiences to match emerging challenges, and they must appraise internal environmental conditions by determining how much these conditions affect the program planning process. They must be able to assess learning needs by distinguishing learning from nonlearning needs and pinpointing issues of genuine concern to stakeholders, and they must be able to accommodate adult learner characteristics by designing instruction to be congruent with what is known about effective adult learning experiences.

To demonstrate competence in Quadrant 3, "Designing the Program," program planners must be able to set goals and objectives by clarifying desired program results or outcomes with stakeholders; they must be able to plan process and outcome evaluation by converting program goals and objectives into program targets (in other words, goals and objectives are the basis for evaluation, the process of placing value on program results); they must be able to formulate instructional design by selecting, modifying, or preparing materials and experiences to achieve desired results; and they must be able to designate learning procedures, to select appropriate ways to deliver planned learning experiences.

To demonstrate competence in Quadrant 4, "Managing Administrative Aspects," program planners must be able to create an environment that is supportive of planned learning experiences. To achieve that end, program planners must be able to recruit and retain program participants, to induce and preserve participation; they must be able to promote and market programs to establish credibility for their efforts; they must be able to budget and finance programs by planning for and working within existing resource constraints; and they must be able to effectively select, supervise, train, and evaluate instructors.

The LEPP model offers a means for both coaching new program planners and developing experienced planners. It provides a flexible frame of reference for describing what the program planning process is and what competencies are key to success in that process.

The CBPP model, also presented in Chapter One, helps program planners apply the LEPP model and enact their roles. It describes *how* the program planning process is carried out, while the LEPP model describes *what* the steps are in the process. In keeping with the book's theme of adapting program planning approaches to particular situations, participants, and settings, the CBPP model suggests that the program planning process can be carried out either directively, collaboratively, or nondirectively.

Directive approaches make program planners serve as directors of learning, controlling and directing what others learn. In such approaches, program planners oversee each step of the program planning process. Collaborative approaches are participatory. They make program planners learning facilitators and call for negotiation, dialogue, and cooperation among program planners, learners, and other stakeholders. Nondirective approaches are carried out by the learners themselves and call for program planners to serve as resource and enabling agents as well as learning consultants. In such approaches, learners assume responsibility for their own instructional, personal, and professional development, and for their own learning.

Applying the LEPP and CBPP Models

Program planners can obtain valuable clues for applying the LEPP and CBPP models from such sources as the organizational or institutional culture, the project constraints, the importance of predictable outcomes, and the nature of the learning experience—all aspects of the setting; or from stakeholder preferences and program planners' values and preferences.

Generally speaking, directive approaches may be appropriately applied in settings where decisions are made from the top down, time frames are tight, participants are inexperienced with the subject matter, and outcomes must be predictable. Nondirective approaches may be appropriately applied in settings where decisions are made from the bottom up, time frames are not as important as the quality of the results, participants are experienced with the subject matter, and creative outcomes (such as discovery of new information or new insights) are desired. Collaborative approaches may be appropriately applied in settings in which some decisions are made from top down and others are made from bottom up with participants who represent both the experienced and inexperienced.

Words of Inspiration

Program planners face daunting challenges in the years ahead. While the LEPP and CBPP models provide guidance, they are not panaceas. Program planners must ply their trade with creativity and flexibility. If nothing else, that is the central message of this book: that program planners *can* make a difference, and their ability to apply what they do with sensitivity to the surroundings in which they function is the key trait that will lead to their future success.

Yet despite the daunting challenges that program planners face in an age when work is being restructured, job security seems to be a thing of the past, and the focus of attention in many settings is doing more with less as quickly as possible, program planning remains exciting and enjoyable. Those program planners who have the stamina to thrive in the chaotic conditions prevalent in so many settings face rich rewards: appreciation for what they do from learners and from other stakeholders, increasingly challenging and fast-paced assignments, and mastery of new technological applications. Never has program planning been such a worthwhile endeavor. For that reason, the authors can only offer these parting words to the readers: *enjoy yourselves!*

PROGRAM PLANNING FOR LIFELONG EDUCATION COMPETENCY SELF-ASSESSMENT FORM

This form is designed to help you assess your level of competence and identify professional development needs related to the Lifelong Education Program Planning (LEPP) model. This information can in turn be used to identify learning experiences for building the professional competencies required to plan effective programs.

For each component of the LEPP model listed in the left column please check the box in the right column that indicates the most relevant self-rating. Use the following scale in the right column:

DK   You do not know the relation between the listed area and your current level of competence but you would like to explore it through discussion, reading, or independent study.

LO   Your current competence related to the listed area is especially low but could be raised toward a desired level through specific learning experiences.

MD   You believe that past experiences have provided part of the desired competence and that some learning experiences would develop the remainder.

HI   You believe that you have established substantial competence in the listed area.

After you have completed the self-assessment, you may wish to devise a strategy for increasing your competence in whatever areas you did not check as "HI." You may wish to begin by studying or reviewing the chapter in the text that corresponds to that area. To make specific improvements, you may wish to solicit feedback from and/or discuss the competency with coworkers and other colleagues, study references, participate in a course, or take part in an action learning project.

Self-Rate Your Competency	DK	LO	MD	HI
1. *Terminology:* familiarity with various terms and concepts related to technical procedures of program planning.	☐	☐	☐	☐
2. *Program planning process:* ability to utilize a sequence of steps in planning and conducting a training or education program.	☐	☐	☐	☐
3. *Working effectively:* ability to work well with others, maintain a clear sense of direction and control over multiple responsibilities, exercise time management, maintain health and vitality, and demonstrate effective communication skills, initiative, and leadership.	☐	☐	☐	☐
4. *Roles of the lifelong educator:* ability to engage in critical self-reflection about the various roles assumed by the planner to plan education and training programs.	☐	☐	☐	☐
5. *Philosophical foundations of one's practice:* ability to articulate the elements of your own working philosophy that underlie your planning practice.	☐	☐	☐	☐
6. *Ethical responsibility:* ability to discern ethical dilemmas in one's own practice and articulate ethically responsible responses.	☐	☐	☐	☐
7. *Analysis of external context:* ability to identify a variety of issues and conditions external to the organization that impact your education and training programs.	☐	☐	☐	☐
8. *Advisory groups:* ability to involve target participants in program design.	☐	☐	☐	☐
9. *Analysis of internal context:* ability to identify a variety of organizational and institutional contexts in which program planning occurs.	☐	☐	☐	☐
10. *Accommodation of education or training to adults:* ability to take into account the unique traits of adult participants.	☐	☐	☐	☐
11. *Needs assessment:* ability to define personal, institutional, and societal needs that serve as a basis for planning and setting objectives for an agency or program.	☐	☐	☐	☐
12. *Negotiating political interests:* ability to identify different kinds of interests of various individuals/groups who have differential access to power and who have a stake in the programs being planned.	☐	☐	☐	☐
13. *Setting priorities:* ability to order identified needs to determine specific program objectives.	☐	☐	☐	☐
14. *Formulating objectives:* ability to identify, select, and write various types of objectives to use in program planning.	☐	☐	☐	☐

15. *Planning evaluation:* ability to differentiate between evaluation procedures and measures to determine effectiveness of programs at different levels, as well as program impact. ☐ ☐ ☐ ☐
16. *Collection of evaluation data:* ability to construct instruments for data collection. ☐ ☐ ☐ ☐
17. *Instructional design:* ability to articulate the critical considerations of curricular design and to plan the sequence of learning in connection with specific training and education programs. ☐ ☐ ☐ ☐
18. *Learning procedures:* ability to select methods, materials, and instructional resources appropriate and relevant to the needs, abilities, and interests of program participants. ☐ ☐ ☐ ☐
19. *Promotion and marketing:* ability to enable specific target audiences to relate to the program and program sponsor. ☐ ☐ ☐ ☐
20. *Recruitment and retention:* ability to plan programmatic elements to raise motivation of target learners to begin as well as to continue their participation in education or training programs. ☐ ☐ ☐ ☐
21. *Budget and financing:* ability to establish program budgets; to project program costs, benefits, and income; and to calculate program revenues. ☐ ☐ ☐ ☐
22. *Selection, supervision, and evaluation of instructors:* ability to select and contract with instructional personnel as well as to provide on-going supervision and evaluation. ☐ ☐ ☐ ☐

If you have additional needs, please describe them in the following rows and estimate your level of competence.

23. ☐ ☐ ☐ ☐

24. ☐ ☐ ☐ ☐

25. ☐ ☐ ☐ ☐

GUIDELINES FOR DEVELOPING AND IMPLEMENTING A CODE OF ETHICS FOR ADULT EDUCATORS

These guidelines were developed by the board of directors of the Coalition of Lifelong Learning Organizations (COLLO) and were adopted by the board at its June 11, 1993, meeting. Formally established in 1973, COLLO consists of national organizations and groups that share a common interest in enhancing the field of adult and continuing education throughout the United States. These organizations represent public schools, institutions of higher education, industries, labor groups, professions, providers of learning resources for adults, and most important, the learners themselves.

Definition and Purpose

A code of ethics is a statement of principles that are intended to help define the moral and highest professional responsibilities of adult educators in their relationships with learners, employers, the public, and each other. It is not a list of standards or minimum competencies. Rather, a code of ethics stems from a vision of what ought to be the very best aspirations for right conduct by members in the profession.

Multiple legitimate purposes exist within the practice of adult education. In so diverse a universe, no code of ethics can take into account all the moral issues that will be encountered. Honest differences about what constitutes ethical behavior will occur in discussions among reasonable people. Still, there are central issues of ethics that need to be addressed even in the face of controversy.

These guidelines contain provisions that the COLLO board believes ought to be considered by member organizations in developing codes of ethics appropriate for their sectors of the field of adult education. Not all provisions will be relevant to all organizations. Neither will the language in the various provisions exactly fit the needs of every group. Great caution should be exercised, however, to see that important ethical principles are not compromised in deciding upon omissions or word changes. Good codes of ethics are assertive and aim at firm occupancy of the moral high ground.

Classification of Ethical Principles

The provisions for a code of ethics are grouped in three nonmutually exclusive categories: those that are (1) participant focused, (2) employer or sponsor focused, and (3) profession focused.

1. Participant Focused

a. Qualified persons are admitted to programs without discrimination as to race, gender, age, disability, sexual orientation, religion, or national origin.
b. The dignity and worth of all program participants is recognized, protected, and, where possible, enhanced.
c. Participants are informed in advance about planned content, grading or pass/fail procedures, course add/drop deadlines, methods of instruction, assessment, and support services.
d. Policies governing award of credit for successful completion, continuing education units (CEUs), or certificates are disclosed in advance.
e. The amount and structure of fees and expenses for program participation, as well as refund policies, are disclosed in advance.
f. Participants have freedom of expression as guaranteed by the First Amendment.
g. Participants accepted for enrollment in a course or program have the right to have their personal and cultural values acknowledged and understood within the context of course or program objectives.
h. Program participants have the right to evaluate the appropriateness of the planned course or program content, performance of their instructors and other resource personnel, and effectiveness of support services, and to have such evaluations carefully reviewed by the program sponsor.

2. Employer or Sponsor Focused

a. "Competing" programs are not misrepresented or unfairly disparaged.
b. Course and program advertising is accurate in terms of the sponsor's purposes and objectives and in good taste.

c. Credentials, competence, education, training, and experience of instructors and program leaders are accurately represented.

d. Competencies and intentions of instructors and program leaders are matched with requirements of the course or program and with expectations of the anticipated participants.

e. Possible conflicts of interest bearing on course or program objectives for instructors and program leaders are fully disclosed in advance of participant enrollment and again at the onset of instruction.

f. Instructors and program leaders have freedom of expression except as limited by other code of ethics provisions (such as selling of products or services) or explicit contract provisions with the sponsor.

g. All courses and programs offered are within the mission of the institution or sponsoring agency.

h. The prerequisite skills and knowledge, planned content, and purposes of courses and programs are accurately represented in syllabi, as well as in informational materials.

i. Methods for assessing learning are appropriate for the skills and knowledge being taught and the backgrounds and experiences of the learners.

j. Records of programs and course enrollments and successful completion are accurately kept and are appropriately reported.

k. The sponsor has in place a policy on cheating and plagiarism by program participants and enforces that policy systematically and fairly.

l. Grant and related extramural funds are used in accord with budget and other agreements with the granting organization.

m. Regulations governing the award of CEUs and academic credit are scrupulously followed.

n. Within an institution or agency, adult educators are not marginalized; neither are adult learning programs developed at an inferior level of quality for the purpose of using the fees they generate to subsidize programs considered more central to a sponsor's mission.

o. Employers and sponsors have explicit arrangements that enable them appropriately to protect the integrity of individuals who call attention to alleged ethical violations within the organization itself.

3. *Profession Focused*

a. The research and efforts of others are properly acknowledged not only in scholarly books and papers but also in program presentations and course handouts.

b. In preparing materials, instructors and program leaders comply fully with all appropriate copyright laws and document their efforts.

c. Possible conflicts of interest vis-à-vis participants or other agencies and institutions are disclosed by an instructor or program leader in advance of employment or involvement in a program or course.

d. Only persons who have the qualifications and prerequisites to succeed in a credit course or program are recruited and enrolled. Counseling, guidance, and/or supplementary or refresher instruction are provided for persons who desire to enroll but are not yet qualified.

e. Course or program applicants who clearly could better achieve their goals through enrollment in programs of other sponsors are informed about the availability of such programs.

f. Class time is not used to sell a product or service or to distribute flyers and business cards that are oriented to the financial interests of an instructor or program leader (unless the explicit and preannounced purposes of the class include explaining a product or service with the objective of encouraging sales).

g. Class time is not used to solicit contributions or support for political, religious, civic, or social causes (unless the explicit and preannounced purposes of the class include generating funds or support for such causes).

h. Privileged information is maintained in confidence and trust.

i. Instructors or program leaders explicitly identify their educational philosophies at an early stage of work with individuals and groups and likewise identify their personal beliefs or philosophies if they become a point of educational direction or emphasis during the course of instruction.

j. Instructors or program leaders do not use credentials or organizational memberships to make false claims of competence.

k. Instructors or program leaders make it clear that they are open to competing ideas during the course of instruction.

l. Instructors or program leaders engage in professional development to assure that their knowledge, skills, and competence are continuously updated.

m. Instructors or program leaders speak out against abuses in practice and in society that adversely affect adult learners.

REFERENCES

American Society for Training and Development. *Resource Guide: Return on Investment.* Alexandria, Va.: The American Society for Training and Development, 1994a.

American Society for Training and Development. *Who's Who in Training and Development.* Alexandria, Va.: American Society for Training and Development, 1994b.

Andrews, D., and Goodson, L. "A Comparative Analysis of Models of Instructional Design." *Journal of Development,* 1980, *3*(4), 2–16.

Apps, J. W. *Toward a Working Philosophy of Adult Education.* Syracuse, N.Y.: Syracuse University and ERIC Clearinghouse on Adult Education, 1973.

Apps, J. W. *Leadership for the Emerging Age: Transforming Practice in Adult and Continuing Education.* San Francisco: Jossey-Bass, 1994.

Babbie, E. *The Practice of Social Research.* Belmont, Calif.: Wadsworth, 1995.

Banathy, B. H. *A Systems View of Education.* Englewood Cliffs, N.J.: Education Technology Publications, 1992.

Bengtson, B. "An Analysis of CEO Perceptions Concerning Trainer Roles in Selected Central Pennsylvania Manufacturing Firms." Unpublished doctoral dissertation, The Pennsylvania State University, 1994.

Bennett, C. *Analyzing Impacts of Extension Programs.* Report ESC-575. Washington, D.C.: Extension Service, U.S. Department of Agriculture, 1976.

Bloom, B. S. (ed.). *Taxonomy of Educational Objectives: The Classification of Education Goals. Handbook I: Cognitive Domain.* New York: McKay, 1956.

Boshier, R. "Motivation for Adult Education: A Summary of Discussions." In J. Knoll (ed.), *Motivation for Adult Education.* Bonn: German Commission for UNESCO, 1985.

Boshier, R. "Recent Developments in Motivational Orientation Research: A Rejoinder." *Australian Journal of Adult Education,* 1990, *29*(2), 33–40.

Boud, D., and Feletti, G. (eds.). *The Challenge of Problem-Based Learning.* London: Kogan Page, 1991.

Boyle, P. G. *Planning Better Programs.* New York: McGraw-Hill, 1981.

Bradford, L. "Group Formation and Development." In L. Bradford (ed.), *Group Development.* (2nd ed.) San Francisco: Pfeiffer, 1978.

Broad, M., and Newstrom, J. *Transfer of Training: Action-Packed Strategies to Ensure High Payoff from Training Investments.* Reading, Mass.: Addison Wesley Longman, 1992.

Brookfield, S. *Understanding and Facilitating Adult Learning: A Comprehensive Analysis of Principles and Effective Practices.* San Francisco: Jossey-Bass, 1986.

"Business Students Cheat Most." *Fortune,* July 1, 1991, p. 17.

Caffarella, R. S. *Planning Programs for Adult Learners: A Practical Guide for Educators, Trainers, and Staff Developers.* San Francisco: Jossey-Bass, 1994.

Campbell, R., and Monson, D. "Building a Goal-Based Scenario Learning Environment." *Educational Technology,* 1994, *34*(9), 9–14.

Carnevale, A. P., Gainer, L. J., and Villet, J. *Training in America: The Organization and Strategic Role of Training.* San Francisco: Jossey-Bass, 1990.

Casey, D. *Managing Learning in Organizations.* Buckingham, U.K.: Open University Press, 1993.

Cervero, R. M. "The Politics of Responsibility: A Theory of Planning Practice for Adult Education." *Adult Education Quarterly,* 1994, *45*(1), 249–268.

Cervero, R. M., and Wilson, A. L. *Planning Responsibly for Adult Education: A Guide to Negotiating Power and Interests.* San Francisco: Jossey-Bass, 1994.

Collins, A., Brown, J., and Newman, S. "Cognitive Apprenticeship: Teaching the Craft of Reading, Writing, and Mathematics." In L. Resnick (ed.), *Cognition and Instruction: Issues and Agendas.* Hillsdale, N.J.: Erlbaum, 1989.

Cookson, P. S. "Recruitment and Retention of Adult Students: The Viewpoint of Practice." In P. S. Cookson (ed.), *Recruitment and Retention of Adult Students.* New Directions for Adult and Continuing Education, no. 41. San Francisco: Jossey-Bass, 1989.

Cookson, P. S., and Rothwell, W. J. *A Survey of the Program Planning Practices of Continuing Education Professionals.* Unpublished survey results. University Park: The Pennsylvania State University, 1995.

Cunningham, I. *The Wisdom of Strategic Learning.* New York: McGraw-Hill, 1994.

Dickinson, G. *Teaching Adults: A Handbook for Instructors.* Toronto: New Press, 1973.

Dixon, V., Conway, K., Ashley, K., and Stewart, N. *Training Competency Architecture* and *Training Competency Architecture Toolkit.* Toronto: Ontario Society for Training and Development, 1995.

Egan, K. "What Is Curriculum?" *Curriculum Inquiry,* 1978, *8*(1), 65–72.

Elias, J., and Merriam, S. *Philosophical Foundations of Adult Education.* Malabar, Fla.: Krieger, 1994.

Flanagan, J. "The Critical Incident Technique." *Psychological Bulletin,* 1954, *51,* 327–358.

Foshay, W., Silber, K., and Westgaard, O. *Instructional Design Competencies: The Standards.* Iowa City, Iowa: The International Board of Standards for Training, Performance and Instruction, 1986.

Galagan, P. "Reinventing the Profession." *Training and Development,* Dec. 1994, pp. 20–27.

Gardner, R. E. "Community Relations: Promotion, Marketing, and Publicity." In P. D. Langerman and D. H. Smith (eds.), *Managing Adult and Continuing Education Programs and Staff.* Washington, D.C.: National Association for Public Continuing and Adult Education, 1979.

Garratt, B. "The Power of Action Learning." In M. Pedler (ed.), *Action Learning in Practice.* (2nd ed.) Aldershot, Hants, U.K.: Gower, 1991.

Geis, G. "Human Performance Technology: An Overview." In M. Smith (ed.), *Introduction to Performance Technology.* Washington, D.C.: The National Society for Performance and Instruction, 1986.

Gilley, J., and Coffern, A. *The Role of the Internal Consultant: Where Do You Fit?* Alexandria, Va., and New York: American Society for Training and Development and Business-One, 1993.

Griffith, W. "Recruiting and Retaining Adult Students: A Marketing Perspective." In P. S. Cookson (ed.), *Recruiting and Retaining Adult Students.* New Directions for Adult and Continuing Education, no. 41. San Francisco: Jossey-Bass, 1989.

Grotelueschen, A. "Program Evaluation." In A. B. Knox and Associates, *Developing, Administering, and Evaluating Adult Education.* San Francisco: Jossey-Bass, 1980.

Guba, E. G., and Lincoln, Y. S. *Effective Evaluation: Improving the Usefulness of Evaluation Results Through Responsive and Naturalistic Approaches.* San Francisco: Jossey-Bass, 1988.

Hale, J. *Training Manager Competencies: The Standards.* Batavia, Ill.: The International Board of Standards for Training, Performance and Instruction, 1989.

Hart, L. *Faultless Facilitation: A Resource Guide for Group and Team Leaders.* Amherst, Mass.: Human Resource Development Press, 1992.

Havighurst, R. *Developmental Tasks and Education.* New York: McKay, 1961.

Head, G. E. *Training Cost Analysis: A How-To Guide for Trainers and Managers.* Alexandria, Va.: The American Society for Training and Development, 1994.

Hennessy, D., and Hennessy, M. *Instructional Systems Development: Tools and Procedures for Organizing, Budgeting, and Managing a Training Project from Start to Finish.* Frederiksted, St. Croix, Virgin Islands: TRC Press, 1989.

The Higher Education Directory. Washington, D.C.: Higher Education Publications, 1994.

Houle, C. *The Inquiring Mind.* Madison: University of Wisconsin Press, 1961.

Houle, C. O. "The Education of Adults." In R. M. Smith, G. F. Aker, and J. R. Kidd (eds.), *Handbook of Adult Education.* New York: Macmillan, 1970.

Houle, C. *The Design of Education.* San Francisco: Jossey-Bass, 1972.

Houle, C. "Structural Features and Policies Promoting (or Inhibiting) Adult Learners." In J. Knoll (ed.), *Motivation for Adult Education.* Bonn: German Commission for UNESCO, 1985.

Inglis, S. *Making the Most of Action Learning.* London: Gower, 1994.

Jensen, G. "Social Psychology and Adult Education Practice." In G. Jensen, A. Liveright, and W. Hallenbeck (eds.), *Adult Education: Outlines of an Emerging Field of University Study.* Washington, D.C.: Adult Education Association of the U.S.A., 1964.

Jonassen, D., Hannum, W., and Tessmer, M. *Handbook of Task Analysis Procedures.* New York: Praeger, 1989.

Jones, M. "Action Learning as a New Idea." *Journal of Management Development,* 1990, *9*(5), 29–34.

Jonsen, R. "The Environmental Context for Postsecondary Education." In P. Callan (ed.), *Environmental Scanning for Strategic Leadership.* San Francisco: Jossey-Bass, 1986.

Kast, F., and Rosenzweig, J. *Organization and Management: A Systems Approach.* (2nd ed.) New York: McGraw-Hill, 1974.

Katz, D., and Kahn, R. *The Social Psychology of Organizations.* (2nd ed.) New York: Wiley, 1978.

Kirkpatrick, D. *Evaluating Training Programs.* San Francisco: Berrett-Koehler, 1995.

Knowles, M. *The Modern Practice of Adult Education: From Pedagogy to Andragogy.* River Grove, Ill.: Follett, 1980.

Kotler, P. *Marketing for Nonprofit Organizations.* Upper Saddle River, N.J.: Prentice-Hall, 1975.

Kotler, P., and Fox, K. *Strategic Marketing for Educational Institutions.* Upper Saddle River, N.J.: Prentice-Hall, 1985.

Krathwohl, D., Bloom, B. S., and Masia, B. B. *Taxonomy of Educational Objectives: The Classification of Educational Goals. Handbook II: Affective Domain.* New York: McKay, 1956.

Laird, D. *Approaches to Training and Development.* (2nd ed.) Reading, Mass.: Addison Wesley Longman, 1985.

Lauffer, A. *The Practice of Continuing Education in the Human Services.* New York: McGraw-Hill, 1977.

Lombardo, M., and Eichinger, R. *Eighty-Eight Assignments for Development in Place: Enhancing the Developmental Challenge of Existing Jobs.* Greensboro, N.C.: The Center for Creative Leadership, 1989.

Longnecker, J., McKinney, A., and Moore, C. "The Generation Gap in Business Ethics." *Business Horizons,* Sept.-Oct. 1989, pp. 9–14.

Mager, R. *Preparing Instructional Objectives.* (2nd ed.) Belmont, Calif.: Fearon-Pitman, 1975.

Mager, R., and Pipe, P. *Analyzing Performance Problems or You Really Oughta Wanna.* (2nd ed.) Belmont, Calif.: Lake, 1984.

Marsick, V. "Experience-Based Learning: Executive Learning Outside the Classroom." *Journal of Management Development,* 1990, *9*(4), 50–60.

Marsick, V., and Watkins, K. "Towards a Theory of Informal and Incidental Learning in Organizations." *International Journal of Lifelong Education,* 1992, *11*(4), 287–300.

Marsick, V., and others. "Action-Reflection Learning." *Training and Development,* 1992, *46*(8), 63–66.

Maslow, A. *Motivation and Personality.* (2nd ed.) New York: HarperCollins, 1970.

Matkin, G. W. *Effective Budgeting in Continuing Education.* San Francisco: Jossey-Bass, 1985.

McGill, I., and Beaty, L. *Action Learning: A Practitioner's Guide.* London: Kogan Page, 1992.

McLagan, P. *Models for HRD Practice.* 4 vols. Alexandria, Va.: The American Society for Training and Development, 1989.

McLagan, P., and McCullough, R. *Models for Excellence: The Conclusions and Recommendations of the ASTD Training and Development Competency Study.* Alexandria, Va.: The American Society for Training and Development, 1983.

McLane, S., Rothwell, W. J., and Schechter, S. "Major Findings." *Human Resources Management: Ideas and Trends in Personnel,* June 19, 1996, p. 2.

McMahon, E. *Needs—Of People and Their Communities . . . and the Adult Educator: A Review of the Literature of Need Determination.* Syracuse, N.Y.: Educational Resources Information Center, 1970. (ED 038 551)

Mead, M. (ed.). *Cultural Patterns and Technical Change.* New York: NAL/Dutton, 1955.

Mumford, A. "Learning in Action." *Personnel Management,* 1991, *23*(7), 34–37.

Nadler, L. "A Study of the Needs of Selected Training Directors in Pennsylvania Which Might Be Met by Professional Education Institutions." *Dissertation Abstracts International,* 1962, *24*(2).

Nadler, L. (ed.). *Designing Learning Programs.* New York: Wiley, 1985.

Nadler, L., and Nadler, Z. *Designing Training Programs: The Critical Events Model.* Houston: Gulf, 1994.

Norton, R. *The DACUM Handbook.* Columbus: The Ohio State University, 1985.

Ontario Society for Training and Development. *Core Competencies for Training and Development.* Toronto: Ontario Society for Training and Development, 1976.

Overfield, K. "Nonlinear Approach to Training Program Development." *Performance and Instruction,* July 1994, pp. 26–34.

Pedler, M. (ed.). *Action Learning in Practice.* Aldershot, Hants, U.K.: Gower, 1983.

Pedler, M. (ed.). *Action Learning in Practice.* (2nd ed.) Aldershot, Hants, U.K.: Gower, 1991.

Phillips, J. J. *Handbook of Training Evaluation and Measurement Methods.* (2nd ed.) Houston: Gulf, 1991.

Phillips, J. J. *In Action: Measuring Return on Investment.* Vol. 1. Alexandria, Va.: The American Society for Training and Development, 1994.

Pinto, P., and Walker, J. *A Study of Professional Training and Development Roles and Competencies.* Alexandria, Va.: The American Society for Training and Development, 1978.

Piskurich, G. *Self-Directed Learning: A Practical Guide to Design, Development, and Implementation.* San Francisco: Jossey-Bass, 1993.

Pitt Community College. *A Model for Recruiting the New Community College Student.* Greenville, N.C.: Pitt Community College, 1985. (ED 267 187)

Powers, B. *Instructor Excellence: Mastering the Delivery of Training.* San Francisco: Jossey-Bass, 1992.

Prahalad, C., and Hamel, G. "The Core Competence of the Corporation." *Harvard Business Review,* May–June 1990, pp. 79–91.

Ramsey, D. "Making the Most of Free Promotions." In R. Conter and W. Procelli (eds.), *Removing Barriers to the Adult Learner Through Marketing, Management, and Programming: Proceedings of the NUCEA Region VI Conference.* Tucson: University of Arizona, Continuing Education, 1982.

Reigeluth, C. (ed.). *Instructional Theories in Action: Lessons Illustrating Selected Theories and Models.* Hillsdale, N.J.: Erlbaum, 1987.

Revans, R. *Developing Effective Managers: A New Approach to Business Education.* New York: Praeger, 1971.

Revans, R. *The Origins and Growth of Action Learning.* Bromley, U.K.: Chartwell-Bratt, 1982.

Revans, R. "Action Learning: Its Origins and Nature." In M. Pedler (ed.), *Action Learning in Practice.* Aldershot, Hants, U.K.: Gower, 1983.

Richey, R. C. "Trends in Instructional Design: Emerging Theory-Based Models." *Performance Improvement Quarterly,* 1995, *8*(3), 96–110.

Rogers, E. *Diffusion of Innovations.* New York: Free Press, 1962.

Rosenberg, M. "The ABCs of ISD (Instructional Systems Design)." *Training and Development Journal,* Sept. 1982, pp. 44–46.

Rosenfeld, S. "Business Crime: Just a Few Bad Apples, or the Barrel?" *The Commercial Appeal,* Dec. 15, 1985, p. C2.

Rothwell, W. J. *A Survey About Training Needs Assessment: Summary of Survey Results.* Unpublished survey results. University Park, Pa.: The Pennsylvania State University, 1995a.

Rothwell, W. J. *A Survey About Training Evaluation Practices: Summary of Results.* Unpublished survey results. University Park, Pa.: The Pennsylvania State University, 1995b.

Rothwell, W. J. *The ASTD Models for Human Performance Improvement: Roles, Competencies, Outputs.* Alexandria, Va.: The American Society for Training and Development, 1996a.

Rothwell, W. J. *Beyond Training and Development: State-of-the-Art Strategies for Enhancing Human Performance.* New York: AMACOM, 1996b.

Rothwell, W. J. *The Just-in-Time Training Assessment Instrument and Administrator's Handbook.* Amherst, Mass.: HRD Press, 1996c.

Rothwell, W. J. *The Self-Directed On-the-Job Learning Workshop.* Amherst, Mass.: HRD Press, 1996d.

Rothwell, W. J., and Cookson, P. S. *A Survey of the Program Planning Practices of Human Resource Development Professionals.* Unpublished survey results. University Park, Pa.: The Pennsylvania State University, 1995.

Rothwell, W. J., and Kazanas, H. C. "Curriculum Planning for Training: The State of the Art." *Performance Improvement Quarterly*, 1988, *1*(3), 2–16.

Rothwell, W. J., and Kazanas, H. C. *Mastering the Instructional Design Process: A Systematic Approach.* San Francisco: Jossey-Bass, 1992.

Rothwell, W. J., and Kazanas, H. C. *The Complete AMA Guide to Management Development.* New York: AMACOM, 1993.

Rothwell, W. J., and Kazanas, H. C. *Human Resource Development: A Strategic Approach.* (rev. ed.) Amherst, Mass.: Human Resource Development Press, 1994a.

Rothwell, W. J., and Kazanas, H. C. *Improving On-the-Job Training: How to Establish and Operate a Comprehensive OJT Program.* San Francisco: Jossey-Bass, 1994b.

Rothwell, W. J., and Sredl, H. J. *The ASTD Reference Guide to Human Resource Development Roles and Competencies.* (2nd ed.) 2 vols. Amherst, Mass.: Human Resource Development Press, 1992.

Rothwell, W. J., Sullivan, R., and McLean, G. (eds.). *Practicing Organization Development: A Guide for Consultants.* San Francisco: Pfeiffer, 1995.

Schein, E. *Process Consultation: Its Role in Organization Development.* Vol. 1. (2nd ed.) Reading, Mass.: Addison Wesley Longman, 1988.

Schmidt, J. "The Leader's Role in Strategic Planning." In R. G. Simerly and Associates, *Strategic Planning and Leadership in Continuing Education: Enhancing Organizational Vitality, Responsiveness, and Identity.* San Francisco: Jossey-Bass, 1987.

Senge, P. *The Fifth Discipline: The Art and Practice of the Learning Organization.* New York: Doubleday, 1990.

Sork, T. J. *Determining Priorities.* Unpublished manuscript. British Columbia: Ministry of Education, Division of Continuing Education, 1982.

Steele, S. "Program Evaluation: A Broader Definition." *Journal of Extension*, Summer 1970, p. 8.

Steele, S. "Eight Key Mental Skills in Evaluation." *Adult Learning*, 1991, *3*(2), 11–12, 26.

Stein, F., and Hutchison, C. *Instructor Competencies: The Standards,* Vols. 1 and 2. Batavia, Ill.: The International Board of Standards for Training, Performance and Instruction, 1988.

Strother, G., and Klus, J. *Administration of Continuing Education.* Belmont, Calif.: Wadsworth, 1982.

Stufflebeam, D. "Evaluation as a Community Education Process." *Community Education Journal*, Mar./Apr. 1975, p. 7.

Stufflebeam, D. "Principal Evaluation: New Directions for Improvement." *Peabody Journal of Education*, 1993, *68*(2), 24–46.

Stufflebeam, D. "Empowerment Evaluation, Objectivist Evaluation, and Evaluation Standards: Where the Future of Evaluation Should Not Go and Where It Needs to Go." *Evaluation Practice*, 1994, *15*(3), 321–338.

Stufflebeam, D. "Toward a Science of Education Evaluation." *Educational Technology*, 1975, *7*(14).

Tough, A. *The Adult's Learning Projects.* (2nd ed.) Toronto: Ontario Institute for Studies in Education, 1979.

Tyler, R. *Basic Principles of Curriculum and Instruction.* Chicago: University of Chicago Press, 1949.

U.S. Civil Service Commission. *The Employee Development Specialist Curriculum Plan: An Outline of Learning Experiences for the Employee Development Specialist.* Washington, D.C.: U.S. Civil Service Commission, 1976.

Usher, J., Simmonds, D., and Earl, S. "Industrial Enhancement Through Problem-Based Learning." In D. Boud and G. Feletti (eds.), *The Challenge of Problem-Based Learning.* London: Kogan Page, 1991.

Verner, C. "Definitions." In G. Jensen, A. Liveright, and W. Hallenbeck (eds.), *Adult Education: Outlines of an Emerging Field of University Study.* Chicago: Adult Education Association of the U.S.A., 1964.

Vince, R., and Martin, L. "Inside Action Learning: An Exploration of the Psychology and Politics of the Action Learning Model." *Management Education and Development*, 1993, *24*(3), 205–215.

Von Bertalanffy, L. "General Systems Theory: A New Approach to the Unity of Science." *Human Biology*, 1951, *23*, 302–361.

Von Bertalanffy, L. *General Systems Theory: Foundations, Development, Applications.* New York: Braziller, 1968.

Wallace, M. "Can Action Learning Live Up to Its Promise?" *Management Education and Development*, 1990, *21*(2), 89–103.

Warren, M. *Training for Results: A Systems Approach to the Development of Human Resources in Industry.* (2nd ed.) Reading, Mass.: Addison Wesley Longman, 1979.

Watkins, K., and Marsick, V. *Sculpting the Learning Organization.* San Francisco: Jossey-Bass, 1993.

Watkins, R., and Kaufman, R. "An Update on Relating Needs Assessment and Needs Analysis." *Performance Improvement*, 1996, *35*(10), 10–13.

Wedman, J. F., and Tessmer, M. "'The Layers of Necessity' ID Model." *Performance and Instruction*, 1990, *29*(4), 1–8.

Wedman, J. F., and Tessmer, M. "Adapting Instructional Design to Project Circumstance: 'The Layers of Necessity' Model." *Educational Technology*, 1991, *31*(7), 48–52.

Wedman, J. F., and Tessmer, M. "Instructional Designers' Decisions and Priorities: A Survey of Design Practice." *Performance Improvement Quarterly*, 1993, *6*(2), 43–57.

Wiggs, G. "Designing Learning Programs." In L. Nadler (ed.), *The Handbook of Human Resource Development.* New York: Wiley, 1985.

Winer, L., and Vázquez-Abad, J. "The Present and Future of ID Practice." *Performance Improvement Quarterly*, 1995, *8*(3), 55–67.

Wortham, F. *An Examination of Program Planning in Management Career Development Programs in Corporations: The Theory-Practice Dimension.* Unpublished doctoral dissertation, The Pennsylvania State University, 1992.

Zemke, R. "The Systems Approach: A Nice Theory But. . . ." *Training*, Oct. 1985, pp. 103–108.

Zemke, R., and Zemke, S. "Adult Learning: What Do We Know for Sure?" *Training*, 1995, *32*(6), 31–40.

INDEX